Care and Education in Early Childhood

The authors draw on their extensive early years expertise to provide a comprehensive and up-to-date review of the key issues in the field of early childhood care and education. In this fully updated and revised new edition, rewritten to include the new Early Years Foundation Stage, students will find that this text now meets the needs of students on Foundation degrees, Early Childhood degrees and the new Early Years Professional qualification.

Topics covered in this essential textbook include:

- an overview of the principles of effective practice discussions on equal opportunities and children's rights;
- an update of the latest theories relating to brain development and how children learn, and the difficulties children may face in their learning;
- investigations into what working with parents really means;
- consideration of the different early years systems in operation;
- summaries of key management issues and useful information on how to address them;
- comparison with European perspectives on early years care and education;
- the importance of play in children's early learning.

Readers of this new edition will also find the expansion of existing chapters in order to include topics such as inclusion, transitions, child protection in relation to the internet and partnerships with parents. The book covers the whole age range from birth to eight years with a special section on the birth to three years age group. Each chapter is fully referenced and has case studies or reflective practice sections within the text.

Informative and engaging, the book challenges the reader to think about how underlying theory may be reflected in practice. It will be essential reading for all students who are studying for early childhood qualifications at levels 4, 5 and 6.

Audrey Curtis was formerly World President of OMEP (World Organisation for Early Childhood Education) and now acts as a consultant.

Maureen O'Hagan was formerly Director of Quality Assurance at CACHE (Council for Awards in Children's Care and Education). She now works as a freelance consultant.

Care and Education in Early Childhood

A student's guide to theory and practice

Second edition

Audrey Curtis and Maureen O'Hagan

Routledge
Taylor & Francis Group

LONDON AND NEW YORK

First edition published 2003
by Routledge
Second edition published 2009
by Routledge
2 Park Square, Milton Park, Abingdon, Oxon OX14 4RN

Simultaneously published in the USA and Canada
by Routledge
270 Madison Ave, New York, NY 10016

Routledge is an imprint of the Taylor & Francis Group, an informa business

© 2003, 2009 Audrey Curtis and Maureen O'Hagan

Typeset in Sabon by Wearset Ltd, Boldon, Tyne and Wear
Printed and bound in Great Britain by TJ International Ltd, Padstow, Cornwall

British Library Cataloguing in Publication Data
A catalogue record for this book is available from the British Library

Library of Congress Cataloging in Publication Data
Curtis, Audrey.
Care and education in early childhood: a student's guide to theory and
practice/Audrey Curtis and Maureen O'Hagan. – 2nd ed.
  p. cm.
Includes bibliographical references and index.
1. Early childhood education–Great Britain. 2. Child care–Great Britain. I.
O'Hagan, Maureen. II. Title.
LB1139.3.G7C87 2009
372.210941–dc22   2008025216

ISBN10: 0-415-45757-2

ISBN13: 978-0-415-45757-6

Contents

Introduction to second edition

In this new edition of *Care and Education in Early Childhood*, there have been substantial re-writes of a number of chapters due to significant changes that the UK government has brought in since the first edition was written. It is a very positive feeling to realise that early childhood, care and education continue to remain on the agendas of governments and politicians in many parts of the world, not just in the UK. International organisations such as UNICEF and UNESCO continue to stress the importance of providing quality early-childhood education and care for all children, not just those from disadvantaged backgrounds. Research evidence has shown the long-term benefits of offering young children high-quality care and education during their early years.

UK government initiatives such as Sure Start, Every Child Matters and more recently the Early Years Foundation Stage, have all been important developments within the framework of improving the quality of early years provision. However, in some areas a major setback has been the complicated processes that have to be negotiated in order to implement and fund continuing projects once the start-up funding has expired.

The UK Effective Provision of Pre-school Education Project (EEPE) showed that the quality of the staff who work in the provision was significantly linked with the quality of the care and education the children received. This has led to more and more staff members seeking to enhance their existing qualifications by undertaking an early-childhood degree course. It is with this in mind that the authors have upgraded the level of the book in order to make it relevant to students on the early-childhood degree courses. The book is able to offer the reader a sound theoretical and practical basis for working in the early-childhood care and education sector. It offers sound underpinning theory and practice for those working with children in the birth to eight years age range. The book may also prove useful to those who are also undertaking the Early Years Professional Status qualification. Both authors have a great deal of experience in both the academic and practical fields of early-childhood care and education, so they are able to link theory and practice in an interesting and up-to-date way. At the end of each chapter there is a 'Reflect upon …' activity related to the chapter content.

The first chapter examines the principles and values that underpin effective practice. It also emphasises other areas such as equality of opportunity, anti-bias practice and, most importantly, the why and how of becoming a reflective practitioner.

Chapter 2 investigates the whole issue of children's rights, particularly the arguments for and against relating rights with responsibilities. There are issues in this chapter that may also be raised in other chapters of the book as the authors have tried, throughout the book, to address other matters such as race, religion, sex and gender.

Chapters 3 and 4 relate to how children learn and communicate and both provide the reader with information and discussion about the current research in these fields. Consideration is given to the development of memory and concentration skills and the role these play in learning. Attention is also drawn to the role of emotional intelligence in the areas of learning and development. The chapter on language and language development explores the development of verbal and non-verbal skills and highlights ways in which social and cultural factors affect language and learning. There is also discussion about the challenges in situations where children and their families are operating in more than one language and how the needs of these families can be met.

Chapter 5 is about working with the under-threes, which has now become an important part of the role of many early years practitioners. Most recent research on brain development before and after birth, and how the adult is able to stimulate children's development during the early years, is a major section of this chapter. The curriculum for three-year-olds is new material as it is part of the Early Years Foundation stage which covers the birth to five years age range.

Chapter 6 explores children's feelings and relationships and suggestions are given as to the best ways to help children develop positive relationships with adults and other children.

Working in partnership with parents is a very important aspect of the role of the early years practitioner. Chapter 7 explores the differences between working in partnership with parents and parental involvement, and the reasons why, by default, these terms seem to have become interchangeable. There is also a section on working with and involving fathers in partnerships, and gives ideas on the interesting ways this can best be achieved.

For decades, play has been recognised as a conduit for learning, however, within society as a whole, the role of play is not always fully understood. The crucial role of play has been threatened by recent curriculum developments as we move from a process model of learning to one that is concerned with end products (outcomes). Chapter 8 aims to provide readers with firm evidence with which to argue the case for play to be an integral part of the early years curriculum. This chapter also looks at the role of computers in relation to children's learning and development.

Chapter 9 relates to management and leadership issues within the early years; an area that has become more important as parents become customers, looking for quality service for their children and more and more centres have multi-disciplinary teams. This chapter also looks at the role of the new Early Years Professional Status (EYPS).

Chapters 10 and 11 have been the subject of extensive updating in order to bring the book in line with the most recent developments. The Early Years Foundation Stage and the changes to the curriculum in Key Stage 1 have made all previous information redundant as they have dramatically changed the learning outcomes for children from birth to eight years of age. These chapters include the core curriculum and the curriculum subjects.

The early years of education are of crucial importance to children, so it is vital that all those who work with them have an understanding of early-childhood theory and practice. Of course, it is impossible to put all information into one book but, where applicable, the authors have included useful websites where additional information can be obtained.

1 Principles and values of effective practice

This chapter examines the underlying principles that underpin early years practice including the National Occupational Standards Principles and Values. It also looks in depth at other areas such as equality of opportunity, anti-bias practice, celebrating diversity and the reflective practitioner.

One of the most important aspects of the early child care and education worker is that they should be able to operate effectively within their job role. All underlying principles of practice should reflect the requirements of the Children Act 1989 as a minimum. In addition to this there are basic rights for the child as laid down in the United Nations Convention on the Rights of the Child 1989 and the Human Rights Act 1998. Effective practice must be an underlying principle for all workers, not just the managers of the setting. It is only by ensuring that practice is effective can you be certain that the children are receiving the best quality of care possible. This chapter will examine the underlying principles of good practice and the reflective practice, which is needed if the child care and education worker is going to deliver a high-quality service. It is important that all practitioners reflect on their practice so that they can assess how things have gone and whether there is room for improvement. Practitioners also need to be aware of the different sets of underlying principles and values that affect their day-to-day practice.

A good starting point is the Early Years Foundation Stage principles that are fundamental to the work of all early years practitioners. These are grouped under the following themes:

- *A Unique Child* – every child is a competent learner from birth who can be resilient, capable, confident and self-assured.
- *Positive Relationships* – children learn to be strong and independent from a base of loving and secure relationships with parents and/or a key person.
- *Enabling Environments* – the environment plays a key role in supporting and extending children's development and learning.
- *Learning and Development* – children develop and learn in different ways and at different rates and all areas of Learning and Development are equally important and inter-connected.

(Practice Guidance for the Early Years Foundation Stage 2007)

The Practice Guidance which accompanies these principles offers very clear ways in which these can be implemented by the practitioner.

There is also the Statement of Underlying Principles and Values, which are incorporated into the National Occupational Standards (NOS) in Children's Care, Learning and Development. These have been written and published by the Children's Workforce Development Council (CWDC). There are three principles and eight values; the principles are part of the NOS and the values are demonstrated by practitioners in their day-to-day work.

The *principles* are as follows:

1   *The welfare of the child and young person is paramount.*
    The Children Act 1989 makes it very clear that the welfare of the child is paramount. Therefore children must come first. Children must be listened to and their opinions respected and treated seriously. In managing children's challenging behaviour, the child care and education worker should emphasise the positive aspects of behaviour and physical punishment must never be used.

2   *Practitioners contribute to children's care, learning and development, and safeguarding, and this is reflected in every aspect of practice and service provision.*
    The first five years of a child's life is a period of rapid growth and learning. Therefore children need activities that will stimulate their social, physical, intellectual, linguistic, emotional and moral development. The early years curriculum should be linked with a child's stage of development that can be ascertained by careful observation of the child and discussions with the parents and family. From September 2008, the Early Years Foundation Stage will ensure that children's learning is not only appropriate for their stage of development but is stimulating and meets the needs of all children. The child's progress will be monitored, recorded and shared with the parents.

3   *Practitioners work with parents and families who are partners in the care, learning and development, and safeguarding of their children, and are the child's first and most enduring carers and educators.*
    Early years care and education workers must respect a child's parents and family and work with them in planning the care for their child. It is to be remembered that the parents and family will know more about the child than anyone else and, in addition to respecting opinions, etc. of parents and carers, they must also be given regular information about the child's development and progress. Child-care workers must comply with parent's wishes for their child and family, cultural and religious values must be respected.

The values are intended for practitioners in order to inform them of what they should be actively demonstrating in their work. As they stand, the values would appear to represent the practical implementation of a number of different pieces of legislation such as the UN Convention on the Rights of the Child and the Children Act 1989.

The *values* are as follows:

1   *The needs, rights and views of the child are at the centre of all practice and provision.*
    It is important that all child-care practitioners are familiar with the legislation that relates to the rights of the child. They also need to be aware of the needs of

individual children and how these can be met within the setting and by individual practitioners. Part of children's rights is to be treated with respect by adults actively seeking and listening to their views.

2 *Individuality, difference and diversity are valued and celebrated.*
   The UK is a pluralistic society and as such it is important that cultural diversity is appreciated and viewed positively, no one culture should be viewed as superior. Children should be helped to develop a sense of their own identity within their race, culture or social group. Children should be introduced to other cultures in a positive way and be encouraged to sample food, art, stories and music from different cultures.

3 *Equality of opportunity and anti-discriminatory practice are actively promoted.*
   The individuality of each child must be recognised and each child should be treated according to its needs. Each child should have the same opportunities to play, learn and develop according to their potential. Every child should be treated with equal concern, thus avoiding stereotyping and labelling on the basis of gender, religion, culture, race, class or ability. Early years care and education workers must not discriminate against any child or group/family. They must respect a child and their family's race, religion, gender, culture, class, language, ability, etc. Expressions of prejudice by staff members, children or adults must be challenged and the victims should be supported. Early years care and education workers must work within the requirements of the laws, i.e. Children Act, Race Relations Act, Human Rights Act and the policies of the setting.

4 *Children's health and well-being are actively promoted.*
   Children's health and well-being are presently at the forefront of much of the work being undertaken in early years settings and schools, particularly in relation to a healthy diet and exercise. Childhood obesity is becoming an important area of concern and practitioners must encourage healthy eating and exercise. Practitioners themselves should set an example by eating with the children and participating in outdoor activities.

5 *Children's personal and physical safety is safeguarded, whilst allowing for risk and challenge as appropriate to the capabilities of the child.*
   It is the responsibility of every child care and education worker to ensure that the setting is safe for the children and fellow workers. Daily work practices should ensure the prevention of accidents and the protection of health. Familiarity with emergency procedures and the recording of accidents must be adhered to. It is also part of the role of the child care and education worker to protect children from abuse.

6 *Self-esteem and resilience are recognised as essential to every child's development.*
   Lilian Katz (1995: 21) defines self-esteem as being 'best characterised as deep feelings of being loved, accepted and valued by significant others'. Katz goes on to say that self-esteem is derived from the feelings that are linked with the individual's evaluations of self. Children not only need to feel that they are loved and secure but also to know that they are respected and accepted by adults outside the family. Having a good level of self-esteem enables children to cope with criticism and negative comments about themselves. Practitioners are able to nurture a child's self-esteem by having realistic expectations of the individual child and encouraging children to reach these expectations.

Resilience is linked with self-esteem, as how well children can cope with change, stress, uncertainty, etc., depends on how secure they feel in themselves. Brooks and Goldstein (2002) offer ten ways in which parents, early years practitioners and teachers can help develop and strengthen a child's resilience (bear in mind that this list was originally written for parents, although the content is pertinent to all those working with children):

1   Be empathetic. See the world through your [the] kid's eyes.
2   Communicate with respect. Don't interrupt, or put them down. Answer their questions.
3   Be flexible. If we want kids to be flexible we must model that behaviour.
4   Give undivided attention. Kids feel loved when we spend one to one time with them.
5   Accept your kids for who they are. When kids feel appreciated for who they are, they'll feel more secure reaching out to others and learning how to solve problems.
6   Give kids a chance to contribute. When we enlist children in helping others, we communicate our faith in their ability to handle a variety of tasks and give them a sense of responsibility.
7   Treat mistakes as learning experiences. Kids whose parents over-react to mistakes tend to avoid taking risks and end up blaming others for their problems.
8   Stress your child's strengths. Their sense of accomplishment and pride gives them the confidence to persevere the next time they face a challenge.
9   Let your kids solve problems and make decisions. Instead of always telling children what to do encourage them to come up with solutions to problems.
10   Discipline to teach. Do not discipline in a way that intimidates or humiliates your child.

7   *Confidentiality and agreements about confidential information are respected as appropriate unless a child's protection and well-being are at stake.*
Policies in the setting relating to confidentiality must be adhered to. Information relating to a child and/or their parents or family must not be disclosed unless it is in the interests of child protection. In the latter circumstances any disclosure should only be to other professionals involved in the case. Confidentiality policies should also ensure that information about working colleagues is not disclosed without permission.

8   *Professional knowledge, skills and values are shared appropriately in order to enrich the experience of children more widely*
In order to ensure the best interests of the child, when appropriate, early child care and education workers should confer with colleagues and other professionals from outside the setting for support and advice. Respect for other professionals' opinions should be maintained and confidentiality observed at all times.

A number of the above principles and values overlap with other chapters in this book; however, there are other areas, such as the following, that are worth expanding upon.

Equality of opportunity is an expression that is used very easily but not always properly understood when it comes to integrating it into one's own practices. All early years settings are required to have an equal opportunities policy but in many cases it sits in a folder on a shelf and is never monitored in terms of how it is being implemented. Equality of opportunity means that each child is given the opportunity to develop to his/her maximum potential. However, each child's potential will be different, therefore each child should be treated according to their own individual needs. Some children's needs may be greater than others and may, therefore, require greater input from the staff caring for them. In this context, 'needs' does not refer to children with special needs but to any need that a child may have, i.e. the need for outdoor play if they live in a high-rise flat. When a child is accepted into a day-care establishment, the first thing that should happen is that their needs are assessed and a plan is drawn up to ensure ways of meeting those needs. All of the staff caring for the child should have a copy of the assessment and the plan for addressing the areas where there may be need. In this way the staff team will be working together in the best interests of the child. There should be frequent reviews of each child's needs and assessment carried out on a regular basis, as needs will change over time.

Anti-discriminatory/anti-bias practice is an area that directly affects the delivery of care that the child is getting. As human beings, we all have our own biases or areas that we do not feel comfortable about and therefore hold prejudices against. However, whatever these are they must not be allowed to affect the way in which care/education is delivered to the children. Staff must never voice or enact their prejudices when dealing with children, parents or other staff. Respect must be shown for all parents, even those you may regard as abysmal. Most parents strive to do their best for their children in spite of very difficult circumstances and some of these parents may not have the knowledge and skills to distinguish what is the right thing to do in a particular circumstance. The last thing that these parents need is a lack of understanding from the people who are caring for their children. Situations such as poverty, temporary housing, poor diet, obesity, etc., may not be the fault of the parents as they may be the victims of society. These circumstances require the early years practitioner to have empathy and understanding so that a relationship can be formed that is beneficial to the child and parent. In the same way, the early years practitioner must ensure that they are not behaving in a biased fashion towards children because of the parents' behaviour, after all the child is not able to control his/her parents. An integral part of maintaining an anti-bias early-years setting is taking action when incidents occur. Siraj-Blatchford and Clarke (2000) offer the following short-term action strategies that can happen immediately the incident takes place, such as:

- explaining to the person/child making the remarks that they are offensive and hurtful;
- explaining why the remarks are hurtful and trying to tease out the feelings of the person who made the remark and the receiver;
- explaining why the comment was wrong and correct any misconceptions that the remark may convey;

and long-term action strategies such as:

- working with parents whose children have made the remarks and ensuring they understand the setting's equal opportunities policy;
- creating an ethos in the setting that promotes and values diversity;

- developing topics and reading stories that raise issues of similarities and differences in language, gender and ethnicity;
- encouraging children to talk about their feelings.

In their book *Anti-bias Training Approaches in the Early Years* (1997), Gaine and van Keulen offer the following list of attitudes that early years practitioners need to develop.

Students/workers will show through their practice that they:

- respect and value the individuality of children, their families and other members of staff;
- are willing and able to learn from others;
- are willing and able to think critically about child development theory and are able to recognise the bias of theorists;
- are willing and able to reflect on their own ethnic and cultural experiences;
- are committed to implementing a culturally relevant anti-bias approach;
- are actively engaged in resisting discrimination;
- are able to empathise, i.e. to put themselves in other people's shoes and feel them pinching;
- feel confident about their own ethnic and cultural identity.

MacNaughton (1999) states that staff should be aware of the need to provide a wide range of opportunities for all children, regardless of social class, ability, gender or culture, and even challenging children to cross gender or cultural boundaries through play. Staff need to facilitate this play by encouraging children to join in with their peers and supporting the interactions without controlling them. With this advice, MacNaughton is able, very succinctly, to offer an example of good practice that covers both equal opportunities and anti-bias practice. In her book *Combating Discrimination* (2001), Babette Brown offers ways in which early years practitioners are able to challenge children's hurtful remarks to other children through the use of Persona Dolls. Persona Dolls are a tool that can be used with children in order to help them empathise with a child or what is happening to a child. Early years practitioners use the dolls as vehicles to facilitate powerful storytelling sessions. Children are able to talk about how the doll was feeling when a hurtful remark was made about them, such as when being called names or being bullied. The children are able to empathise with the feelings of the doll and offer solutions for helping the doll feel better and regain their self-esteem. Thus Persona Dolls empower children.

Following on from equal opportunities and ant-bias working it would seem logical to move on to the second 'value', and look at the part that relates to *celebrating diversity*. This area concerns children developing a feeling of worth and self-esteem within the setting regardless of their cultural background. This can be achieved by the staff presenting a variety of cultures in such a way that they are viewed by the children and adults as positive images that are valued and integrated into the ethos of the setting. However, Siraj-Blatchford and Clarke (2000) do offer a warning about well-meaning but poorly informed practice in this area. They point out that token measures, such as multilingual posters, black dolls, puzzles and books with positive gender role models are rarely the focus of attention. Misplaced are the energies of staff who provide a thematic approach such as 'Greek Week' or 'Chinese

New Year' without recognising that diversity should be reflected across the curriculum. If a setting is going to celebrate festivals, then these should be part of an overall multi-faith/multicultural curriculum programme. It is debatable as to what children learn about the real story of Easter from bunnies, chicks and chocolate eggs. In fact, these ideas probably stem from the traditions of the Christian Church, when all eggs were used up on Shrove Tuesday (hence the pancakes) to enable the fasting period required through Lent, and eggs came back into circulation on Easter Sunday. However, I am unable to find any reference to how bunnies came into the picture! Celebrating festivals with children can be fun and may help them to learn something about other cultures, but as Brown (2001) points out, they are unlikely to have much effect upon their attitudes towards adults and children from these cultures. There is a need to examine why we celebrate particular festivals and a need to ensure the cooperation of the parents as they may not wish the early years establishment to celebrate something that is usually confined to their own community. Bisson (1997) offers the following goals for celebrating festivals:

- to promote connections among children, families and practitioners;
- to learn about important events in the lives of all children and families;
- to support and validate the experiences of children, their families and practitioners;
- to reinforce connection to cultural roots;
- to celebrate both similarities and differences in children's lives;
- to stretch children's awareness and empathy.

(from Bisson 1997: 36–7)

Confidentiality is an integral part of the work of the early years practitioner. The *Oxford English Dictionary* offers the following definitions of confidential:

1 spoken or written in confidence;
2 entrusted with secrets.

Confidentiality therefore means being entrusted with information that the discloser does not want to be passed on to anyone else.

Because of the nature of the work, the early years practitioner will often find themselves in a position whereby a parent/family member/carer is disclosing information that needs to be kept confidential. Such disclosure may be given in order for the parent/family member/carer to ensure that those caring for the child are aware that there are particular circumstances that may affect the child's behaviour or emotions. The early years practitioner must then decide whether the disclosure is of such a level of seriousness that it needs to be passed on to a more senior member of staff. The benchmark for any judgement in this area must be the welfare of the child. Certain information may need to be passed on in order to protect the child. Once the practitioner has passed on the information they have broken confidentiality with the person who disclosed the information. This is a common dilemma for many early years practitioners.

Most early years settings have a policy relating to confidentiality and this must be adhered to at all times. In the first instance, when the original disclosure is being made, if the practitioner judges that it is information that may have serious consequences, they should try to persuade the discloser to talk to a senior member of staff. The practitioner may also, gently but firmly, explain to the discloser that they, the practitioner, will have to pass the information to a senior member of staff as this is the policy of the setting. This decision may be met with hostility from the discloser who may need to be reminded that the child's welfare is paramount.

In addition to information relating to children, the practitioner may also have members of staff who may disclose confidential information to them. Once again, there may be information that could affect the children in the care of the discloser and the practitioner must make a decision as to whether they should pass this on. For example: what do you do if a fellow worker reveals to you that they have a drug addiction problem, or that they have forged cheques or that they are having an affair with a parent of one of the children? Once again, the welfare of the child/children is paramount and it is always best if you can persuade the discloser to speak to a senior member of staff themselves. If they are not amenable to this, then you may have to explain to them that you will have to reveal the information to a senior member of staff as it could affect the welfare of the children in the setting.

In addition to verbal disclosures of information, there are other ways in which practitioners can breach confidentiality. Child studies/observations, which may be placed in portfolios or dissertations, require the permission of the child's parents before they can be used outside the setting. It is also necessary to change the child's name and/or only use a first name or initial for the child. Photographs in such studies are not a good idea (even with a parent's permission to use them) as they immediately identify the child/children to the reader of the study/observation who may know the child. Particular care must be taken that a dissertation or child study ensures that the identity of the child is totally anonymous.

Another situation in which practitioners may break confidentiality is when talking about a child/family to another member of staff in a public place, such as on a bus or train, or in a bar. You never know when someone nearby is listening or is able to overhear the conversation, and may know the child or people you are talking about. You also never know whether the person next to you may be related to the child/family, or is a neighbour. It is not professional behaviour to discuss such matters in a place where you can be overheard. Discussing the matter in the first place may, in itself, be a breach of confidentiality. In more recent years it has become a familiar sight to see people on trains or in other out-of-office locations working on laptop computers. There seems to be a belief that no one else is able to read the screen of the laptop, however, sitting behind the operator puts someone in a perfect position to read what is on the screen. It is therefore not a wise move to catch up on confidential documentation whilst working outside of the office. Many people also find it easy to read handwriting from a position upside-down to them. A breach in confidentiality, however it happened and whether it was intentional or accidental, is a serious lapse of professionalism.

The reflective practitioner

Whilst this is number nine on the list of underlying values, it is also an integral part of this chapter. One of the basic tenets of effective practice is the ability to reflect on one's own practice. Reflection is becoming a core skill in the profession of early years care and education. Reflection on one's practice is one of the important differences between the professional child-care practitioner and the non-professional 'mums army' worker. Professionals claim to contribute to social well-being, put the clients' needs before their own and hold themselves accountable to standards of competence and morality. Professionals also claim a body of knowledge that shapes the profession, in early years care and education this has been legitimised by the Early Years Foundation Stage and the National Framework of Qualifications that offer the underpinning knowledge for the profession. Practitioners are frequently embroiled in conflicts of values, goals, purposes, interests, etc. For example, teachers are faced with pressures for increased efficiency whilst at the same time being expected to work within ever-decreasing budgets. Such dilemmas, which are outside the control of the teachers, make them disturbed, as they cannot account for the processes they have come to see as central to their professional competence.

The term 'Reflective Practitioner' was first coined by Donald Schön (1983) as a way for the professional to be able to resolve problems that did not just rely upon their professional knowledge. Schön refers to work by Edgar Schein that states that there is a gap between the application of knowledge, what he refers to as being 'convergent', and practice, which he refers to as 'divergent'. Therefore professionals in the areas of social work, teaching, nursing, etc., need divergent thinking skills in order to resolve problems, as resolution cannot be solved by theory alone. Professionals have to analyse particular circumstances in order to assess how best to respond to them, what may be referred to as 'thinking on your feet' or 'keeping your wits about you'.

Schön maintains that a professional practitioner is a specialist who encounters certain types of situations over and over again, hence the word 'case' is used by them to describe units that go together to make up practice. Practitioners may reflect on practice whilst they are in the midst of it, what Schön calls 'reflection-in-action'. Reflection-in-action is central to the practitioner coping with 'divergent' situations. This process of reflecting and analysing particular circumstances is what is referred to as reflective practice.

Megarry (2000) gives the following very good simple example of how using theory alone to analyse a problem can fail to take in all the variables and thus come to the wrong conclusions.

> A child consistently behaves badly when he comes to the childcare setting. There has recently been a new baby in the family and his mother tells you that she does not have time to give the child breakfast before he comes to the childcare setting. Using the knowledge of theory would tell you that children need a balanced breakfast before they start the day. Based on this theoretical knowledge the child's behaviour must be due to the fact that he is nutritionally deficient – hungry. So if you give the child breakfast his behaviour will improve.

Reflection-in-action would not draw this conclusion as it would enable the early years practitioner to take a holistic approach in order to consider all the variables, i.e. new baby, harassed mother, lack of attention to older child, etc. Schön points out that in the real world problems do not present themselves as givens. They must be constructed from the materials of problematic situations that are puzzling, troubling and uncertain, what Schön refers to as problem-setting. Problem-setting is a process in which we select what we will treat as the 'things' of the situation, set the boundaries of our attention to it and impose upon it a coherence that allows us to say what is wrong and in what directions the situation needs to be changed. In short, we define the problem, the end and the means to the end.

According to Schön, to be an effective reflective practitioner it is necessary to be able to recognise:

* knowing-in-action;
* reflecting-in-action;
* reflecting-in-practice.

Knowing-in-action

This is the kind of knowing that is inherent in intelligent action; the know-how is in the action. Skilful action often involves knowing more than we can say. Schön (1991: 21) gives the following properties of knowing:

* There are actions, recognitions, and judgements, which we know how to carry out spontaneously; we do not have to think about them prior to or during their performance.
* We are often unaware of having learned to do these things; we simply find ourselves doing them.
* In some cases, we were once aware of the understandings, which were subsequently internalised in our feeling for the stuff of action. In other cases, we may never have been aware of them. In both cases, however, we are usually unable to describe the knowing which our action reveals.

Reflecting-in-action

Much of reflecting-in-action hinges on surprise. This is the 'thinking on your feet', 'keeping your wits about you' situation. It shows that we can think about something whilst we are doing it. (This seems to describe a very familiar situation for early years practitioners who are good at this type of thinking.)

Reflecting-on-action

Schön (1991) does point out that in some situations reflecting-in-action may be not only difficult but it may be dangerous to stop and think. He gives as examples someone in the midst of traffic, or in the firing line or on a playing field. It is not difficult to think of situations when the early years practitioner may find it difficult, such as children fighting or children in a dangerous situation. These are not appropriate times to undertake reflection of what you might or might not do, as at this point the reflection would interfere with the action. In order to overcome these situations, Schön puts forward the idea of 'reflecting-on-action', which has the benefits of taking place after the event and reflecting on the action that was taken at the time. Reflecting-on-action has become more relevant to the early years field as many situations require immediate action and there is only time for reflection after the event.

Reflecting-in-practice

This involves reflecting on and questioning the above categories, on the way in which we acted and responded to different situations and on our own role in the workplace.

A practitioner's reflection can serve as a corrective to over-learning. Through reflection, the practitioner can surface and criticise tacit understandings that have grown up around repetitive experiences of a specialised practice and can make new sense of the situations of uncertainty or uniqueness that he may allow himself to experience. The practitioner needs to be open to their own practice and ready to see ways in which they can learn to improve on both knowing-in-action and reflecting-in-action.

Jill Rodd (1994) uses the term 'action research' to refer to a way of thinking that uses reflection and enquiry as a way of understanding the conditions that support or inhibit change. This is very different from Schön's thesis as it is not 'thinking on your feet' but a six-point plan carried out as a team activity over a period of time. However, there does seem to be a valid place for both the Rodd and Schön theses within the early years care and education settings. Rodd points out that in action research the problem needs to be meaningful for the team and the team leader, it must be manageable within a realistic time frame and appropriate for the research skills of the people involved. There also needs to be a healthy attitude within the team to problem solving and risk taking.

Rodd (1994: 144–5, citing Wadsworth 1984; Kemmis and McTaggert 1988) gives the following seven steps in the action-research process cycle:

1   Identifying the problems of mutual concern – the present problems are brought into focus through the processes of observation and reflection by all members of the team.
2   Analysing problems and determining possible contributing factors – the ability to diagnose the determinants of a problem is required. The existing situation is monitored using recorded uncensored and uninterpreted observations from the members of the team.
3   Forming tentative working hypotheses or guesses to explain these factors – at this point, questionable assumptions are eliminated. Decisions are made about the form and method of the interpretation of the data which are to be collected.
4   Collecting and interpreting data from observations, interviews and relevant documents to clarify these hypotheses and to develop action hypotheses – accurate details of events need to be recorded in order to avoid erroneous or superficial influences.
5   Formulating plans for action and carrying them out – plans are experimental, prospective and forward looking and may involve the acquisition of new skills or procedures in order to implement the plans.
6   Evaluating the results of the action – the processes of observation and reflection are used to critically assess the effects of the informed action and to make sense of the processes and issues that unfolded during the implementation phase. Collaborative reflection provides an opportunity to reconstruct meaning out of the situation and establishes a basis for a revised plan.
7   Introducing a revised cycle from step 1 to step 6.

In addition to the above, there are the stages that go towards promoting reflection in general, as cited in Megarry (2000). These are outlined below.

Stage 1 Returning to experience

This is where the experience is revisited by recollecting what has taken place and replaying the experience in the mind's eye, to observe the event as it happened and to notice exactly what occurred and one's reaction to it in all its elements.

This description provides the data for subsequent processes and can help to ensure that our reflections are on the basis of the actual events as we experienced them at the time rather than in terms of what we wished had happened.

The description should as far as possible:

- be clear of any judgements;
- observe the feelings evoked during the experience, both positive and negative.

Stage 2 Attending to feelings experienced

Emotions can be a signification source of learning, as they can form barriers to learning that need to be recognised and removed before the learning process can proceed.

Stage 3 Re-evaluating the experience

Elements of the whole process are:

- association – relating of new data to that which is already known;
- integration – seeking relationships among the data;
- validation – determining the authenticity of the ideas and feelings that have resulted;
- appropriation – making knowledge one's own.

The outcomes of reflection may include:

- a new way of doing something;
- the clarification of an issue;
- the development of a skill;
- the resolution of a problem.

The changes and benefits of reflection may be small or large but unless they are linked to action they are worthless. Actions may not necessarily be observed or recognised by others but what is important is that the learner makes a commitment to action on the basis of their learning.

Post-structuralist thinkers such as Foucault offer another way of reflection that is related to the reflector being critical of themselves. This is called 'critical reflection' and involves the practitioner looking back and not only reflecting on what has happened but also questioning their own actions. MacNaughton (2005: 5) points out that, in using this methodology, 'The critical reflector risks fragmenting her *know-*

ings of what she does and who she "*is*". She risks the peril of uncertainty.' By undertaking this critical reflection the practitioner is able to question themselves about the ways in which power can both enable and marginalise the service users and the workers. Critical reflection has no particular methodology and the practitioner has to develop their own ways for producing questions, however, MacNaughton offers a possible list of questions:

- Think of an interaction, event or episode you experienced.
- Describe what happened – this might include the context, space, time people, conversations, nonverbal interactions, etc. It is important to specify what you did in the situation.
- How did you feel?
- How did you come to be in this situation?
- What kind of choices did you make to be in this situation?
- Why did you choose to act or approach the situation in this way?
- What do you think this might mean for you, others and the context?
- What if you were to explain this situation to someone else (colleague, parent, child, manager, bus driver etc.)? What would you say? How would you say it?
- Why did you choose these ways? What might that mean for you, them, others, and the context? – Use many perspectives and theories, and consider the ways some perspectives and choices can privilege, silence and marginalise social and cultural groups.
- Who is it about? What is it for?
- Share these reflections with others.
- Develop some possibilities for social action!

(MacNaughton 2005: 54)

Finally, although leadership is discussed in more detail in Chapter 9 of this book, it is useful to briefly look at the relationship between reflective practice and leadership. The ability to reflect on one's own practice or to promote action research within a team is one of the qualifications for leadership as put forward by Hodgkinson (1991, cited in Rodd 1994: 4), who states that leadership is:

- an art rather than a science;
- focused on policy rather than execution;
- concerned with values rather than facts;
- to do with generalism rather than specialism;
- the use of broad strategies rather than specific tactics;
- concerned with philosophy rather than action;
- reflective rather than active;
- concerned with human as opposed to material resources;
- focused on deliberation rather than detail.

Reflect upon …

1   Brooks and Goldstein (2002) offer ten ways in which early years practitioners can help to develop and strengthen children's resilience. Write a recent example of an occasion when you had to exhibit empathy by seeing a situation through the eyes of a child.

2   Describe three ways in which your setting reflects diversity across the curriculum.

3   Re-read the short 'case study' from Megarry (2000) that appears earlier in this chapter and illustrates reflection-in-action. Devise a case study of your own that illustrates reflection-in-action and that you could use with staff in order to explain the way in which they can implement this methodology in their daily work.

References

Bisson, Julie (1997) *Celebrate: An Anti-bias Guide to Enjoying Holidays*, St Paul, MN: Redleaf Press.

Brooks, R. and Goldstein, S. (2002) *Raising Resilient Children*, New York: McGraw-Hill.

Brown, Babette (2001) *Combating Discrimination: Persona Dolls in Action*, Stoke on Trent: Trentham Books.

Boud, D., Keogh, R. and Walker, D. (1985) *Promoting Reflection in Learning: Reflection: Turning Experience into Learning*, London: Croom Helm.

Children's Workforce Development Council (2005) *Draft Principles and Values Statement. Principles and Values Underpinning all Induction Standards*, available online: http://cwd-council.org.uk/ resources/inductionstandards.asp.

Council for Awards in Children's Care and Education (CACHE) (1998) *Candidate Handbook NVQ in Early Years Care and Education*, Herts: CACHE.

Derman-Sparks, Louise (1989) *Anti-Bias Curriculum. Tools for Empowering Young Children*, Washington, DC: National Association for the Education of Young Children.

DfES (2007) *Practice Guidance for the Early Years Foundation Stage*, Nottingham: DfES Publications.

Gaine, Brenda and Van Keulen, Anke (1997) *Anti-Bias Training Approaches in the Early Years: A Guide for Trainers*, Utrecht and London: Agency MUTANT/EYTARN.

Hodgkinson, C. (1991) *Educational Leadership. The Moral Art*, Albany, NY: State University of New York Press (cited in Rodd 1994).

Katz, L. (1995) 'The distinction between self-esteem and narcissism: implications for practice', in Katz, L., *Talks with Teachers of Young Children. A Collection*, New York: Ablex Publishing.

MacNaughton, G. (1999) cited in Siraj-Blatchford and Clarke 2000 p. 80.

MacNaughton, G. (2005) *Doing Foucault in Early Childhood Studies*, Abingdon: Routledge.

Megarry, Bridget (2000) 'Reflection' and the 'Reflective practitioner', unpublished lecture notes, OMNA Early Years Training.

Rodd, Jillian (1994) *Leadership in Early Childhood. The Pathway to Professionalism*, Buckingham: Open University Press.

Schön, Donald (1991) *The Reflective Practitioner. How Professionals Think in Action*, Aldershot: Ashgate Publishing.

Siraj-Blatchford, Iram and Clarke, Priscilla (2000) *Supporting Identity, Diversity and Language in the Early Years*, Buckingham: Open University Press.

2   Children's rights

This chapter debates the issues of Children's Rights and Responsibilities. It is referenced to the various relevant UK Acts and the UN Convention on the Rights of the Child on which there is a full debate and explanation of some of the relevant Articles of the Convention.

The idea that children have rights is a fairly new phenomenon in the UK and probably first appeared in 1924 when the League of Nations drafted the first Declaration of the Rights of the Child. However, it was not until 65 years later that we saw the rights of the child incorporated, in part, into UK law in the form of the Children Act 1989. Enabling children to exercise their rights empowers them and enables them to participate in controlling their lives. However, Seraga (1998: 160) states that '"rights" like "needs" is a highly contested concept particularly when applied to children'. Seraga goes on to say that children depend on the adults who care for them to assert their rights for them and that rights are limited by the child's vulnerability and dependency. Gerison Lansdown (1996) points out that adults are confused about the issue of children's rights for a number of reasons: it is thought that children cannot have rights until they are capable of exercising responsibility; children are not competent to participate; rights for children threaten the stability of family life; the imposition of rights takes away children's opportunities for childhood. Lansdown would argue that the UK has a long way to go in order to meet the requirements of the Convention on the Rights of the Child. There is also the debate about how far such rights should be the child's entitlement and whether a child's rights should be considered at the expense of the rights of the adults. What cannot be disputed is that the Children Act 1989 clearly states that the 'Welfare of the child is paramount'. In the world of 'good practice' in child care and education, the rights of the child should be considered when making decisions about a child, whether this is for social, developmental or other reasons.

As Phillipe Aries (1960) has pointed out, childhood has always been constructed by society rather than being defined by nature. There is no natural state defined as childhood. In modern sociological terms it is what Seraga describes as a social construct.

This chapter will look at specific situations and practical issues that may impinge upon children's rights, such as domestic violence, child abuse and family breakdown.

The United Nations Convention on the Rights of the Child 1989

As previously stated, the first Declaration the Rights of the Child was instigated in 1924 by Eglantyne Jebb, British founder of Save the Children. This version was superseded by the 1959 United Nations Declaration on the Rights of the Child. The Convention on the Rights of the Child was adopted by the United Nations General Assembly in 1989 and came into force as part of international law in 1990. There are 191 countries that have ratified the Convention (the two countries that have not are the United States and Somalia), and the UK ratified it in December 1991. Once a country has ratified the Convention it is obliged to incorporate into its own laws the articles within the Convention. Muscot (1999) points out that ratification creates an opportunity for public scrutiny of government performance. The United Nations has a Children's Rights Committee, which is responsible for monitoring how countries are complying with the convention. Each country that has ratified the Convention must produce a report after two years, and then every five years, which is presented to the UN Children's Rights Committee. The Convention states the need for countries to work together cooperatively in order to implement the articles to the maximum, with richer countries helping poorer countries. There are 45 articles in the Convention, which cover many different areas of children's rights; the following are a few examples:

- Article 1 defines a child as every human being under 18 years of age;
- Article 2 concerns discrimination;
- Article 3 concerns best interests of the child;
- Article 8 concerns preservation of identity;
- Article 9 concerns separation from parents;
- Article 12 concerns the child's opinions;
- Article 14 concerns freedom of thought, conscience and religion;
- Article 18 concerns parental responsibilities;
- Article 19 concerns protection from abuse;
- Article 23 concerns disabled children;
- Article 24 concerns health and health services;
- Article 32 concerns child labour;
- Article 34 concerns sexual exploitation;
- Article 38 concerns armed conflicts;
- Article 40 concerns administration of juvenile justice.[1]

In some countries the implementation of the Convention has resulted in the appointment of a Children's Commissioner or Children's Ombudsman to oversee the rights of children. At about the same time as the 1989 Convention, the UK had amalgamated most of its laws relating to children into one comprehensive Children Act. This Act went a long way towards incorporating a number of the articles of the Convention, however, there are some areas that remain unrecognised or neglected. For example, Article 31 deals with the child's right to play, leisure and recreation, yet this seems to be in conflict with government policies that advocate selling local playing fields for housing and retail development. Newell (1991) points out that a major obstacle to the implementation of the Convention in the UK is the lack of monitoring regarding the state of the UK's children. This results in there being a lack of information to enable researchers to draw conclusions on how well or how badly the Convention is being implemented. Whilst the UK would appear to be meeting many of the articles contained in the Convention, there are still issues concerning the numbers of children living in poverty and the way children can be excluded from school with no opportunity to defend themselves or express their views. In 1992 the UK set up the Children's Rights Development Unit (CRDU) to promote the implementation of the UN Convention, funded by major charitable trusts and child welfare organisations. In 1994, the government submitted its first report to the UN Committee citing the Children Act 1989 as the evidence of its compliance. Lansdown and Newell (1994: xiii) point out that the CRDU described the report as complacent and stated, 'whether for reasons of poverty, ethnicity, disability, sexuality, immigration status or geography, many children are denied fundamental rights in the Convention'.

Whilst the articles of the Convention go a long way towards stating what all the world's countries need to do in order to ensure a better lifestyle for their children, there is a necessity to monitor whether this is happening in reality. Like many other documents of this type there are anomalies, not least in Article 38 that deals with the rights of children in situations of armed conflict. Whilst the Convention defines the age covered by 'childhood' as 0–18 years, in Article 38 it refers to not recruiting children under the age of 15 years into the armed forces. In recent years we have seen a number of armed conflicts in which children, mostly boys, are recruited as fighters and taught to use arms. In the UK you can join the Armed Forces at the age of 16 and are legally able to carry arms at the age of 17. It is surprising that in this article the Convention did not recommend the age of 18 as the recruitment age, in line with the recommendations in all the other articles. There is a significant difference between a child's (as defined by Article 1) development at age 15 and at age 18, which does not seem to have been acknowledged.

The articles could offer a set of underpinning values for those who work with children all over the world. In order to bring the articles into context with the UK situation, wherever possible and appropriate the relevant article will be quoted in full at the beginning of each section heading in the chapter.

The Children Act 1989

The Children Act 1989 was a major piece of legislation that not only brought together existing pieces of legislation but also formulated them into a cohesive whole. The Act ensured that the welfare of the child was paramount and allowed children's opinions to be taken into account. Franklin (1995) sees the Children Act as marking a shift in defining children, whereby they moved from being objects of concern to people with rights, thus acknowledging that children have the ability to make decisions. When a child is very young they are assigned an independent guardian *ad litem* who acts as an advocate for the child and is responsible for ensuring that the welfare of the child comes first. Adults were not left out of the Act, and some groups of adults who, in the past, had no laws to protect their interests in the child, i.e. grandparents, fathers who were not married to the mother, other family relatives who are part of the child's primary-care network, are now able to apply for residency orders, etc., in order to legitimise their positions.

The quality of children's care was taken into consideration by the Act as it brought in a registration and inspection regime for all settings where children were looked after, apart from in their own homes (which made nannies exempt from registration). Local Social Services Departments were made responsible for registering and inspecting care settings, e.g. childminders and family centres; and the Office for Standards in Education (OFSTED) was responsible for inspecting educational establishments. (From 2001 OFSTED became responsible for all inspection and registration in all settings [Part X Registrations].)

On paper, the Children Act gave hope that at last children's rights would be high on the agenda, however, in practice that was not necessarily the case. One of the first disappointments was the issue of a childminder smacking a child in her care. The local authority, adhering to the Guidelines to the Children Act, which said that childminders must not use physical punishment on children in their care, removed the childminder's registration. The childminder then took the local authority to court for removing her registration, which in effect removed her livelihood. The childminder's lawyers argued that the parents had given their permission for the childminder to smack their child. The judge ruled that the Guidelines were not part of the Act and therefore only what was written in the Act was legally binding. Thus the Act did not say that physical punishment could not be used on children and therefore the Local Authority were obliged to reinstate the childminder's registration.

Seraga (1998) argues that the Children Act was more concerned in giving rights to parents than with the rights of children, citing the fact that there are no procedures in the Act to enable the child to complain about their parents or other maltreatment they may receive from the system.

Human Rights Act 1998

Although this Act was passed in 1998 it was not implemented until 2 October 2000. Prior to this Act litigants had to apply to the European Court of Human Rights in Strasbourg. In implementing the Human Rights Act 1998, judges and lawyers will need to refer to the precedents that have come from the European Court of Human Rights as a guide to their case law and decision making. The Human Rights Act has taken as its model Articles 2–12 and 14 of the European Court of Human Rights and Articles 1–3 of the First Protocol. It is too soon to know whether the Human Rights Act will be beneficial to the rights of children, although it has been reported that children who have been excluded from school may be able to bring a case under the heading of a 'right to education' (First Protocol Article 2).

Rights and responsibilities

As previously mentioned, there is a great deal of confusion among early years academics, practitioners and the general public as to whether children should have rights without also having responsibilities. Lansdown (1996: 7) puts forward the following arguments that are commonly used to support the idea that children should not have rights:

1   Children cannot have rights until they are capable of exercising responsibility
2   Children are not competent to participate in decision making

3   Rights for children threaten the stability and harmony of family life
4   The imposition of rights takes away children's opportunities for childhood.

These four arguments do not really stand up as reasons why a child cannot be listened to, involved in decision making and be respected. Mayall (2002: 2) points out that:

> It is not that we should base the arguments for children's rights on the fact that they carry responsibility; it is that recognition of their responsibilities may help raise their social status, and thence provide an arena for serious consideration of their rights.

Lancaster (2006: 62) highlights the importance of listening to young children and advocates this as a 'rights-based approach in relating to children'. By giving children the opportunity to take part in matters that affect their lives we are not only respecting them but giving them the opportunity to indicate or speak about their own feelings. Dahlberg and Moss (2005: 30) believe that rights should be put into 'perspective, treating them more as a tool than an icon. Rights have a tactical value within the political arena, increasing the agency of those with less power and providing a modicum of protection against oppression'.

In the final months of 2007 there were two important government reviews relating to children. The Labour Party produced the *Children's Plan – Building Brighter Futures* in December and the Conservative Party produced its *Childhood Review* in September. In neither of these documents are there any references to children's rights or the importance of listening to children and consulting with children. Both reports are based upon the well-being of children. It would appear that the impetus behind both of these reports was the UNICEF Children Review of Rich Countries 2007, in which the United Kingdom came at the bottom of the list. Whilst it is to be welcomed that both political parties are interested in improving conditions for children and their families, at the same time it would appear that the notion of children's rights has either not reached them or is not viewed as an important subject. Alternatively, it is possible that, as the UK is signed up to the UN Convention on the Rights of the Child, this area is no longer a subject requiring political discussion.

Maria Montessori is one of the people who believed that children were very capable of being responsible and taking on responsibility from a very early age. As Mooney (2000) points out, 'Montessori thought teachers should: give children responsibility for keeping the community space clean and orderly; provide large blocks of time for free work and play and allow children to structure their own time' (p. 29). Montessori believed that having these types of responsibility helped children to become more competent. Thus in the Montessori nursery children are encouraged to choose what they want to play with, take it from the shelf, play with it and then when they are finished put it back on the shelf in the same place where they found it. This does not just apply to older children as children in the toddler room are also able and expected by the staff to do this on a daily basis.

In order to help adults to understand more about the types of responsibility children have, UNICEF's website has a leaflet entitled *Children's Rights and Responsibilities*. Some examples of these are as follows:

If children have a right to be protected from conflict, cruelty, exploitation and neglect, then they also have a responsibility not to bully or harm each other.

If children have a right to a clean environment, then they also have a responsibility to do what they can to look after the environment.

If children have the right to be educated, then they have the obligation to learn as much as their capabilities allow and, where possible, share their knowledge and experience with others.

There is also another leaflet produced by Childline, Gauteng, South Africa, which is written to inform children of their rights and responsibilities. It has simple illustrations, as can be seen in the examples in Figure 2.1.

From all the above evidence it is true to say that children can be made aware of their rights and responsibilities from an early age and this can be done in such a way that it is fun, non-threatening, part of everyday routines and helps children become more competent and resilient.

Child protection

> **Article 19 Protection from abuse and neglect**
>
> States Parties shall take appropriate legislative, administrative, social and educational measures to protect the child from all forms of physical or mental violence, injury or abuse, neglect or negligent treatment, mal-treatment or exploitation, including sexual abuse, while in the care of parent(s), legal guardian(s) or any other person who has the care of the child.
>
> Such protective measures should, as appropriate, include effective procedures for the establishment of social programmes to provide necessary support for the child and for those who have the care of the child, as well as for other forms of prevention and for identification, reporting, referral, investigation, treatment and follow-up of instances of child maltreatment described heretofore, and, as appropriate, for judicial involvement.
>
> Articles 33, 34, 35 and 36 deal with protecting children from drug abuse, sexual exploitation, selling and trafficking of children and other forms of exploitation.

Protecting children from abuse and neglect is a major responsibility for all societies. Child abuse is not a new phenomenon in our society; you only have to read the novels of Dickens to find out what was happening in the nineteenth century. What is new is society's decision to take the maltreatment of children seriously and to legislate in order to protect children. In addition to this, the improvement in media communications has placed serious incidents of child abuse in the public domain, heightening people's awareness and to a certain extent their anxiety relating to their own children's protection. In recent years, a new global form of child abuse has appeared via the Internet where children are depicted in pornography. This is proving much more difficult to stop as it involves numerous people across a large number of countries.

The Children Act clearly states that local authorities have a clear duty to protect children who are at 'risk of harm' under the category of 'children in need'. The decision as to whether a child is 'at risk' and the course of action that should be taken to protect that child is a matter of complex professional judgement. However,

**Children have the
right to be taken
seriously**

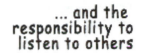

**... and the
responsibility to
listen to others**

**Children have the
right to quality
medical care**

**... and the
responsibility to
take care of
themselves**

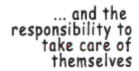

**Children have the
right to a good
education**

**... and the
responsibility to
study and respect
their teachers**

Figure 2.1 Children's rights and responsibilities (source: taken from Childline South Africa
website (2008) www.childlinesa.org.za).

there have been a number of cases that have been the subject of government enquiries, which have concluded that wrong or inappropriate judgements had been made, for example, the Maria Colwell case, the Kimberley Carlile case and the Cleveland case.

The Department of Health has produced definitions of child abuse and neglect, although individual local authorities are allowed to interpret these in order to fit in with their own child-protection policies. The categories of abuse used by the Department of Health and by local authorities, however, remain the same: physical abuse; sexual abuse; emotional abuse; neglect; and grave concern. Article 19 of the Convention does go further than the Children Act as it states that children must be protected from 'all forms of physical and mental violence'. It is interesting to note that the Department of Health definitions do not include other forms of abuse such as bullying and psychological abuse.

Emotional abuse is defined in the Department of Health document *Working Together* (1991) as 'the actual or likely adverse effects on the emotional development and behaviour of a child caused by persistent or severe emotional ill treatment or rejection. All abuse involves some emotional ill-treatment'. O'Hagan (1993) discusses the difficulties in defining emotional abuse and proving that it has occurred, because the evidence must show the lack of awareness, understanding and intentionality on the part of the carers to be abusive. Often, emotional abusers are not aware that what they are doing is a form of abuse. Behaviour such as ignoring the child, not interacting with the child verbally or non-verbally, being over-critical of the child, never giving praise for the child's accomplishments and using other members of the family as a threat, for example, 'wait until your father gets home', as a form of control. Whilst any one of the above list may have been used by a carer or within the family in a 'one-off' situation, it is when it becomes the normal day-to-day treatment of the child that it would constitute abuse. O'Hagan states that emotional abuse is not perceived as creating a crisis in the same way that physical or sexual abuse does and is therefore given less attention by those who have a role in child protection.

Bullying is a form of emotional/psychological abuse and in recent years employees' organisations, teachers and others have become far more aware of the damage caused by bullying. Children are open to bullying by other children (older or peer group), other family members and those who care for them. The child who is being bullied loses their self-esteem as they feel the shame of being called names or of always being the victim and unable to fight back. Eventually they may reach a point of believing that the names they are being called are a true description of themselves and this can add to their suffering and feelings of humiliation and shame. Bullies often pick on the most vulnerable children, such as those with disabilities, those who are different in some way in looks (e.g. wear glasses), have a different skin colour or those who are visibly poor or needy. Many schools now have anti-bullying policies but there is still an expectation that bullying is a school phenomenon and could not happen in the playgroup or nursery. As most early years workers know, children will often copy behaviour they have learnt from their parents, primary carer or older siblings and if this was of a bullying nature then it is likely that the child will also take on a bullying role. If this happens it is important that the child-care worker is aware of the situation and is able to deal with it in a positive way. To ignore bullying behaviour is to condone it and in doing this the welfare of the child who is being bullied is not being taken into consideration.

In November 1993 the Commission on Children and Violence was set up in the UK by the Gulbenkian Foundation. The aims of the Commission were to:

i   provide as accurate a picture as possible of the level of all kinds of violence to and by children and young people.
ii propose ways of challenging social and legal endorsement of any form of inter-personal violence and policies and practices which tend to increase violence involving children and young people.

The Commission defined violence as 'behaviour by people against people liable to cause physical or psychological harm'.

Children themselves are not naturally violent, it is behaviour that is learnt from parents, carers, older siblings, etc., or exposure to inappropriate media via videos and television. The Commission's report, *Children and Violence* 1995, states that the behaviour of children who themselves are violent is inextricably linked to having themselves been the victims of violence. The report not only explores children as victims of violence but children as violators. There is no doubt that it is a good idea to begin working towards a non-violent society from the moment children enter an early years setting. Children have the right to be looked after in a safe environment and this will require all staff to be vigilant and have procedures for dealing with physical violence, bullying, name calling, etc. Finch (1994) has produced a checklist for early years establishments to enable them to work towards a non-violent society.

Where domestic violence is concerned, the children in the family often suffer violence from the person who is abusing the parent. Domestic violence is usually the man physically abusing the woman and children; however, it is to be remembered that there are a small number of cases where it is the woman who is the violent person. It was not until 1990 that the Home Office issued a circular to all police forces informing them that domestic violence was no less serious than any other type of civil assault. Police forces were asked to set up Domestic Violence Units and train staff in the correct ways of dealing with such cases. The Women's Aid Federation came into being to set up refuges for abused women and their children in order to remove them from the violent situation. Refuge workers supported the non-abusing parent in order to empower them to be in a position to promote the welfare and safety of themselves and their children. Recently, the present government has declared a position of zero tolerance on domestic violence.

Refugee children

Article 22 Refugee children

States Parties shall take appropriate measures to ensure that a child who is seeking refugee status or who is considered a refugee in accordance with applicable international or domestic law and procedures shall, whether unaccompanied or accompanied by his or her parents or by any other person, receive appropriate protection and humanitarian assistance in the enjoyment of applicable rights set forth in the present convention and in other international human rights or humanitarian instruments to which the said States are Parties.

For this purpose, States Parties shall provide, as they consider appropriate,

co-operation in any efforts by the United Nations and other competent intergovernmen-
tal organisations or non-governmental organisations operating with the United Nations
to protect and assist such a child and to trace the parents or other members of the
family of any refugee child in order to obtain information necessary for reunification
with his or her family. In cases where no parents or other members of the family can be
found, the child shall be accorded the same protection as any other child permanently
or temporarily deprived of his or her family environment.

(Other articles which can be used to promote the welfare and rights of refugee children include Article 2, Article 8, Article 9, Article 10 and Article 20.)

The UK has numerous applications for refugee status each year (around 20,000 per
year at present) from people arriving from countries such as Somalia, Uganda,
Kosovo and Afghanistan. Rutter and Hyder (1998) succinctly explain that the term
'refugee' has a legal meaning:

> a person must be judged to have left his or her own country or be unable to
> return to it 'owing to a well-founded fear of being persecuted for reasons of
> race, religion, nationality, membership of a particular social group or political
> opinion'.

The term 'asylum seeker' is used to describe someone who has crossed an international
border in search of safety and refugee status in another country. All children have
refugee status or exceptional leave to remain and therefore have access to education
and early years facilities. Asylum-seeking families with children under 18 years of age
are able to be supported by Social Services under Section 17 of the Children Act 1989.
Asylum seekers and refugees tend to be the younger generation of a society and therefore are more likely to have young children. Many children and families seeking
asylum or refugee status have experienced great trauma before reaching the UK and
few will have a good command of the English language. The children and their families will be suffering from traumatic experiences, loss of the wider family and friends
and the effects of change from having left their own country and the expectations of
the new country. Due to the negative publicity in the UK media relating to asylum
seekers, many families have been subject to racial discrimination from the local population where they are living. This only compounds their already traumatised situations
that made them leave their own country in the first place. Asylum seekers/refugee
families are often moved around a great deal; in fact the government's white paper on
Asylum and Immigration (Home Office 1998) advocates a policy of dispersal.

Research has shown that the uptake of early years provision by asylum
seekers/refugees is very low. Rutter and Hyder (1998) offer the following reasons for
this:

- frequent moves of the families through a series of temporary accommodation;
- lack of knowledge of the local Social Services;
- unemployment and low income means that some provision is beyond their
  means;
- cultural factors such as viewing child care as an activity that takes place within
  the extended family or community;

- inaccessibility of some services, such as places offered in nursery or playgroup that are too far away from where the family lives;
- unwelcoming services – playgroups, One O'clock Clubs, etc., may be used by a regular group of parents who do not welcome new members, particularly asylum seeker/refugees.

It is a sad indictment that the children who need the services most are not able to get them for a variety of reasons. In London there have been a small number of projects that have been targeted at children living in temporary accommodation. The voluntary sector has also proved to be responsive and enabled community organisations to run playgroups and sessional nurseries, for example, An Viet Foundation, Hackney; Armenian Community Playgroup, Acton; Minik Kardes Day Nursery, Hackney; Windmill Project for Refugee Women and Children.

Early years care and education establishments need to devise plans as to how they can help asylum seekers/refugees to make better use of their facilities. This may be by undertaking outreach work, employing interpreters, producing information in a number of languages or offering facilities for the parents to have language support.

Non-discrimination

> **Article 2 Non-discrimination**
>
> States Parties shall respect and ensure the rights set forth in the present Convention to each child within their jurisdiction without discrimination of any kind irrespective of the child's or his or her parents' or legal guardians' race, colour, sex, language, religion, political or other opinion, national, ethnic or social origin, property, disability, birth or other status.
>
> State Parties shall take all appropriate measures to ensure that the child is protected against all forms of discrimination or punishment on the basis of the status, activities, expressed opinions, or beliefs of the child's parents, legal guardians or family members.

The Children Act 1989 clearly states that 'child care provision must take into account the religious, racial, cultural and linguistic needs of the child'. This means that all early years workers must take into account these aspects of the child when planning meals and activities and in their dealings with parents/carers. Not to do so would constitute discrimination against a particular family, child or group of children. The UK is a pluralistic society and as such its members should be aware and respect each other regardless of differences in race, religion, culture, ability, class, etc. Unfortunately we are often made aware that such tolerance and respect does not always exist in our society and there is bias among people and within institutions.

If early years workers are going to be strategically effective in combating discrimination in their work settings, they first have to examine and address their own biases. Everyone is biased against something; to err is to be human! However, it is important that every worker is aware of their biases and able to ensure that these do not influence decisions made about children and their parents. Bias is often based upon misinformation or unproven information, sometimes incited by the media. One must not condemn a whole group on the basis of the behaviour of one or two members of that group. For example, because your dealings with the opposite sex may not have been friendly and congenial you cannot attribute the same behaviour to all members of that sex. To do this would be making stereotypical judgements, which are then transferred into the labelling of individuals. Sadly, much labelling can go on in staff rooms of child-care establishments, for example, 'Beware of Ms Dodds the new parent you know she is a cousin of Ms Harper and you must all remember what she was like, the parent from hell!'. Poor Ms Dodds and her child probably stand little chance of proving that they are not like their cousin. How did Ms Harper get such a reputation? Maybe no one was listening to her and she became frustrated and tried to make herself understood using language that was not acceptable to the staff. Whatever happened, the actions of Ms Harper have now been attributed to the whole family, however distant the relationship. Research such as that by Rosenthal and Jacobson (1968) and the Swann Report 1985 shows how teacher expectation reflects on how well a child will succeed within the education system. If teacher expectation is based upon discrimination and bias then certain children will stand very little chance of success.

Siraj-Blatchford and Clarke (2000) put forward four main conditions that need to be satisfied if a child is to learn:

- the child needs to be in a state of emotional well-being and secure;
- the child needs a positive self-identity and self-esteem;
- the curriculum must be social/interactional and instructive;
- the child needs to be cognitively engaged.

These points need to be considered when planning the early years curriculum, particularly 'positive identity and self-esteem', as the foundations of these attributes are laid down very early in children. Milner (1983) found that children learned positive and negative feelings at a very early age and by the age of three they are able to demonstrate an awareness of racial feelings that mirrored the current practices of the adults around them.

The UK has a policy of inclusion for children who have disabilities. Inclusion should be a very positive experience for these children but can easily turn into a negative model if the other children call them names, leave them out of their games and generally marginalise them from the social interaction of the setting. It is important that the staff in early years settings are aware of what is happening in their setting and are trained in how to deal with incidents in a way that is sensitive to all the children involved.

Travellers' children are another group that suffer discrimination in the UK and elsewhere in Europe. Children from these families may be transient, moving from area to area and only attending the early years setting for a number of weeks before moving on. Some travellers live on permanent trailer sites and others may live in houses. The children from these families will probably be regular attendees. Travellers' families are very close-knit, extended families sharing a rich culture, beliefs, values and history. Part of their history has been their survival under some of the most traumatic circumstances, not least of which was the large number of gypsies who were victims of the Holocaust. There is still a deep-rooted prejudice in our culture towards travellers; perhaps this is because we know so little about them, their history and their lifestyle.

Brown (1998) points out that children who live in trailers may find the nursery or school a very daunting prospect. It may be the first time that they have been in such a large indoor space with running water, flushing toilets and a plethora of play materials and books. Brown suggests that setting up a trailer-home corner and using themes such as transport, working animals or homes can help these children feel more safe and secure in the nursery setting. Talking to the children and their parents can offer the best source of information staff and other children.

It is important that if other children in the group come to school voicing their parents/carers prejudices against travellers this is dealt with by the staff in a positive way. Many local education authorities have specialist teachers who work with travellers' children and who may be able to offer positive ways to enable these children to be accepted by the rest of the group.

On a positive note, Michael McDonagh (1996: 62, quoted in Brown 1998), a traveller's child, writes:

> I like this school. I have lived in thirteen houses and a lot of sites, one in Dublin. I had two big dogs, Lassie and Wolf. My sisters go to school and my big sister goes to secondary school and her reading is good. I live in a house in Tottenham and I have been in this school for a year now. I have lots of friends, Jamil, Kelvin, Mattie, Michael and Daniel. They know I am a Traveller and they like me. I play football with them. I have a good teacher and a teacher for Travellers comes in to see me every week. A lady called Ivy helps me as well. I am better at reading and I have good writing. I can sound letters and make words. I like the computer. In my last school the children were not nice to me and I was fighting a lot. Here I have learned to get on better with other children. I like school.

International Decade for a Culture of Peace and Non-violence for the Children of the World Explanation and Implementation

In November 2000 in Paris the International Decade for a Culture of Peace and Non-violence for the Children of the World was launched by UNESCO and Living Values (an educational programme). The launch took the form of a conference on the theme of a 'Framework for Action on Values in Education in Early Childhood'. Led by UNESCO and supported by the Living Values education programme, there was a commitment to involving as many countries as possible to sign up to and implement a culture of peace and non-violence for their children over the next ten years. Research has shown that there are 800 million children under the age of six in the world and less than one-third of these benefit from any form of early childhood education or intervention. There are five levels of action in order to facilitate implementation of the Framework:

- personal level: adults need to learn to express feelings. Children need to learn to listen, model, acknowledge diversity, to have time, to enjoy, to play, to feel;
- family level: parents need to be supported, helped, educated;
- school level: educators need to be trained to take into account emotional and affective attitudes;

- community level: communities need to have/create places/spaces where children can be welcomed and nurtured, including street children, AIDS children/orphans;
- state level: states have a responsibility to implement the Convention on the Rights of the Child and to provide education.

The guiding principles for action are based upon the fact that every child has the right to early childhood care and education and all programmes should be based upon the values of trust, respect, non-discrimination and the right of the child to grow in an environment of peace. The key organisations involved in using their networks to promote the Framework are UNESCO, UNICEF and Education International, however, in each country there will be additional organisations who will take up the implementation of the Framework at a local level. Each organisation will define its own level of participation. One aspect of educating children for peace is how early years workers can get children to empathise with each other. Levin (1994) offers the following suggestions (adapted):

- the child care and education worker should be a role model and themselves show empathy and compassion;
- the feelings of the child should be validated before correcting behaviour;
- emotions should be given a name;
- interpret emotions of others for the children;
- use visuals to teach children to recognise emotions;
- provide opportunities for children to demonstrate caring behaviours with others;
- notice and value acts of kindness;
- use 'us' puppets to role-play situations.

There is also a need for early years care and education workers to know how to deal with conflict when it does arise. As with adults, the best solution is to ask about the problem, talk to the people concerned and possibly others as to what may be acceptable solutions to the problem, choose the best idea and put it into action. For young children, a system of traffic lights can be used: Red – stop, what's the problem? Amber – what can we do? Green – go ahead with the best plan for a resolution. It is not quite the same as the football penalty cards system but can certainly have the same positive effects!

Reflect upon ...

1   This chapter has highlighted the arguments relating to why children should not only have rights but should also have responsibilities. From your own experience give reasons why you agree/disagree with the argument that rights and responsibilities *must* go together.

2   Look at the illustrations on page 23 and write out four further examples that show how a child can have responsibilities associated with specific rights.

3   The UK has a large number of refugee/asylum seekers' children. Many of these children attend early years settings. Describe some of the ways in which these children can be helped by attending an early years facility.

Note

1 UNICEF has produced a booklet on the Convention Articles in which children have re-written some of the Articles in their own easy-to-understand form.

References

Aries, P. (1960) *Centuries of Childhood*, Harmondsworth: Penguin Education.

Brown, B. (1998) *Unlearning Discrimination in the Early Years*, Stoke-on-Trent: Trentham Books.

Calouste Gulbenkian Foundation (1995) *Children and Violence*, report of the *Commission on Children and Violence*, London: Calouste Gulbenkian Foundation.

Childline, Gauteng, South Africa (2008) *Children's Rights and Responsibilities*, available online: www.childlinesa.org.za.

Conservative Party (2007) *Childhood Review*, London: Conservative Party.

Coppock, S. (1997) 'Families in Crisis', in P. Scratton (ed.), *Childhood in Crisis*, Berkeley, CA: UCLA Press.

Dahlberg, G. and Moss, P. (2005) *Ethics and Politics in Early Childhood Education*, London: Routledge Falmer.

Department for Children, Schools & Families (2007) *The Children's Plan – Building Brighter Futures*, Norwich: HMSO.

Department of Education and Science (1985) *Education for All*, the Swann Report, London: HMSO.

Finch, S. (2000) *Towards a Non-Violent Society: Checkpoints for the Early Years*, London: Forum on Children and Violence.

Franklin, B. (1995) 'The case for children's rights: a progress report', in B. Franklin (ed.), *The Handbook of Children's Rights*, London: Routledge.

Lancaster, Y.P. (2006) 'Listening to young children: respecting the voice of the child', in G. Pugh and B. Duffy (eds), *Contemporary Issues in Early Years*, London: Sage Publications.

Lansdown, G. (1996) The United Nations Convention on the Rights of the Child – progress in the United Kingdom', in C. Nutbrown (ed.), *Children's Rights and Early Education*, London: Paul Chapman Publishing.

Lansdown, G. and Newell, P. (1994) *UK Agenda for Children*, London: Children's Rights Development Unit.

Levin, D.E. (1994) 'Building a peaceable classroom: helping young children feel safe in violent times', *Childhood Education* 70: 267–70.

Mayall, B. (2002) *Towards a Sociology for Childhood*, Buckingham: Open University Press.

McDonagh, M. (1996) 'Michael's story', in *Stories from Travelling Children*, London: Haringey Traveller Education Service (quotation taken from Brown 1998).

Milner, D. (1983) *Children and Race: Ten Years On*, London: Ward Lock Educational.

Mooney, C. (2000) *Theories of Childhood. An Introduction to Dewey, Montessori, Erikson, Piaget and Vygotsky*, St Paul, MN: Redleaf Press.

Muscot, S. (ed.) (1999) *Children's Rights: Reality or Rhetoric*, London: The International Save the Children Alliance.

Newell, P. (1991) *The UN Convention and Children's Rights in the UK*, London: National Children's Bureau.

O'Hagan, K. (1993) *Emotional and Psychological Abuse of Children*, Buckingham: Open University Press.

Rosenthal, R. and Jacobson, L. (1968) *Pygmalion in the Classroom*, New York: Holt Rinehart & Winston.

Rutter, J. and Hyder, T. (1998) *Refugee Children in the Early Years: Issues for Policy Makers and Providers*, London: Refugee Council/Save the Children.

Schwer, B. (2000) *A Guide to the Human Rights Act 1998*, London: Rowe and Maw.

Seraga, E. (1998) Children's needs: who decides', in M. Langan (ed.), *Welfare: Needs, Rights and Risks*, London: Routledge/Open University.

Siraj-Blatchford, I. (1994) *The Early Years: Laying the Foundations for Racial Equality*, Stoke-on-Trent: Trentham Books.

Siraj-Blatchford, I. and Clarke, P. (2000) *Supporting Identity, Diversity and Language in the Early Years*, Buckingham: Open University Press.

UNICEF (1995) *The Convention on Rights of the Child*, London: UNICEF UK Committee.

UNICEF *Children's Rights and Responsibilities*, available online: www.unicef.org.uk.

3   How children learn

I hear and I forget;
I see and I remember;
I do and I understand.

Ancient Chinese proverb

This chapter looks at current brain research and its contribution to our understanding on how children learn. It also considers the ways in which other factors like emotional intelligence, memory and concentration affect learning. There is also a section on the role of major learning theorists in helping educators to understand how to support children's learning.

From conception we all have a different set of experiences and interact with the environment in a unique manner. These affect the content of what we learn and the use to which we can put this knowledge. We also learn in different ways – some children and adults are highly curious and motivated and engage in active experimentation, whereas others are more reflective. The learning styles we develop emphasise some learning abilities over others; we all have some strong and some weak areas. In this chapter we shall be looking at some of the theories that have been put forward to explain how we learn and how internal and external factors affect that learning.

What is learning?

The term 'learning' is one that everyone uses and understands, but how we learn has yet to be fully understood. The *Oxford English Dictionary* defines learning as 'knowledge got by study', a definition that does not cover all aspects of learning. In psychological terms, learning is a process whereby a relatively permanent change of behaviour occurs as the result of prior experience. However, there are difficulties with this definition as it does not cover such activities as learning to stand up. Although not completely comprehensive, a useful definition is that of Kolb (1984), who wrote that 'learning is the process whereby knowledge is created through the transformation of experience'.

What is development?

The other term that will be used a great deal during this chapter is 'development'. Development involves changes over time and is sometimes seen as a gradual, linear, continuous process that is affected by both experiences and physiological changes. Growth and maturation follow a fixed programme that may be either continuous or discontinuous.

One of the major issues relating to development is the relative contribution of nature and nurture to the changes that occur. How much can parents, teachers and others support a child's development and how much is dictated by genetic inheritance? Psychologists agree that development is influenced by the interaction of innate and environmental factors, but the relative importance of each is still being discussed.

Old versus new thinking about the brain

In the past decade there have been advances in our understanding of the brain and its functions and this research has implications for our understanding of how children learn. Until quite recently, neuroscientists believed that the genes we are born with determine the structure of our brains and that fixed structure determines the way we develop and interact with the world. However, new investigations have shown that although heredity may determine the basic number of brain cells (neurons) that children are born with and their initial organisation, this is only a framework. The child's environment has an enormous impact on how the circuits of the brain are 'wired'.

We know that the brain at birth is composed of trillions of neurons and synapses (connections between the brain cells), many more than we actually need. As the child has more and more experiences and learns more skills, the synapses grow and the existing connections are strengthened. In the early years the child's brain forms twice as many synapses as will eventually be needed. Those that are used are reinforced and become a permanent part of the brain. We also know that connections that are not used eventually fade away. Therefore, children's experiences during the first years of life are even more decisive than we had once believed. We now know that by the age of three, children's brains are twice as active as those of adults and that activity levels begin to drop during adolescence.

During the first three years in particular, brain connections develop quickly in response to outside stimulation. The child's experiences, good or bad, directly affect the ways in which the brain is wired and the connections in the nervous system.

Research by Gunnar *et al.* (1996) has demonstrated how 'stress-sensitive' systems in the brain are shaped by outside experiences. For example, one particular stress-sensitive system is activated when children are faced with emotional or physical shock. The system produces a steroid hormone called cortisol, high levels of which cause the death of brain cells and a reduction in connections between the cells in certain areas of the brain. Research on adults who have experienced chronic or intense activation of the system that produces cortisol shows shrinkage of an area of the brain that is important in learning and memory. There appears to be a clear link between physical or emotional trauma and long-term impairment to learning and development. On the other hand, babies with strong emotional bonds to their caregivers show consistently lower levels of cortisol, which will have a positive effect upon their learning.

Critical periods for learning

Are there 'critical periods' in young children's learning and what happens if they do not gain the knowledge or skill at a specific time? Although the human brain has a remarkable capacity to change – the plasticity of the young child's brain is phenomenal – there seem to be 'prime times' when the brain will develop in specific areas and it will grow or strengthen connections most readily at these times. For example, visual and auditory stimuli promote synaptic development most quickly in the second and third months of infancy. Equally, negative experiences or the absence of appropriate stimulation are more prone to serious and sustained effects at these times. Trauma, abuse, neglect and lack of stimulation or social exposure can all interfere with healthy brain development and therefore with learning. Such negative experiences can result in the creation of a brain prone to anxiety, depression and an inability to form social attachments.

Can the early childhood educator influence the brain's growth and learning?

Babies do not come into the world with 'clean slates' but with a number of behaviour patterns that help them to deal with how the world works, but their innate structures are transformed by their experiences with objects and other people. It was Vygotsky who made such a profound contribution to our understanding of human nature when he suggested that nurture, which is how others change us, is part of our nature. If we adopt this approach we can see that there is no real conflict between biology and culture. A unique feature of human learning is that we depend upon other people for learning.

Recent brain research suggests that:

- the brain develops through the interplay of genes and experiences;
- babies and young children have strong learning capacities;
- everything that the baby sees, hears, smells, touches affects the developing network of brain connections;
- children need to make connections between various areas of the brain and gain experience between exploration and experimentation.

There is no doubt that early care and education has a fundamental and long-lasting effect upon how people develop, their ability to learn and their capacity to regulate their own emotions.

Early childhood educators should:

- be offering children emotional and social security;
- be mindful that the brain is the greediest organ in the body for oxygen, as it uses some 20–5 per cent of the body's intake. Fresh air and physical exercise are as essential as a challenging environment for successful learning;
- be aware that children who have a stressful or deprived early environment may experience damage to their brain development.

Factors affecting learning

Memory

Memory plays an important part in our learning and the use that we make of our experiences. Like other areas of brain research, research into memory and the way in which it develops has undergone a major rethink in recent times. A big shift has come in the past two decades with the emphasis on the importance of socio-cultural factors on our cognitive development.

Since the 1980s cognitive and neuro-sciences have shown that the brain has multiple memory systems – two of the systems are explicit (or declarative) memory and implicit (or procedural) memory. Explicit memory relies on the conscious recollection of names, places, events and other information, whereas implicit memory represents a variety of unconscious abilities, including the capacity for learning habits and skills. Declarative memory is characterised as fast and flexible whereas procedural memory is slow and results from gradual learning. We use both systems all the time.

As children grow older, from about seven years of age, they, like adults, learn to organise their memories. It appears that we organise memory for individual events (episodic memory) in chronological order, whereas memory for facts (semantic memory) seems to be organised by meaning.

An important change in both our thinking and the way in which we use our memory comes with the development of metamemory, that is, the knowledge that we have about our memory processes. Very young children have no idea about how their memory works and that they will not remember everything they are told, but from about five to six years of age they come to have some understanding of metamemory. There will of course be individual differences in the age at which they develop this highly important skill. As humans we are good at knowing what we know and what we do not know.

As they develop metamemory, children begin to use memory strategies like rehearsal, organisation or elaboration to help them remember in the same way as adults. Over-confident children often do poorly in memory tasks, as they do not see the necessity to use appropriate strategies. It seems that the more general knowledge children have in their long-term memory the more readily they are able to absorb new information, since we know that familiar and meaningful information is more easily remembered than the unfamiliar. Retrieval processes can be difficult for children, particularly those with learning disorders. Adults often forget how long it takes young children to retrieve information, particularly when they have been asked a question, and become impatient if a response is not immediately forthcoming.

Memory can be divided into sensory, short- and long-term memory. Sensory memory is fleeting, 200–500 milliseconds; short-term memory lasts only a minute or two while the brain sorts out how to store the information in the long-term memory. Children's improvement in short-term memory as they grow older appears to be due to the changes in strategy that they use, rather than an increase in the capacity of the memory store. This does not change much throughout childhood.

However, pre-schoolers are able to use their memory effectively in many situations. For example, if children have mislaid a toy in the playground, they are well able to retrace their steps to try to find it. They can remember where they last saw it and are then able to infer that this is the best place to start searching. If they are so good at this, why are they unable to carry out tasks like carrying messages efficiently?

Basically it seems that memories that arise incidentally as a result of other activities are retained better than activities that require deliberate memorisation. There has been much research to show that when young children are asked to memorise as an end in itself, they do not have the strategies to proceed, whereas when the memorisation is part of an activity in which they are involved the young child is able to cope.

It is therefore most important for educators to offer children strategies to help develop their memory skills. Although no one wants to reintroduce drills and rote learning, nevertheless we should not ignore the role of rehearsal and repetition in learning.

Memory is a complex subject that links closely not only to areas of cognition, like perception, language and representation, but also to our social experiences. Like us, children attend to, concentrate on or memorise information most effectively if it is seen to be pertinent to their lives and interests.

Concentration and attention

Every educator is aware that there are some children who do not appear to be able to concentrate on a task and whose attention flits from one activity to another. However, many of these 'flitters' will focus on a task once they find one of interest and/or there is an adult who is willing to support their learning. There is, though, a smaller group of children who have genuine attention deficits, and the difficulties of these children need to be recognised because the inability to concentrate has serious implications for children's learning. Some of these difficulties will be discussed more fully in a later chapter.

Many educators are now using the two observation scales produced by the Effective Early Learning Project (EELP 1993) to help them assess the level of concentration of the young children in their institutions. The first, the Child Involvement Scale is designed to measure whether or not the child is really involved deeply in an activity or whether the involvement is superficial. The second scale, the Adult Engagement Scale, aims to help adults look at their involvement with the children. Are they providing appropriate materials to meet the needs of the children and helping them to become independent, autonomous learners? There may be a number of reasons for the child's behaviour and careful observation may help the educator solve or ameliorate the problem and improve the quality of their teaching.

Cognitive styles

Just as some adults are more effective in the morning and others work better in the evening, so parents recognise early that their children have different biological rhythms. Children, as adults, also have different ways of tackling problems and dealing with challenging situations. It seems that some of us are more analytical in our approach, whereas others take a more holistic view to tackle a problem. It has been argued that an extreme global style produces field dependence, intuitive and emotional thinking that involves a simultaneous processing of many aspects of experience and a tendency towards impulsive behaviour. At the other end of the scale there is a total field-independence style that involves the dispassionate noting of detailed objectives, critical and logical thinking and a focus on learning step-by-step, rather than taking a comprehensive overview. In most instances, people do not adopt either extreme but rather use a balance of the two. It has been argued that these differences come about as a result of parenting strategies. However, modern research has demonstrated that cognitive style is not a stable trait and that motivation is also an important factor to be taken into account.

Intelligence

The argument as to whether intelligence depends upon learning and experience (nurture) or is fixed because it is inherited (nature) has dominated the thinking of scholars until recent times. During the first half of the twentieth century the nature/nurture argument was one of the most controversial topics in psychology. But it was not just an academic issue; there were deep political implications to the question of whether intelligence depends upon learning and experience or whether it is inherited and fixed. Educational policies were designed based on the belief that intelligence could be measured accurately and decisions about children's education were made dependent upon their scores on intelligence tests. IQ tests such as the Stanford-Binet (1905) or Merrill-Palmer (1931) scales were developed and widely used. These tests were developed by a white male, middle-class group of psychologists, many of whom saw intelligence testing as a way of identifying the 'innate feeble minded' who in their eyes were the source of many of the social problems of the time. Terman, writing in 1916 in the introduction to the first version of the Stanford-Binet test, stated that:

> In the future, intelligence tests will bring tens of thousands of these high grade effectives under the surveillance of society, this will ultimately result in curtailing the reproduction of feeble-mindedness and in the elimination of an enormous amount of crime, pauperism and industrial inefficiency.
>
> (Terman 1916: 6–7)

In spite of the reservations of many psychologists concerning the validity and reliability of intelligence testing, the 1944 Education Act introduced verbal reasoning and other tests based on number and memory to decide whether children should go to grammar schools, technical schools or secondary modern schools at the age of eleven. Opportunities for higher education were effectively closed for any child who did not make 'grammar school'. It soon became very apparent that testing at the age of eleven favoured male, middle-class children. It also became very apparent that there were big discrepancies throughout England and Wales as to the number of grammar school places available in different parts of the country.

Not only was there criticism that the intelligence tests favoured children from a white, middle-class culture, but they also looked at intelligence from a very limited point of view and did not take into account abilities in music, creativity or interpersonal skills. This approach continued even though the question that intelligence might consist of a number of different, independent skills (multiple intelligences) had already been raised.

By the 1960s, the writings of Piaget were becoming more generally known and his ideas about how children construct their view of the world helped to raise questions about the nature of intelligence and the importance of the environment to children's learning.

He defined intelligence as a basic life function that helps the organism to adapt to its environment. Piaget believed that:

- all children are active learners trying to make sense of their world;
- all children go through discrete stages of learning and development;
- children think differently from adults;
- children play a crucial role in their own development;
- children vary in the age at which they reach a particular stage;
- each stage rests firmly on the preceding one;
- no stage can be omitted;
- children can be at different levels of attainment within a stage at the same time;
- children use first-hand and prior experiences in order to learn.

Educators began to realise that a stimulating environment could increase intelligence. This led to wide-scale programmes of compensatory education in the UK and throughout the rest of the Western world, as well as major changes in our secondary schooling.

Intelligence tests have a part to play in the assessment of children, particularly those with special educational needs, but they fail to provide a whole picture of the individual. Observations and other forms of assessment are also necessary before a full analysis of a child's needs can be made.

Gardner's (1983) theory of multiple intelligence has implications for education. He proposed that within the brain there is a system of discrete information-processing operations that deal with the different kinds of information that humans encounter during their everyday lives. These modules include:

- linguistic intelligence: the ability to use language effectively either orally or in writing;
- logical/mathematical intelligence: the ability to use numbers correctly; to think inductively or deductively; to classify, generalise and categorise;
- musical intelligence: the ability to understand and use musical concepts; to develop an appreciation for music;
- spatial intelligence: the ability to represent spatial information effectively;
- bodily kinaesthetic intelligence: the ability to use physical means to represent ideas and feelings;
- interpersonal intelligence: the ability to relate to others;
- intrapersonal intelligence: the ability to understand oneself and to have self-discipline.

These processes are genetically pre-programmed, but are subject to cultural influences. Therefore, in his view individuals may differ in the strength of their intelligences and therefore possess personal 'profiles of intelligence'. Gardner has suggested that children already enter school with distinctive profiles of intelligence and that these need to be cultivated through suitable activity-centred curricula.

Writers since Piaget have argued that intelligence needs to be defined socially.

Cross-cultural studies have shown that Western definitions of intelligence are at variance with those in other cultures. For example, the Baoulé argue that technological skills have to be integrated with social skills as the child's abilities are useless unless they are applied to the well-being of the social group.

Emotional intelligence

Another aspect of intelligence has been put forward by Goleman (1995), who stressed the importance of children becoming what he termed 'emotionally literate' – a skill that he and others have considered vital for later learning and development.

The key components of emotional literacy are:

- emotional awareness: understanding the cause of feelings, being able to name and recognise emotions, recognising the difference between feelings and actions;
- managing emotions: the ability to manage anger, frustration and sadness, avoiding aggressive or self-destructive behaviour, monitoring self-criticism;
- communication: being able to talk about one's feelings effectively, being a good listener, being able to ask appropriate questions;
- personal decision making: examining your actions and understanding their consequences, distinguishing between thoughts and feelings when making decisions;
- empathy: being sensitive to others' feelings, having the ability to see things from another person's point of view;
- handling relationships: the ability to analyse, understand and solve problems in relationships, being considerate, being able to work as part of a group, share, cooperate, negotiate and solve conflicts.

Goleman and others have argued that emotionally intelligent people who can motivate themselves, know and manage their emotions and recognise emotions in others are more likely to be able to handle relationships effectively and use their cognitive abilities to the full. The evidence for emotional intelligence is compelling and has definite implications for how we support children's learning.

Theories of learning

In this section we shall consider some different approaches to learning and their effectiveness in helping our understanding of how children learn.

Behaviourist approaches

Classical conditioning

The founder of this school of thought was the Russian 1904 Nobel Prize winner Ivan Pavlov, who based his learning principles upon the notion of conditioning. From his experiments with dogs, Pavlov developed a set of principles, three of which are of particular importance for educators.

- The principle of reinforcement: Pavlov demonstrated that the act of achieving success, or of getting a response right, means that it is more likely to be repeated.

- The principle of extinction: the response stops when there is no reinforcement.
- The principle of generalisation: Pavlov found that it is possible for both animals and humans to generalise their responses from one situation to a similar situation.

A number of behavioural programmes have been based upon these principles, particularly in relation to extinction and reinforcement. Educators are encouraged to ignore children when they are attention seeking as it is argued that if the behaviour is ignored, it will either fade or disappear entirely.

An instance of conditioning occurs in many schools in the morning when children first arrive in the playground. They will be playing or talking to each other until they see their teacher come into the playground and stand in a certain place. The children will immediately line up in front of their teacher ready to go into school.

Operant conditioning

Skinner (1904–90) was a behaviourist who advocated a form of conditioning or learning that he termed 'operant conditioning'. He worked with rats and pigeons, rewarding them with food if they did what was required (positive reinforcement) and punishing them if they did not behave appropriately (negative reinforcement), thus extinguishing undesirable behaviour. Skinner argued that desirable human behaviour can be shaped by his operant conditioning techniques as undesirable behaviour is ignored and desirable behaviour is reinforced.

Contribution of behaviourism

The major contribution to our understanding of learning by the behaviourists is that they carried out strict experiments to test behaviour and found that their theories worked. The principles of reinforcement and extinction are used in child-rearing practices, particularly in relation to discipline, but they have weaknesses in that they do not explain how all learning occurs or take into account motivation. Most of the early work was carried out on animals, but a child's life is rather more complex. It may also be argued that the behaviourists have too simplistic an approach to learning as they do not take into account situations such as when children are experimenting with sand and water for fun and enjoyment and do not receive any form of reinforcement. Skinner can explain how existing behaviour becomes repeated but does not adequately explain where new behaviour comes from. For example, learning to stand is not the result of previous experience. Like learning to walk and talk, this is a skill that has to be practised before it is fully acquired.

Observational learning

Observational learning results from observing the behaviour of other people. Almost anything can be learned from watching (or listening to) others.

Social-learning theorists, of whom Bandura (1977) is one of the most important, accept that children learn a great deal from reinforcement and punishment, but argue that children acquire large parts of their behaviour by observing and imitating.

Children model their behaviour upon those whom they hold in high esteem, such as parents, teachers, peers and famous people.

Bandura argues that there are two main ways in which this modelling takes place.

Modelling behaviour: children often copy new pieces of behaviour that they did not previously know. Children do not seem to need to practise this behaviour or learn it by trial and error. Bandura carried out a famous experiment in which he showed children a film in which adults acted in a very aggressive manner. After seeing the film, the children quickly began to exhibit aggressive behaviour without any prompting or suggestion of any kind. He argued that watching the behaviour of a role model can result in some children changing their usual way of behaving by either strengthening or inhibiting their usual responses. This is one of the ways in which children learn 'how far they can go' and find the level of tolerance that other people will accept in particular situations. For example, if there is a new member of staff who allows children to carry out normally unacceptable behaviour, the children will produce a higher level of undesirable behaviour than they would with a more established member of staff. If the behaviour goes unchecked, then the children are more likely to repeat the deviant behaviour. Some would argue that if the deviant behaviour is ignored it will be extinguished.

Eliciting effect: behavioural changes can take place from what is termed the 'eliciting effect'. The behaviour can be initiated by cues given by the model. This behaviour is not inborn, but it is argued that the child merely copies the behaviour she sees in others with behaviour or actions that she already possesses but had previously suppressed. For example, she had refrained from hitting another child at school but came home and saw her father, her model, hitting her brother. Immediately she believes that this is acceptable behaviour and on a subsequent occasion will strike another child.

Role models can have a positive effect and help to make learning more efficient. They can also account for why some people are more influential than others over what children learn and how their personalities develop.

However, criticisms can be made of this approach:

* children are all different and even if they see the same role model they may react differently;
* children do not always copy the behaviour of people who seem influential. Their behaviour may be the result of trial and error or have no apparent cause at all;
* it fails to take into account that children are active in their own learning;
* it fails to accept that children are capable of learning different things at different ages.

In the first half of the twentieth century this approach to learning had a powerful influence upon educators and education. Children were exposed to vast amounts of rote learning and intermittent schedules of reinforcement – irregular periods of practice. Lessons were all pre-planned and there was little or no scope for questioning or investigation by the children. Even reading was taught in this fashion.

Gradually it was realised that traditional learning theories, based upon principles of stimulus and response, could not account for all aspects of children's learning and other psychologists were putting forward the idea that the thinking of young children was qualitatively different from adults. It was not only lack of experience that produced such unexpected responses to adult questioning.

In spite of the criticisms, behaviour theories still play an important part in behaviour-modification programmes and the underlying principles are important in many aspects of early childhood education. Furthermore, there are early childhood programmes flourishing in various parts of the world that are based entirely upon these approaches to learning.

The next three theorists to be discussed have all had a profound influence upon early childhood education today.

Constructivism

Jean Piaget (1896–1980)

The writings of Piaget had a great impact upon educational thinking in many parts of the world during the second half of the twentieth century. He emphasised the link between cognitive/intellectual development and learning, believing that the child constructs her own understanding about things. However, unlike the two other theorists mentioned in this section, he did not emphasise the role of social relationships in learning.

Assimilation and accommodation

Piaget argued that as young children experience new activities or events, they try to make sense of them by assimilating this knowledge into existing schemas (organised patterns of thought or actions that we construct in order to interpret our experiences). This process, which he called assimilation, is balanced by accommodation. During accommodation children try to adapt their previous knowledge to the new experience. Learning takes place when a state of equilibrium (balance) has been reached.

Children are constantly adapting to new situations and in so doing move from a state of equilibrium to a state of disequilibrium. Piaget gives the term equilibration to the overall interaction between assimilation and accommodation.

For example, most children between the ages of four and six think that animals are the only living things. On hearing that plants are also alive the child may become confused and unsure as to how you know something is alive. In Piagetian terms she is in a state of disequilibrium. Gradually the child begins to discover similarities between plants and animals in that they both need water and food. The new knowledge about plants and animals helps to achieve a state of equilibrium as the child now realises why both animals and plants are living things.

Early concepts

Children learn about the world around them through their senses and perceptions. The feedback from these senses helps babies to develop ideas about objects and people. Research has shown us that babies begin to develop concepts about themselves and the world around them at a very early age, gradually linking past experiences with present ones. Piaget termed these early concepts 'schemas'. These are linked patterns of behaviours from which the child can generalise and use in different situations.

Schema approach to learning

Athey (1990) carried out a research project over a five-year period from 1972 to 1977 to investigate the use of schema in children's learning. As a result of her observations she suggested that children possess patterns or schemas that grow in complexity and become coordinated with one another. Athey describes a schema as a pattern of repeatable and generalisable actions that can be applied to objects or events.

According to the research, the following schemas were found to be present in children's behaviour between the ages of three and five:

- transporting, e.g. moving objects from one place to another;
- trajectory, e.g. throwing, jumping, horizontal, vertical and oblique;
- dynamic vertical, e.g. flying a kite;
- dynamic back and forth/side to side, e.g. moving on the climbing frame;
- dynamic circular, e.g. hopping round in circles;
- going over and under, e.g. taking cars over and under a bridge;
- going round a boundary, e.g. building a block boundary around toy cars, taking the cars around it;
- enveloping and containing space, e.g. wrapping a teddy bear in a blanket;
- going through a boundary, e.g. building a boundary around toy cars, taking the cars through it.

Schemas were also observed in one-to-one correspondence, ordering and connection. Each schema was considered under four headings:

- *motor level* – senses and movements;
- *symbolic level* – graphic representation, action and speech;
- *functional level* – cause and effect;
- *thought level* – anything children can talk about without a reminder (i.e. internal representation).

According to the researchers, the marks and actions relating to these descriptions of movements can be identified in young children's drawings, play and thinking. They argued that these schemas form the basis for later learning as they become incorporated into more complex concepts and can be related to Piaget's stages of cognitive development.

Piaget's stages of cognitive development

1   Sensori-motor stage: from birth to around 18 months to two years. This is characterised by the child exploring her world through her physical actions. She recognises and explores objects with her senses. By the end of the first year most children understand object permanence, that is, that objects and people continue to exist even when they are no longer in sight. Children also develop some understanding of cause and effect. This stage comes to an end with the development of language and thought.

2   Pre-operational stage: from around 18 months to seven years. This period begins when children begin to represent actions with symbols and we see the

beginnings of pretend play and the use of props to symbolise other objects, for example, a stick may represent a doll. It is also the time when children may begin to invent imaginary playmates. At this stage children are moving towards operational thinking but are still not able to link schemas in a logical way. There are inconsistencies in their reasoning as children at this stage have rather primitive concepts compared with older children and adults. One of these Piaget termed 'animism', that is, attributing life to inanimate objects, for example, a child may think the wind is angry because it blows so hard.

Another inconsistency he termed 'transductive reasoning', which means the child reasons from the particular to the particular. When any two events occur together the child will assume that the one has caused the other. For example, Piaget quoted his daughter who stated 'I haven't had a nap, so it isn't afternoon'. In this case, the child had missed her normal lunch-time sleep and so could not understand that it could be the afternoon.

Another limitation to the child's thinking is associated with what Piaget terms 'egocentric thinking'. The child sees the world from her own view-point and fails to take into account the perspective of others.

Children of this age have a different perception of right and wrong. For example, a child who accidentally drops a glass when carrying it to the kitchen will be perceived as naughtier than a child who has deliberately taken a glass from the cupboard after being told not to touch, even though it has not been broken. For the young child, what is right or wrong is based on what happens rather than on the motive. Piaget called this 'moral realism'.

Towards the end of this phase children begin to show a decrease in egocentricity. Many children can now sort by shape, size and colour although they are still dominated by their perceptions and classify objects according to their perceptual attributes. This is referred to as the 'intuitive period' because thinking is still centred on the way things appear, rather than on a rational thought process. Piaget uses the term 'centration' to describe this inability to focus on more than one feature of a situation.

3 The concrete operational period: from approximately seven to 11 years. During this period the child becomes less egocentric and can take on the views of others. She is able to classify and organise objects but is still dependent upon concrete experiences. Not only do children develop 'conservation' of time, mass, number, volume, shape, size and area throughout these years but they also develop the concept of 'reversibility'. This is the ability to mentally undo an action they have witnessed. For example, they can look at a ball of clay, watch it made into a sausage shape and then see it turned into a round ball and appreciate that there is the same amount of clay. The development of reversibility is crucial in the child's cognitive development.

4 The formal operational stage: from approximately 12 years onwards. Thinking about abstract ideas and hypothetical issues becomes possible. In practice, children no longer require concrete reality to understand and manipulate ideas and relationships between things. Abstract concepts like peace and justice can be understood and problems can be solved. This ability to handle abstract concepts and ideas is not necessarily reached by all adults and many people use both abstract and concrete thinking throughout their lives.

For Piaget, development is sequential and each period is dependent upon the previous stage. However, he recognised that children may master certain tasks at different rates and therefore be at the concrete operational stage for one task and pre-operational in another. This is termed 'décalage'.

Criticisms of Piaget

- Piaget used clinical interviews to gather his information and these have been criticised as they were seen as too subjective;
- Piaget relied heavily upon children's language and memory skills. Later research has shown that he underestimated the ability of children under five years;
- It was also argued that his model drew attention to what children could not do rather than what they could do;
- He argued that young children are egocentric and unable to see another person's point of view;
- Piaget failed to take account of the effects of the social context upon children's development.

Susan Isaacs (1930) was one of the first critics of Piaget. She argued that young children were not only less egocentric than he had suggested, but that they were capable of logical thought at a much earlier age. Many years later the research of Margaret Donaldson and her colleagues (1978) led to a major shift in thinking about Piaget's stage theory. The main thrust of Donaldson's argument was that if children were asked to undertake activities or problems within a familiar context they would be able to think and reason at a higher level than that suggested by Piaget. She argued that some of the failure to respond came from either children's lack of understanding of the question or the reason for asking the question; neither of which suggested that the children did not understand the task.

Donaldson and her researchers decided to repeat some of Piaget's tasks with some changes in the methods of administration. She showed that if children were provided with tasks that made sense to them, they could draw upon their previous experience and be able to undertake more complex activities. Donaldson believed that the knowledge we bring with us to a particular learning task is of crucial importance and suggested that the meaning of the activity was embedded in the actual situation. Donaldson, as had Isaacs, demonstrated that children were not as egocentric as Piaget suggested and that they could certainly empathise with people, particularly younger children, which cast doubt upon the view that they were unable to take another person's point of view.

Piaget's views on object permanence have also been challenged as researchers have shown that babies achieve this understanding much earlier than he had recognised.

However, in spite of the criticisms that have been made of his work, it appears that he was largely right in his description of the ways in which children develop cognitively.

Social constructivists

Jerome Bruner (1915–)

Bruner is a cognitive psychologist who has exercised considerable influence upon the early years curriculum. Like Piaget, Bruner believed that children are active learners and need first-hand experiences to help them develop their ideas. He suggests that we develop skills that enable us to represent the environment to ourselves in three main ways:

- enactive representation;
- iconic representation;
- symbolic representation.

Enactive representation

By this term Bruner suggests that the human represents many things through motor experiences and actions. He argues that such activities as riding a bicycle, driving a car or swimming become represented in our muscles. Automatic patterns of activity are built up and we can reproduce them as needed.

Iconic representation

Iconic representation is a development from enactive representation and occurs when we are able to build up a series of mental pictures or images of things we have experienced. Usually these images are formed from a variety of similar experiences. Bruner argues that it is essential for us to have a great deal of motor skill before we can form an image to represent a sequence of acts. We have to have a lot of practice at riding a bicycle before the actions become automatic. He considers that it is difficult for an educator to distinguish between enactive and iconic representation, but stresses the importance of talking with children and discussing actions and events with them so that they have the words to build images.

Symbolic representation

Symbolic representation occurs when children are able to translate their experiences into symbolic form. To help the child with this, the educator and child must continually be talking together, asking and answering questions and explaining the meanings of words and actions.

A radical difference between the two theorists is that whereas Piaget expected children to reach a particular stage of development before moving on to the next, Bruner believes that we should help the child move forward in her thinking, not wait for a particular stage. To support this view, he made his now-famous statement in his book *The Process of Education* (1960), writing 'any subject can be taught effectively in some intellectually honest form to any child at any stage of development'.

Bruner speaks of a 'spiral curriculum' where the child learns first through actions, then through images and pictures of the world and finally through the symbols of numbers or words. In his view, we use all three modes of representation throughout our lives as and when it is appropriate.

Bruner, like Vygotsky, suggests that the adult has a key role to play in supporting or 'scaffolding' the child's learning in a way that will enable the child to go beyond the immediate information or experience and reflect and produce new ideas and ways of looking at the world.

Scaffolding includes:

- gaining the attention and interest of the child;
- simplifying the number of responses the child needs to make;
- maintaining the child's interest by giving encouragement and feedback;
- identifying the key points of the task so the child knows what is needed;
- providing a model to the task, e.g. demonstrate how it might be done.

The most important aspect of Bruner's work has been to emphasise the importance of the adult in children's learning. Many early childhood education programmes have, with good effect, adopted the notion of the adult as a 'scaffold' for children's learning.

Lev Vygotsky (1896–1934)

The Russian psychologist Vygotsky has also made a considerable contribution to the discussion on learning and of how young children learn. He focused on the effects of society on children's learning and development. He criticised Piaget for apparently ignoring the context of situations and the cultural and historical factors that he believed affected children's learning.

Whereas Piaget was convinced that children learn as individual learners striving to make sense of their world, Vygotsky argued that only through interaction with adults and peers can we extend our experience. Children do not grow up in isolation and therefore the social groups in which they mix have an important effect upon their knowledge and understanding of the world. Like Bruner, Vygotsky believed that children would be able to attempt more complex tasks if they had some support from others. In his view, when a child carried out a task independently, like building with Lego bricks, she was performing at an 'actual level of development', but with the help of an older child or an adult, the child's ability could be stretched and a more sophisticated model would be constructed. This he termed the 'zone of proximal development' (ZPD), or the next area of development that could only be achieved with the help and support of others.

The ZPD is the gap between what the child can do alone and what she can do with the help of others. For Vygotsky, adult interactions and the quality of those interactions were crucial, and he therefore argued in favour of cooperative or supported learning. Vygotsky, unlike Piaget, highlighted what children could do, rather than what they could not do, starting from their own knowledge and building on it. Wood (1988) has pointed out that cooperatively achieved success lies at the foundations of learning and development. Cooperative learning is very important in play situations and by playing together and trying out new ideas and combinations of skills, children are able to come to understand many of the skills and behaviours that are expected of them by the adult world.

Leading on from the work of Vygotsky and his colleagues, the newer approaches to learning stress the importance of looking at the role of society and culture in children's learning. We have moved away from the traditional theories that focus on the individual in a decontextualised way. In the social-cultural approach, development and learning are assumed to take place through the child's participation with others in activities that constitute daily life within the child's cultural community. This stress on the importance of the family and community in young children's learning is having an impact on early childhood programmes throughout the world and requires educators to see learning within a broader framework.

Reflect upon ...

1   What are the implications of the new research on the brain for educators?
2   Discuss the social factors that may affect a child's learning.
3   How can the learning environment encourage the development of children's concentration?

References

Athey, C. (1990) *Extending Thought in Young Children: A Parent-Teacher Partnership*, London: Paul Chapman Publishing.
Bandura, A. (1977) *Social Learning Theory*, Englewood Cliffs, NJ: Prentice Hall.
Bruner, J. (1956) *Studies in Cognitive Growth*, New York: Wiley.
Bruner, J. (1960) *The Process of Education*, Cambridge, MA: Harvard University Press.
Cowan, N. (ed.) (1997) *The Development of Memory in Childhood*, Hove: Psychology Press.
Donaldson, M. (1978) *Children's Minds*, London: Fontana/Collins.
Gardner, H. (1983) *Frames of Mind: Theory of Multiple Intelligences*, New York: Basic Books.
Goleman, D. (1995) *Emotional Intelligence*, New York: Bantam.
Gunnar, M.R., Broderson, L. and Rigatus, R. (1996) 'Dampening of behavioural and adreno-cortical reactivity during early infancy: normative changes and individual differences', *Child Development* 67, 3: 877–89.
Isaacs, S. (1930) *Intellectual Growth in Young Children*, London: Routledge.
Kagiçibasi, C. (1996) *Family and Human Development across Cultures*, New York: Basic Books.
Kolb, D. (1984) *Experiential Learning*, Englewood Cliffs, NJ: Prentice Hall/London: Paul Chapman.
Nutbrown, C. (1998) *Threads of Learning*, London: Paul Chapman Publishing Co.
Pascal, C. and Bertram, A.D. (1997) *Case Studies in Effective Early Learning*, London: Hodder and Stoughton.
Piaget, J. (1962) *Play, Dreams and Imitation in Childhood*, London: Routledge & Kegan Paul.
Piaget, J. and Inhelder, B. (1969) *The Psychology of the Child*, New York: Basic Books.
Roberts, R. (2002) *Self Esteem and Early Learning*, London: Paul Chapman Publishing Co.
Shore, R. (1996) *Rethinking the Brain*, New York: Families and Work Institute.
Terman, L.M. (1916) *The Measurement of Intelligence*, Boston: Houghton Mifflin.
Vygotsky, L.S. (1978) *Mind in Society*, Cambridge, MA: Harvard University Press.
Whalley, M. (2001) *Involving Parents in their Children's Learning*, London: Paul Chapman Publishing Co.
Wood, D. (1988) *How Children Think and Learn*, Oxford: Blackwell.

4   Language and language development

This chapter provides a general introduction into the theories and development of language and thought in young children from birth. It also considers the part played by social factors as well as the role of the adult in children's language development; there is also a section on bilingualism and how it affects children's language development.

This chapter deals with the ways in which young children develop non-verbal and verbal communication skills and the factors that affect this development.

Communication is the process by which messages are imparted and exchanged. It can take many forms such as speech, writing, hand gestures and even objects such as traffic lights. From birth, babies try to communicate with others, at first through crying and using various body movements that are often difficult to interpret and then with simple gestures. As children grow older, they, like adults, use facial expressions (a smile, a frown or eye contact) and body language to convey feelings. The type of body movement and gesture will vary according to the culture. Many of our movements are regulators, for example nodding to imply 'yes' or 'no', and these are often culturally based. Children and adults from different cultures need to understand how to interpret these so that they do not misread the signals.

Besides gestures and facial expressions there is also 'voice communication'. The way we use our voices can convey many different messages, for instance a shout, a whisper, a particular emphasis on a word or sentence are all effective ways of stressing the message. The intonations and nuances are frequently cultural and children have to learn to the meaning of these messages.

What is language?

The one truly remarkable achievement that sets man apart from the rest of the animal kingdom is our ability to use language. There is considerable evidence to show that animals can communicate with one another with a limited number of sounds and calls, but the adult human being is able to produce from a small number of individually meaningless sounds a vast number of words and messages. Language is creative and everyone who knows our language will be able to understand our ideas as long as we stick to the rules and conventions of the language we are speaking.

Languages are highly complex and abstract and yet children from all cultures come to understand this intricate form of communication, some long before they are able to walk.

How can this occur? Are all infants biologically programmed to acquire language? What relationship is there between a child's cooing, babbling and gesturing and the later production of meaningful words? How do infants come to attach meaning to words? Do all children in all cultures pass through the same stages in order to acquire their native language? What is the role of the adult in developing these language skills?

First of all, let us consider what children have to know and understand before they can use language effectively. They need to know that there are four components to language: knowledge of phonology, semantics, syntax and pragmatics.

Language is a small number of individually meaningless symbols (sounds, letters and gestures) that can be combined according to agreed rules to produce an infinite number of messages.

Language development involves both listening and speaking. Listening is a receptive system that involves:

- the physical aspect of hearing;
- the attention of the learner;
- the ability to process auditory information.

Speaking is an expressive language system that involves:

- the production of speech sounds (phonology);
- the ability to produce meaningful sentences and use grammar rules;
- the ability to use speech for a range of purposes.

In order to develop linguistic proficiency, researchers are agreed that four kinds of knowledge are required: *phonology*; *semantics*; *syntax* and *pragmatics*.

Phonology is the sound system of a language and the rules for combining these sounds to produce meaningful units of speech. *Phonemes* is the name given to the basic units of sound that are used in a spoken language.

Each language uses only a small proportion of the sounds that a human being is capable of making. For example, the English language uses 45 phonemes and no language uses more than 60. Each language has rules for combining these phonemes and for pronouncing these combinations. For example, an English speaker would understand that it is permissible to begin a word with *st (stop, study)* or *sk (skull)*, but not *sb or sg*. In other languages there are other acceptable combinations. Each child has to learn to discriminate the sounds acceptable to its mother tongue.

Semantics refers to the meanings expressed in words and sentences. The most basic meaningful units of language are called *morphemes*; they include words and grammatical markers such as the suffix *-ed* to denote the past tense and *s* to indicate the plural noun. There are many suffixes and prefixes, which children learn about over time. Later in this section, when we look at children's development of the past tense, we shall see how this occurs.

Syntax is the structure of a language, the rules specifying how words and grammatical markers are to be combined to produce meaningful sentences.

Consider the following sentences:

The dog bit John.
John bit the dog.
The dog John bit.

Even very young speakers of English would recognise that the last sentence violates the rules of English, although this word order would be acceptable in some other languages. The first and second sentences, however, are grammatical although they convey different meanings.

Pragmatics is the term given to the principles that underlie the effective and appropriate use of language in a social context. Even very young children have to learn the pragmatics of language if they are to communicate effectively. For example, six-year-old Emma is trying to explain to her two-year-old sister how she wants her to play a game, and already knows that she has to adjust her speech if she wants to be understood.

Pragmatics also involves sociolinguistic knowledge, that is, knowledge about how you use language in a particular social context. A three-year-old may not yet have learned that the best way of getting a sweet from Grandma is to say 'May I have a sweet Grandma please', rather than 'I want a sweet', but in a very short time she will have learned the strategy.

Besides the enormous task of coming to understand the necessary knowledge about pragmatics, phonology, semantics and syntax, the young child has to learn about the non-verbal communication that plays such an important part in our conversations. Young children hear what is said to them but do not read the accompanying body language. For example, a mother may have grumbled at a child for some misdemeanour, but her facial expression is not that of a very angry person even though her voice sounded cross. An older child or an adult would have read all the signals and understood the true message, that although her mother was cross, her eyes showed that she was not as angry as she sounded.

Tables 4.1 and 4.2 summarise the main factors that affect language acquisition and development.

Table 4.1 Factors affecting language acquisition

In order to acquire language

Factors affecting language input:
1 An environment in which language is spoken by competent speakers in a variety of communicative situations
2 An ability to hear spoken language

Factors affecting language processing:
3 An ability to process the language heard and the context in which it takes place in order to 'make sense' of the information

Factors affecting language output:
The ability to form units of spoken language with the organs of speech so that they can be understood by others

---

Table 4.2 Factors affecting input of language

---

1 Factors affecting input:
  a Environmental factors
    i social circumstances
    ii bilingualism
  b sensory deprivation
    i hearing loss
    ii visual problems

2 Factors affecting language processing:
  a general cognitive deficiencies
  b specific affective deficiencies (autism)
  c specific language deficiencies

3 Factors affecting language output:
  a disorders of oro-motor control
  b structural abnormalities

The pre-linguistic period

The period of a child's language development for the first ten to 13 months of life is often termed the pre-linguistic period, as this is before the child speaks its first meaningful words. However, that is not to say that children do not communicate before that time. They are responsive to language from the moment they are born. Research has shown that by the age of three days an infant already recognises the mother's voice and clearly prefers it to the voice of a stranger (Crystal 1986). By one month it has been found that children are as capable as adults at distinguishing the consonant sounds such as 'ba' and 'pa' or 'da' and 'ta', and by two months the baby can discriminate certain vowel sounds.

All normal healthy babies are capable of vocalising at birth and they communicate in a predictable sequence. Neonates cry to signal distress and by three to five weeks of age babies begin to coo; a few weeks later babbling commences (usually between four and six months). This involves the baby making vocal/consonant combinations such as 'dada' or 'mama'. These may sound like words but are not used meaningfully even though proud parents believe the child is saying something recognisable. Early babbling worldwide is very similar, which makes researchers believe that it is influenced by maturation of the brain. However, environmental factors soon come into effect as by six to nine months deaf infants do not continue babbling. By eight months, hearing babies have the ability to listen carefully to the adults around them and match the pitch and intonation of their babbles to the language they hear. They actually begin to sound as if they are speaking a language. Although children are born with the ability to make every sound required for any language, by listening to the language of the adults around them they practise the sounds they hear and gradually the other sounds are dropped from their repertoire. As this occurs the 'language' of the future English-speaking child will become different from the 'language' of the future Chinese-speaking child.

Even at this stage babies know about language and communication. For instance, during the first six months babies often coo or babble while their caregivers are speaking, but by seven to eight months they are generally silent when their companion speaks and will wait to respond until their partner has finished talking. At a very early age they have learned turn taking. The game of 'peek-a-boo', a firm favourite with many children and their caregivers, is an example of the way in which children learn to take turns in conversation. Moreover, by nine months the child will make noises or gestures to encourage the adult to continue the exchange if the adult fails to respond.

The importance of this kind of interaction between children and adults will be drawn upon later in the chapter.

By eight to ten months the child is using gestures and other non-verbal responses to communicate. These are mainly of two kinds: declarative gestures, in which the child points or touches objects; and imperative gestures, in which the child tries to persuade others to carry out her wishes. For example, a child will tug at the leg of the caregiver and put up her hands in the hope of being picked up. It is at this age that adults can be deceived into thinking that a child understands particular words, when in reality, the child obeys commands by correctly interpreting the speaker's non-verbal gestures. In the same way, the child appears to understand the meaning of the word 'no' when in fact it is the intonation which the child has understood.

By the beginning of the second year the child is able to understand a great deal more than she can say. Receptive language is ahead of expressive language.

A breakthrough in children's language development comes once the child understands that words can be used as labels. For example, a young child has seen the dog in the house, but it is not until she realises that the word 'dog' refers to an actual object and is not just a meaningless sound that she has meaningful speech. This awareness is called referencing. The first stage of meaningful speech has been termed the 'holophrastic' phase. This is the phase when children use one word to convey a sentence of meaning. For example the child may say 'ball', but it will convey a variety of meanings according to the context of the situation. It may mean 'give me the ball', 'I have a ball' or 'throw the ball'.

Between 18 and 24 months the child's vocabulary increases rapidly, anything from ten to 40 words a week, the typical two-year-old may now have a vocabulary of around 80 words and understand a great many more.

What types of words do they use? Nelson (1973) studied the first 50 words of 18 children and found that 65 per cent of utterances were object words referring to unique objects like Mummy or Katy, or to classes of objects like 'doggie', 'car', 'man'. Action words like 'go', 'bye-bye' and 'up', were used 13 per cent of the time, while 9 per cent of the children's utterances referred to what she termed modifiers, that is words that refer to the property or quantity of things like 'mine', 'hot', 'bit'. Personal and social words like 'no', 'please', 'ta' accounted for 8 per cent of the language while the remaining language referred to function words, i.e. words that have a grammatical function such as 'what', 'for' and 'where'.

Telegraphic speech

Around 18 to 24 months children begin to combine words and produce simple sentences such as 'daddy go', 'mummy milk', 'no car' (see Table 4.3). These early sentences are called 'telegraphic speech' because they contain only the critical content words – nouns, verbs and adjectives – and leave out the less meaningful parts of speech, e.g. prepositions, pronouns, auxiliary verbs. Although it is not grammatical to say 'no wet', the meaning is clear. This development of spontaneous two-word utterances has been found to occur in other languages, for example, German,

Table 4.3 Examples of two-word utterances

Some examples of two-word utterances	
To locate or name	'there book'
To demand	'more milk'
To negate	'no go', 'no wet'
To indicate possession	'my shoe'
To modify/qualify	'big dog'
To question	'where ball'

Finnish and Samoan. However, it is not universal as researchers (De Villiers and De Villiers 1992) have found that Russian and Turkish children use short reasonably grammatical sentences from the very beginning.

It is interesting that, although these early sentences are incomplete, they are always in the correct word order of the language being learnt.

Language development from two to five years

During the period between the ages of two-and-a-half to five years, children make enormous strides in language development. They not only increase their vocabulary at a rapid rate but they also master basic syntax. They develop the use of morphemes, modifiers that give more precise meaning to the sentence. It is these that indicate whether the word is singular ('book') or plural ('books') or whether the verb is in the present or the past tense ('help' or 'helped') (see Table 4.4).

Overgeneralisations

Around the age of three years, many children begin to make apparent mistakes in their grammar as they overgeneralise. For example, they have come to understand

Table 4.4 Acquisition of English morphemes

Morpheme	Example
Present possessive -*ing*	She is sit*ting* down.
Preposition 'in'	The doll is *in* the box.
Preposition 'on'	The book is *on* the table.
Plural -*s*	The boy*s* ran away.
Past irregular, e.g. went	The girl *went* home.
Possessive -*s*	The girl*'s* trousers are blue.
Uncontractible copula, e.g. are/was	*Are* they houses?
	Was that daddy?
Articles – the, a	He has *a* toy
Past regular -*ed*	He jump*ed* the stream
Third person regular -*s*	She run*s* fast.
Third person irregular, e.g. has, does	*Does* she play?
Uncontractible copula 'be', e.g. is/were	*Is* he running?
	Were they in the garden?
Contractible copula 'be', e.g. - *'s*, *'re*	That*'s* a man.
Contractible auxiliary 'be', e.g. - *'s*, *'re*	They*'re* running fast.

that one adds an '-ed' ending to make the regular past tense and may use this rule inappropriately. For example, they may say 'I runned' or 'I goed' when a few months earlier they may have been using the correct grammatical form. This is not a sign that they are regressing but rather evidence that the child has learned a new grammatical principle that she applies 'creatively' to her language. In the beginning they had imitated words correctly; now they are using their newly found knowledge. Children continue to make these 'mistakes' well into primary school and, although the adult may model the correct form, the child will ignore the correction. It is interesting that a child who can read and understand that the past tense of the verb 'fight' is 'fought', will continue to use 'fighted' in general conversation.

Asking questions

There are two basic kinds of questions – yes/no and the *wh-* questions.

The simpler yes/no questions are the first to develop. Initially the child indicates a question merely by a change in intonation. Sometimes *wh-* words are placed at the beginning of telegraphic sentences such as 'Where Mummy?'.

The second phase of question form is when the child asks 'What Daddy is eating?'; finally they realise that they have to transform the words and ask 'What is Daddy eating?'.

'What', 'where' and 'who' questions come long before 'why', 'when' and 'how'. This is probably because the first involve referring to concrete things, whereas the others involve abstract concepts like cause and effect, and time, concepts that are not normally used by children under the age of four to five years.

Negative sentences

Just as questions develop gradually, so do children's negative sentences. In the beginning children simply place the word 'no' in front of the word: 'no go' or 'no sock'. Gradually the child begins to extend the sentence with a phrase like 'I not wear mitten'. By the age of four most children can negate sentences in the same way as the adult: 'I am not wearing the shoes'.

Gradually children develop complex sentences, first by joining two simple sentences with 'and', then producing embedded sentences with clauses. By the end of this period most children are using all the grammatical rules of their language and speaking very much like an adult. However, they still have difficulties in interpreting the passive tense. Here is an example of an active sentence, followed by its passive form.

> The girl hit the boy.
> The boy was hit by the girl.

Most young children will understand the second sentence to mean that the boy hit the girl, not the girl hit the boy.

Conversational skills continue to develop and by the age of five most children are good communicators and spend the next few years refining their use of language and using it for more complex tasks like reading, writing and hypothesising. In the next two or three years children begin to develop metalinguistic awareness, that is the ability to think about what they say. Children come to realise that language can be used for purposes other than communicating. There is evidence to suggest that during communication they take into account the sociolinguistic understanding required to make the right kind of speech adjustments so that the message is clear for the listener. Children also become better listeners.

However, although many children reach a high level of language development by the time they enter school, there are many individual differences and a lot of children may still have immature speech and language development.

Speech acts

As children grow up they have to learn to 'read' the linguistic strategies that adults use in general conversation. So often we use expressions and language that we do not expect to be taken literally.

These utterances where we expect the listener to 'read between the lines' are termed speech acts. The child has to interpret the underlying meaning of the statement. For example, the child asks her mother for a sweet and instead of being told 'No', the mother replies that 'It is nearly tea time'. The child has to reconcile the question and response and realise the intent of her mother's answer.

The adult may say to a child, 'There are stains on the carpet'. The child replies 'Yes' and is surprised when she is then told, 'Don't just say yes, tell me how it happened'. The child had responded to the comment but had not taken on board the full implication of the statement.

Most children have been exposed to examples of this type of utterance from an early age and know how to respond, but for some children who have not been exposed to this form of dialogue at home, it can lead to genuine misunderstanding if they meet such statements or questions at school. This type of language presents particular difficulties for second-language learners who are not aware of the cultural implications of the statements.

Young children can also be confused by the different meanings of a word. Perhaps the most famous example is that quoted by Laurie Lee in *Cider with Rosie* where on his first day at school he is told by the teacher to 'Wait there for the present'. The unhappy five-year-old went home and complained to his mother that the teacher had not given him the promised present.

Everyone working with young children can recall instances where their use of language has led to misunderstandings and with second-language learners it is imperative that we use unambiguous language and express ourselves clearly.

Relationship between language and thought

The development of language and thought are closely linked but there has been a great deal of discussion among psychologists as to whether we can think without words. Piaget (1959) argued that language is only one of several possible ways in which children can represent their knowledge. For him, thought is a precursor to language; it is a symbolic system that can be used to express our thoughts and experiences. This belief that thought precedes language led Piaget to the idea that the language children use will reflect their cognitive development. However, other psychologists such as Vygotsky argued that although thinking and language occur together, they do not necessarily have the same origins. He argued that thinking is a cognitive activity that arises as children learn about their world. Language develops because infants hear it around them from their caregivers and other children and adults. Vygotsky believed that at around two years of age there is a crucial moment when the two areas of pre-linguistic thought and pre-intellectual language join together. For him, 'thought becomes verbal and speech rational' (Vygotsky 1962). From now on language has two different functions for the child, an internal function that directs internal thought and an external social function to do with communicating with other people.

For the adult, language has two different functions: inner speech, which we use to monitor our thinking; and the communicative function for speaking or writing. Vygotsky says that young children also use what he terms egocentric speech, when they express their thoughts and ideas out loud without any reference to a listener. Children talk to themselves to organise their thinking, express their feelings or regulate their behaviour. This egocentric speech normally fades as children grow older and they can internalise their thinking more effectively, although, as we know, adults talk to themselves on occasion.

Theories of language development

As we have seen, most children by the time they enter the reception class have an understanding of the grammatical structures of their native language without ever having had a grammar lesson. Psycholinguists and psychologists have raised the question as to how this occurs. Is language learned or is it innate? This was one of the controversies of the twentieth century and the debate still continues.

Learning theory approach

Imitation and reinforcement are the key factors in this approach to language development. The leading exponent of this approach is Skinner, who argued that children learn by imitating adults who shape the child's language by selectively reinforcing the sounds that sound most like speech. During conversations with adults the baby's babble is expanded into words and the child then imitates the sounds she hears. She is then praised for her efforts (reinforced) so makes the sound again. Other learning theorists like Bandura also believed that children gain most of their linguistic knowledge by carefully listening to and imitating the speech of others.

There are problems with this approach. Imitation plays an important part in children's learning but, as research has indicated, if children are not ready to have their grammatical structures shaped then no amount of disapproval will have any effect. If a young child is telling you that she 'sawed a bird', no amount of correction will persuade the child to say she 'saw the bird' until the appropriate linguistic rules have developed and been internalised. Furthermore, the majority of parents do not correct grammatical errors, but will correct statements which involve falsehoods. For example, 'We sawed a bird this morning.' 'No, we saw a bird in the garden yesterday morning.' Skinner's approach may help to explain how children increase single words in their vocabulary but it does not explain the complex original sentences that children generate in such a short time.

Nativist approach

In 1965 Chomsky challenged the behaviourist view of language development and demonstrated that children can generate new sentences that they have definitely not heard before. He argued that children were born with an innate 'language acquisition device' (LAD) that enables the child to structure her language. It provides what Aitchison (1996) terms a 'blueprint for language'. Children learn to talk partly because they are born with this device and partly through the people they meet. It is an innate ability, but requires humans to trigger the process. Researchers studied the errors made by children and found that these gave them important clues about the development of language. However, in 1986 Chomsky abandoned his earlier viewpoint, arguing that this did not account for how children acquired the full grammar of their language with such little information to work on. He now assumes that children are born with a two-tier system of language which is independent of other cognitive abilities. Children are born with a set of language principles and further aspects of language that they learn to 'set switches' to the language to which they are exposed, in order to acquire further aspects of language.

There is support for this theory as there seems to be a sensitive period during which children can learn language more easily. Studies with children deprived of human contact at an early age like the Wild Boy of Averyon and, more recently, the case of the twins in America show that there is a crucial time for language development. Support for the sensitive-period hypothesis, postulated by Lenneberg (1967), also comes from brain-injured children who were found to recover their language almost completely if the accident occurred before the onset of puberty. According to the nativists the sensitive period for language learning is a product of biological maturation.

Recent research has not borne out all of Chomsky's ideas but it seems that there is evidence to show that children seem to be equipped with some sort of innate linguistic device that helps them to extract language from the jumble of sounds around them. As Aitchison writes:

> They have relatively little knowledge about the actual *form* of the language, but seem instead to have a remarkable ability for processing linguistic data. We are still a long way from specifying exactly how the operating principles work. And we do not know how children backtrack in order to correct their wrong assumptions. This is still quite puzzling, since they seem to be impervious to corrections by other people.
>
> (Aitchison 1996: 225)

Therefore, the nativist approach alone does not seem to provide an adequate explanation as to how children learn their language.

Social interactionist approach

Neither learning theory nor the nativist approach is able to provide a complete answer to language development. In recent years, cognitive theorists like Piaget, Vygotsky and Bruner have argued that biological factors, cognitive factors and the linguistic environment interact to affect the development of children's language.

According to interactionist theory, children all over the world may talk alike because they are members of the same species who share common experiences. Bates (1993) has suggested that what is innate is not a special language mechanism but a sophisticated brain that matures very slowly and predisposes children to develop similar ideas about the same age. They then express the ideas in their own speech.

Advocates of the interactionist approach place a general focus on general cognitive development, as well as on the social and communicative factors that promote language learning. For advocates of this approach, other humans, older children as well as adults, contribute to children's understanding by the way in which they tailor the level of language to the child's needs.

Social factors affecting language

Although the vast majority of children develop language, some children enter school with a wider vocabulary and speaking in more complex sentences than others. Research by Bernstein in the UK and many others in the USA argued that children from working-class homes were disadvantaged because they used what has been termed a 'restricted language code' that held them back at school. By contrast, children from middle-class homes used what Bernstein termed an 'elaborated' code that enabled them to achieve more in school. However, as Labov (1969) and others have shown, these children from working-class homes were not impoverished in their language; rather they used a non-standard English that was rich, varied and grammatical. To be fair to Bernstein, he did not say that the children from lower socio-economic groups had impoverished language, rather that children who did not speak standard English were likely to be disadvantaged in school as there standard English was required.

This view has been adopted more recently by researchers who have realised that the problems are more likely to reflect the failure of the schools to recognise that staff may come from different cultures and backgrounds and therefore may not value and respect the language and culture of the children. Furthermore, research by Gordon Wells (1986) has shown that there is no evidence to support the assumption that there is 'verbal deprivation' in families of lower socio-economic status. He has shown that the problem lies in the fact that teachers do not have real everyday conversations with children, talking about what is of interest to the child. When they do, the teachers would find that many 'disadvantaged' children are able to produce a great deal of language. Children have substantially different sets of communication skills at home and school.

Dialects

Children growing up in different areas of a country will speak differently from one another. Sometimes these differences are just in the way they pronounce words, the accent. For example, children in London will speak with a different accent from children in Glasgow or Liverpool. However, people throughout the country also speak with different dialects, in other words not only is the pronunciation different, but the actual words and grammar are different. Many people in the south-east of England speak with a standard English dialect, this is the dialect used mostly on television and radio. However, in, for example, Scotland and parts of the north-east of

England, people may use different words. For example, the word 'bairn' may be used rather than 'child'. This is not standard English, but it is *not* wrong.

It is important to realise that children who do not speak in a standard dialect do not have an incorrect or impoverished language. Yet one of the problems that these children may encounter in school is the prejudice of teachers who use only a standard dialect and view the children's grammar, in particular, as wrong.

Bilingualism/multilingualism

For the majority of the world's population, the ability to speak two or more languages fluently is normal. Only in countries with a very dominant first language, such as English, French or Spanish, do people tend to be monolingual, i.e. speak only one language.

Until the 1960s, linguists from monolingual societies considered that learning two languages rather than one hindered a child's language proficiency or slowed intellectual development. This research has been shown to be flawed. Contrary to popular belief, learning two or more languages rather than one neither hinders a child's language proficiencies nor retards her intellectual growth. Recent research shows that there are cognitive advantages to bilingualism.

Later research shows that children exposed to two languages before the age of three have little difficulty in becoming proficient in both. They occasionally mixed phonologies and sometimes applied the grammar and vocabulary of one language to the second language being acquired, but by the age of three they were aware that the two languages had independent systems and were used in different contexts and situations. By the age of four they displayed normal language proficiencies in the language of their community and had excellent linguistic skills in the second language, depending on how much they had been exposed to it.

Advantages of being bilingual/multilingual:

- the child learns the culture that is linked to the language;
- they can think in different ways about the same thing, for example in Arabic there are many more words for sand than in English, so children can think about sand in greater detail;
- they grow with an understanding of two or more cultures, which should help them to be more tolerant of others;
- they can think more divergently.

Role of the adult in children's language development

From birth, the adult has an important role in the child's language development. It is from the adult, or another child, that the baby hears the language of its environment. It is through hearing that language that the early babbles and coos become language specific and the baby practises the sounds that are part of her mother tongue.

As discussed earlier in this chapter, the caregiver will play games like 'peek-a-boo' with the child, helping to develop an understanding of turn taking and its importance in conversation. In responding to the baby's cries and gestures the adult is helping the baby to understand about communication.

Adults support the early language of children in a number of ways. One way is by the 'expansion of utterances'. When the baby utters a word like 'milk' it is the adult who puts the statement into context and who responds by saying 'You want some milk', 'Here is the milk' or 'You have finished your milk'. As the child progresses to two-word sentences the adult will continue to expand and extend the language so that the child is exposed to new grammatical structures. At the same time, the language used by the adult tends to be simplified, slow and involve a lot of repetition. This has been termed 'caretaker' language. Although it is used in many cultures, the approach is by no means universal as in some cultures the babies are rarely spoken to directly until they are able to respond. Even quite young children will modify their language to an even simpler form when they are talking to a baby.

Adults also help children in both their language and cognitive development when they accompany their language with actions. For example, every time the caregiver lifts the baby out of the high chair she may say 'up we go'. As the child grows more competent in language they still need actions to accompany language as in this way they come to understand language more fully: 'Are we going to make those cakes? Are you going to help me put the mixture into the cake tin?'. When adults respond to children, they will use correct grammatical structures, although normally any correction of the child's language is factual, not grammatical. For example, if the child makes a factually incorrect statement the adult will probably correct it, whereas a grammatical error will not be corrected.

It is through language that we transmit our culture, values and mores. An important role of the adult is to read and tell children the stories and rhymes that reflect the values and customs of society. It is also important that children engage in conversations with adults and their peers, but adults need to remember to talk 'with' not 'at' the child. Bruner refers to the adults as providing the 'scaffolding' for the child. Adults teach children turn-taking skills, but sadly as the children grow older many adults seem to want an extended turn, forgetting that conversations should be two-way. Children are expected to listen and not given the opportunity to put forward their own points of view.

Suggestions for fostering language development:

- give the children something to talk about;
- be prepared to listen to the child;
- tell stories, rhymes and poems;
- help them to understand the world around them;
- engage in genuine dialogue;
- wait for a response – small children often take time to organise their responses;
- help children to express their feelings;
- help children to organise their ideas;
- help children to turn take.

Reflect upon ...

1 How important is non-verbal communication at the pre-linguistic stage?
2 In what ways can adults support children's language development?
3 Discuss the view that children need to be taught to use an appropriate language register in wider social settings.
4 How would you help a child with English as an additional language to integrate into your classroom?

References

Aitchison, J. (1996) *The Articulate Mammal*, third edition, London: Routledge.

Bates, E. (1993) *Nature, Nurture and Language*, New Orleans, LA: Society for Research in Child Development.

Bernstein, B. (1972) 'Social Class, Language and Socialisation', in P.P. Giglioli (ed.), *Language and Social Context*, Harmondsworth: Penguin.

Chomsky, N. (1965) *Aspects of the Theory of Syntax*, Cambridge, MA: MIT Press.

Chomsky, N. (1986) *Knowledge of Language in Nature, Origin and Use*, New York: Praeger.

Crystal, D. (1986) *Listen to Your Child*, Harmondsworth: Penguin.

de Villiers, J.G. and de Villiers, P.A. (1992) 'Language Development', in M.H. Bornstein and M.E. Lamb (eds), *Developmental Psychology: An Advanced Handbook*, Hillsdale, NJ: Erlbaum.

Labov, W. (1969) 'The logic of non-standard English', reprinted in P. Giglioli (ed.), *Language and Social Context*, Harmondsworth: Penguin.

Lees, J. and Urwin, S. (1997) *Children with Language Disorders*, second edition, London: Whurr Publishers.

Lenneberg, E.H. (1967) *Biological Foundations of Language*, New York: Wiley.

Nelson, K. (1973) *Structure and Strategy in Learning to Talk*, monograph of Society for Research in Child Development 38.

Piaget, J. and Inhelder, B. (1969) *The Psychology of the Child*, London: Routledge & Kegan Paul.

Pinker, S. (2000) *The Language Instinct*, Harmondsworth: Penguin.

Vygotsky, L.S. (1962) *Thought and Language*, Cambridge, MA: MIT Press.

Wells, G. (1986) *The Meaning Makers: Children Learning Language and Using Language to Learn*, London: Hodder and Stoughton.

5 Working with the under-threes

This chapter looks at the child's first three years of life including aspects of physiological development such as brain development and how babies communicate with each other. There is also a section on the value of heuristic and other types of play and aspects that may affect their general development. There is also a section relating to young children in day-care. The new Early Years Foundation Stage (EYFS) for the birth–three years age group is discussed in Chapter 10 and Chapter 3 has the most recent information in relation to children's brain development.

The first three years of life are a time of rapid growth and development for young children and therefore prove to be exciting and challenging for the child-care worker or carer. Gopnik *et al.* (1999) state that babies have the best technical support for learning as the adults around them are able to play a powerful role in their development. Therefore anyone who is envisaging working with this age group needs to realise their importance and role in the children's development.

The *Carnegie Task Force Report* (1994) highlights the importance of the first three years of life being the foundation upon which other learning will be built. Goldschmeid and Jackson (1994) refer to 'people under three' in order to reinforce the concept that 0–3 year-olds are not just 'empty vessels' waiting for adults to 'fill them' but people in their own right.

Historically, this has not always been the case as babies were swaddled into inactivity and left to sleep and eat, stimulation and play not being viewed as part of a child's development. One of the most comprehensive accounts of how babies were viewed by society and treated over time can be found in Christine Hardyment's book *Dream Babies – Child Care from Locke to Spock* (1984). One of the most popular texts on babies that did not stem from the religious or medical world was Jean-Jacques Rousseau's *Emile, ou L'Education* (1762). Rousseau followed the belief that children were born 'free, natural and innocent' and should not be swaddled but left free to move and play. John Locke, on the other hand, was of the opinion that babies' minds were a 'blank sheet' (tabula rasa) and it was the responsibility of the adult to 'write' upon this sheet.

Piaget (1952) thought that babies' minds assimilated information in the same way as their bodies assimilated milk, whereas Vygotsky viewed the adult influence on children's minds as part of human nature and stressed the role of language on this area of development. Modern technology such as video has enabled developmental psychologists to study babies' non-verbal behaviour in order to analyse facial expressions, eye movements, etc. As a result of this there is much more research in the field of developmental psychology being carried out on babies and very young children, all in the hope that adults will have a greater understanding of how young children's minds develop.

Physiological development of the brain

As previously stated, babies are not born with a brain that is like an 'empty vessel' or a 'blank sheet' just waiting for the adult to 'fill it up' or 'write upon it'. The baby's brain, like other parts of the body, grows and develops through the nine months of pregnancy. Brain cells begin to form as early as three weeks after conception and multiply at a rapid rate, continuing up until one year after birth. A great deal of foetal development of the brain depends upon the genetic makeup of the child, however, a mother's health and emotional state during pregnancy can have an impact on this development. If the mother has a problem with drugs, alcohol, living in a toxic atmosphere, etc., these factors can all have an effect on the way the brain cells of the foetus develop. Studies carried out on pregnant women seem to suggest that if, during the pregnancy, the mother experiences fear, anger or job stress, this may result in the production of an irritable/bad-tempered infant (Healy 1994). Sadly, trauma during the actual birth process can destroy some brain cells resulting in cerebral palsy or other related conditions.

Once babies are born, the brain's billions of nerve cells become organised into systems and networks we can recognise as thinking, talking, remembering, etc. Activities, environment, adults, etc., stimulate the nerve cells into action, what Healy (1994) refers to as the 'building of neural highways'. Each child's brain is unique and through this process 'each child weaves his own intellectual tapestry, the quality of which depends on active interest and involvement in a wide variety of stimuli' (Healy 1994).

By studying babies' eye movements scientists have found that within a few days of birth babies can recognise human faces and voices and discriminate between them. They also have a well-developed sense of smell that enables them to distinguish between different adults. Whilst it has long been known that newborn babies have a limited visual capacity (about 12 inches) in the early weeks of life, they are able to use hearing and smell to aid their limited sight in order to distinguish between adults and environments.

The brain is divided into four areas:

1   the *occipital lobe*, which relates to vision;
2   the *parietal lobe*, which relates to touch and spatial awareness;
3   the *temporal lobe*, which relates to hearing and language;
4   the *frontal lobes*, which are sub-divided into:
   i the *motor cortex*, which relates to body movements;
   ii the *pre-frontal cortex*, which relates to reasoning, memory, attention, judgement, planning and self-control.

Each lobe/cortex has a right and left side (hemisphere) and in humans the right side of the brain dominates the left side of the body and vice versa. A dominant right side of the brain will result in the child being left-handed.

This can also be seen in people who have strokes, where the paralysis left by the stroke will affect the side of the body opposite to the side of the brain where the stroke has actually taken place.

At birth, the brain is 25 per cent of its adult weight, whereas the baby's body is only 5 per cent of its adult weight. At six months, the brain is nearly half its adult weight. So here we have this tiny baby, with a huge brain and the capacity to build up numerous pathways within the brain through their ability to participate in complex thought patterns. As the baby lies in the cot watching, listening and feeling they build up a picture of people and the world around them. It is therefore important that the child-care worker is aware of this rapid development in the baby's brain and is able to stimulate the child visually and auditorily in order to encourage the 'neural highways' to develop. However, be guarded against over-stimulation, which can be caused by persistent loud noises and a cacophony of sound.

Communication with and between babies

From work undertaken by a number of researchers using video film, we know that babies communicate not only with adults but also with each other. Using this technology the National Children's Bureau were able to produce a training pack called *Communication between Babies in their First Year* (1996) that contains very interesting video footage. Honig (1994) states that children respond appropriately to other children's inviting glances and gestures. Whaley and Rubenstein (1994) made videos of a number of children aged 22–36 months, in day-care settings. They analysed the results and concluded that young children are capable of complex reciprocal relationships and having such relationships helped to develop their self-esteem.

A baby's first communication is with the mother whose voice and heartbeat they learn to recognise in the first days of life. Trevarthan (1995) maintains that infants can, from the age of around four months, learn to join in musical games and body play providing that the adult is able to offer feedback to the baby's actions in the form of mirroring. Babies are then able to make sense of these interactive communications and over a period of time this is internalised and changes the way the baby thinks. Trevarthan maintains that the number of abilities which babies and infants have has long been unrecognised by psychologists. Only recently, and possibly video has aided this development, have psychologists studied and recorded the minutiae of baby's interactions. Trevarthan states that, 'the developing social consciousness of a seven to eight month-old is manifested simultaneously in pretending or joking with "friends", and in sensitivity to incomprehension or ridicule by a stranger' (1995: 11). Trevarthan also refers to something called 'protolanguage', which combines vocalisations, gestures and facial expressions to communicate their interests to other babies and close adults. It is important that babies are able to socially interact with their carers, thus consistency in the relationship between mother and baby/carer and baby is an important aspect of the child's communication.

Bruner (1980) suggests that children learn better when adults support or 'scaffold' children's tasks so that the child's activities are extended. However, Trevarthan sees these activities as more complex than straightforward 'scaffolding' as they are recreated by the child out of the learning situation.

As children grow older they learn language that encodes their previous non-verbal communications. They are able to name objects in addition to understanding the properties of the object, many of which they have probably known long before they could verbalise them. An indication that children have a lot more knowledge than the language they have to express this knowledge is when the frustration in trying to communicate manifests itself as a temper tantrum. This usually begins around 18 months to two years and abates as the child's language abilities develop. At one year of age, a child may understand 40–100 words but can only verbalise 0–20 words (Trevarthan 1995). By the time a child has reached the age of three they are able to communicate in a way that is understood by parents and carers. The development of children's language is well-documented in numerous child psychology/child-development textbooks. However, it must be remembered that the development of a child's language is dependent upon the interactions between the child and the adult.

Factors that may affect children's development

Each child is an individual and develops at his or her own unique pace. However, there are some external factors that may impinge upon their development, such as sex differences, social class and culture.

Since the introduction of ultra-sound scanning expectant parents are now able to get photographs of their child whilst it is still developing in the mother's womb. One aspect of this is that the sex of the foetus can be made known to the expectant parents. In some instances, such as where there is an illness that is carried on a sex-linked gene it may be very important to know the sex of the foetus as soon as possible so that decisions can be made as to whether the pregnancy should be continued or terminated. Expectant parents are asked by the ultra-scan technician whether they wish to know the sex of the foetus; some may wish to know in order to plan, whereas others may be happy to wait until the birth. It appears that the sex of a child makes little difference to the way the child will develop. Neither does it appear are boys more demanding than girls. What does affect development is when a child is encouraged or prevented from developing in certain directions because of their sex. For instance, parents will often have boisterous play with their male offspring whereas they may treat their daughters in a gentler fashion. Expectations of a child's behaviour in relation to their sex may inhibit certain areas of development, for example, it is not uncommon to find that girls are poor map readers or do not feel confident dealing with mathematical or spatial concepts. Such distinctions can start at a very early age with the toys that are presented to children, soft cuddly things for girls, building blocks for boys. Society is becoming more aware of the effects of this type of gender-instigated selection and many parents are making decisive efforts to avoid this happening.

Social class can make a difference to a child's development in terms of environment and financial input. Poor families often live in poor housing in city areas that may be overcrowded and poorly serviced by public transport and amenities. It must not be forgotten that in rural areas the families of farm labourers may also suffer from similar deprivations regarding poverty, public transport and amenities. In terms of child development, poverty is one factor that can inhibit a child's potential.

Infants from poor families are more likely to be born with a low birth weight and the mothers may experience complications in pregnancy and/or delivery. However, Bee (1992) does point out that when you compare healthy babies from middle-class families and healthy babies from poor families in the early months of life, there are no differences in perceptual skills, motor development or learning. Poor diet can result in poor physical development, illness, etc. There is reliance in our present society upon pre-prepared foods that are easily cooked via a microwave, and this can mean that the quality of the food that children are receiving is not always good in terms of nutritional value. The number of cookery programmes on television also seems to indicate that there are large numbers of people who have forgotten how to produce dishes from raw ingredients. Poverty can result in lack of stimulation of the child due to lack of space, few toys and living in an area that is poorly serviced for play groups, nurseries, mother and toddler clubs, etc. In Western cultures there is a reliance on manufactured toys, whereas in many other cultures children may get their stimulation from playing with natural materials found in the immediate environment. Children born into middle-class families do not suffer the effects of poverty, rather they could suffer the effects of too much money and high expectations. Many middle-class women have careers to which they want to return as quickly as possible after giving birth. The baby is then left in the care of a nanny or mother's help. The quality of care that the child will get is very dependent upon the qualifications of the carer. If the carer is not trained to a level whereby they are able to undertake sole-charge posts then the child may not get the stimulation and developmental opportunities it needs. There is also an expression, which has crept into middle-class households, that talks of 'quality time' between the mother and the child. Does one then assume that all other time that the child spends away from the mother is not 'quality time'? Perhaps this expression has arisen in order to reassure the mother that she has some role, however small, in bringing up her child. All interactions between baby and adult (whether the mother or carer) should be of the highest quality. Middle-class parents have high expectations of their child's development. They will have read all the books and will know all the milestones and which toys the child should be given at which stage of development. However, what they often miss is the fact that children's development is an individual process and milestones will happen when the child is ready, not when the book says so. This sometimes leads to stress between the mother and child (and sometimes the nanny) when the child is not developing at a rate that meets the expectations of the mother.

Cultural differences in child development have not been investigated in great depth as there is a danger that misinterpretation of results could lead to racial prejudice. There was a great deal of controversy relating to the research that purported to have found differences in IQ between white and black Americans, particularly as the results mitigated against the black Americans. There are also dangers in how any such research findings may be used; for example research undertaken on Jews in the 1930s was used to justify the Holocaust. In her book on child development, Helen Bee does cite some studies that have investigated cross-cultural differences. Daniel Freedman (1979) observed newborn babies from four different cultures, Caucasian, Chinese, Navaho and Japanese. Of the four, he found that the Caucasian babies were the most active and irritable and the hardest to console. Both Chinese and Navaho infants were relatively placid whilst the Japanese infants responded vigorously but were easier to quieten. Freedman's argument is that as these were newborn children their parents had not yet shaped them. However, as other research has shown, interaction between the mother and their newborn infant is very important. Perhaps this is a dimension that Freedman has not taken into account. Whilst these results are interesting, Freedman does extrapolate a conclusion that says that our idea of what is 'normal' behaviour in a child is strongly influenced by our own cultural expectations. I do not think that anyone would disagree with this conclusion. Certainly research in Africa has shown that black babies are more advanced in their gross motor skills from an early age, however, they are usually living in a spacious outdoor environment with lots of room to move about and lots of stimulation from numerous adults and older children. An area which has been heavily researched is bilingualism. One of the most common questions asked is whether children will become confused if they are spoken to in two different languages. Siraj-Blatchford and Clarke (2000) point out that learning a language is a complex task and that children need to learn the sounds of the language, the vocabulary, the grammar, the way sentences are put together and the rules of the language. It would appear that children cope perfectly well with being spoken to in two different languages from an early age. There are sometimes problems when a second language is introduced much later on. In some cultures a child may be exposed to three languages, for example, most Orthodox Jewish households speak Yiddish, Hebrew and English. Bee cites research into bilingualism by McLoughlin (1984), who states that what would confuse a child is if sentences consist of more than one language, as this will prove much more difficult for the child to understand. In a number of cultures the extended family is the 'norm' and young children may bond with more than one person or just their parents. Where you have people living in small villages that comprise a tribe or clan, then the baby may bond with people who are not members of their direct family. This may also happen in Western societies when the mother returns to work very soon after the birth and the child is left with a childminder or with a key worker in a day-care setting. There does not seem to be any ill effects if the child bonds with a number of people provided they are constant figures in the child's life.

Heuristic play

Heuristic play is a word used to describe how children learn by exploration and discovery. It is linked with the work of Elinor Goldschmeid who developed the 'Treasure Basket' as a tool for heuristic play. The Treasure Basket does not contain toys or objects made from synthetic substances, i.e. plastic. It uses everyday objects made of natural materials in order to stimulate children's senses such as touch, sight, smell and hearing. The child explores the objects in the Treasure Basket and discovers the properties of the objects, such as shape, form, size, hard, soft, cold, warm, squashy, rigid. Children get great pleasure from exploring the contents of the Treasure Basket from an age when they are able to sit unaided.

Goldschmeid suggests that the objects in a Treasure Basket should be able to offer the child the following experiences:

- touch: texture, shape, weight;
- smell: variety of scents;
- sound: ringing, tinkling, banging, scrunching;
- sight: colour, form, shininess, length.

She offers the following suggestions for objects to put in the Treasure Basket:

- natural objects: fir cones, large pebbles, shells, gourds, big feathers, walnuts, lemon;
- objects made from natural materials: woollen balls, bone shoehorn, small raffia mat, wooden nailbrush, shaving brush;
- wooden objects: small boxes, small drum, clothes pegs, cubes, spoon, small bowl, coloured beads on a string;
- metal objects: spoons of various sizes, bunch of keys, small tins, whistle, bells, bicycle bell, lengths of chain, metal egg cup;
- objects in leather, rubber, textile and fur: leather purse, leather bag, velvet powder puff, fur ball, rubber tubing, rag doll, beanbag;
- objects made from paper and card: notebook, tin foil, greaseproof paper, small cardboard boxes, cardboard roll from inside kitchen roll.

(adapted from Goldschmeid and Jackson 1994)

A selection of things from each of these categories can be placed in a wicker basket (not less than 351 mm in diameter). It is important to ensure that all the chosen objects are safe for the baby to be left alone with. The basket is placed near the child who is able to reach out and take things from the basket and explore them. The adult's role in this activity is to organise the collection of the items for the Treasure Basket and keep them in good repair. They are not involved in the child's exploration but are able to observe the child and record/register what the child is learning from the experience. It is also possible to watch two babies exploring one Treasure Basket and note the interaction between the children.

Children over 18 months of age can be introduced to what Goldschmeid calls 'heuristic play with objects'. This is when a group of children are offered a large number of different kinds of objects for a defined period of time in a controlled environment. The children are able to play freely with these objects without adult intervention. The types of objects that can be used are empty tins, woollen pom-poms, table tennis balls, small bags and boxes, old keys tied in a bunch, curtain rings, hair rollers, bottle corks, cockle or snail shells, rubber door stops, cardboard cylinders, etc. The objects are placed in large cloth bags with a drawstring. There should be about 50–60 items in each bag and at least 20 bags for a group of eight children. Each bag should contain only one variety of items and there should be at least 15 varieties of items available for the children. Once again the adult's role is one of facilitator, making sure that the time limit for the activity is kept to and involving the children in the clearing-up process.

Heuristic play is something that can be used with children as part of an activity programme drawn up over a week or a fortnight. It is not envisaged that it should be a daily activity. Holland (1997) states that Hutt *et al.* (1989) put forward two different kinds of play behaviours: 'epistemic' and 'ludic'.

Epistemic play behaviour

- is concerned with acquisition of knowledge, skills and problem solving;
- gathers information;
- is exploratory;

- is productive;
- discovers;
- is invention, task or work-oriented;
- is relatively independent of mood state;
- has constraints that stem from the nature of the focus of attention;
- needs adults to support, encourage, answer questions, supply information, be involved.

Ludic play behaviour

- is playful;
- is fun;
- is lacking in specific focus;
- is highly mood dependent;
- has constraints that (when they exist) are imposed by the child;
- does not need to involve adults;
- requires that adults are sensitive to children's needs;
- has the key features of enjoyment and fantasy;
- is unconstrained;
- is idiosyncratic;
- is repetitive;
- is innovative;
- is symbolic.

Heuristic play would come into the category of epistemic play, although not all the characteristics of this type of play would apply.

Infants/young children in day-care

During the 1950s/1960s and part way through the 1970s it was not the norm for mothers to go to work and leave their children in some type of day-care. The attitude of society was one that discouraged women with children from working, and this was reinforced by psychologists such as John Bowlby. Bowlby (1951) argued that 'an infant and young child should experience a warm, intimate and continuous relationship with its mother'. This began the debate relating to bonding and maternal deprivation in young children. This left many mothers who were forced to return to the workforce for economic reasons feeling very guilty about what they may be doing to their child by placing it in a day-care situation. Around the same time, James and Joyce Robertson made a series of direct-observation films entitled 'Children in Brief Separation'. These films illustrated children being separated from their mothers for short periods either due to hospitalisation or being placed in a residential nursery whilst the mother gives birth to a second child. The visual images of the Robertsons' films served to back up Bowlby's theories on maternal deprivation and attachment and loss. The debate went on through the 1960s and 1970s. Other researchers produced 'evidence' that upheld the Bowlby theory; not least being Harlow's experiments with baby rhesus monkeys that, when taken from their mothers at an early age, bonded with 'terry-towelling' mothers that were placed in their cage.

In an attempt to counteract the maternal deprivation theories a number of American studies were undertaken to compare attachments of children in day-care with those who had remained at home cared for by their mother. From these studies came two important factors: (1) the quality of the substitute care was of great importance, along with (2) the stability of the substitute relationship. British studies undertaken by Mayall and Petrie (1977) and Garland and White (1980) came to similar conclusions as the American studies. Thus a new look was taken at how day-care provision could best provide consistent high-quality substitute care. Small-scale day-care situations such as childminders and nannies came to be viewed as preferable for the care of very young children rather than larger institutions such as day nurseries and family centres. In order to address the issues of staff consistency of those working in baby and toddler rooms, the large institutions were encouraged to introduce a system of key workers. Key workers, usually two per child so that one was on duty at all times, were assigned to work with specific children so that they could offer these children continuity and stability of care.

By undertaking home visits key workers were able to establish relationships with the child and their family prior to them being admitted to the nursery. These visits enabled the key worker to understand the child's home environment and the child's preferences in toys, food, sleep patterns and comfort objects. Key workers were also able to establish relationships with the other children and adults in the family that the baby shared their home with. When a child started at the nursery the key worker represented a familiar person that they could identify with and someone the family could relate to.

Goldschmeid and Jackson (1994) point out that there are difficulties in implementing the key-worker system. First, it is expensive in terms of staffing and is probably not a viable option unless each key worker is responsible for four children. Holidays and illness can result in a child's key worker being away and the child can then experience a sense of loss. One way of overcoming this is to have two key workers attached to each child: one is the predominant carer and the other is a secondary carer who is familiar with the child but does not take the lead role in their care. Another problem is that staff may object to the key-worker system, as it requires them to form a close relationship with one/two children. Too close a relationship can result in the key worker experiencing loss and deprivation when the child becomes old enough to move to a different room in the nursery. Key workers may become upset if the child they care for appears to be neglected at weekends when it is with its parents. Relationships between the key worker and the parents can become strained if the child bonds with the key worker and not the parent. Parents may feel particularly guilty when this happens. A parent may become jealous of the key worker's relationship with their child. The parent may also feel that the key worker is judging their parenting skills and may report the outcome to social workers and others in authority.

However problematic to implement the key-worker system appears to be, it is imperative that centres persevere with it as it is preferable to the child being handled by multiple carers. Research has shown that within our society multiple carers are detrimental to a young child's emotional and cognitive development.

In order to cope with the new demands that being a key worker entails, staff will need to be trained and when necessary have the opportunity to consult a counsellor about their own feelings in times of difficulty.

The present government places great emphasis on women with young children returning to the workforce and has produced a policy it describes as 'wrap-around care' in order to enable mothers to return to work. However, there are very few instances where this 'wrap-around care' can be offered in one establishment; in the majority of cases it may involve a combination of a childminder, a day-care centre and an out-of-school facility. For the two- to three-year-olds this is not a good situation, but for the under-two-year-old it can prove a disaster. For the very young child a placement with a childminder could offer both high-quality care and stability. Childminding is now a profession in its own right. There are qualifications for childminders in the National Qualifications Framework produced by the Qualifications and Curriculum Authority (QCA) and all childminders are encouraged to take these in order to validate their professional status. Childminders must be registered with the local authority/OFSTED. A large number of people become childminders when their own children are small and many were previously teachers, nurses and child-care workers prior to having their own children.

Working in partnership with parents

It is imperative that those caring for children under three years of age work in partnership with parents or the primary carer of the child. In many inner-city areas there is a large selection of full day-care establishments that take children from 0–3 years, however, individual establishments will have different methods of dealing with the 0–3 years age group. For very young children, surveys have suggested that the most popular choice of parents is to leave their child with a relative or a registered childminder. Childminding is able to bridge the gaps that other forms of day-care may be unable to fulfil, for example, where mothers return to work after maternity leave; where parents work shifts or unsociable hours; or where parents are studying at colleges that have no child-care facilities. The small-scale situation is able to offer consistency in terms of the numbers of people a child needs to relate to and much closer links between the carer and the child's parents.

Before admitting a young child to any form of full day-care the parents need to be consulted in order to find out the child's normal routine, such as sleep patterns, food preferences and favourite comforter. This is best done via a home visit or a pre-entry interview with the parent or primary carer.

In recent years we have seen many more fathers choosing to stay at home to look after their children. In many cases their partner may earn a great deal more than they do and so sensible economics result in the father becoming the primary carer. On a recent radio programme that interviewed a number of these fathers it was sad to hear about the prejudices they were encountering. One father had been asked not attend the mother-and-toddler clinic as the mothers objected to him being there when they were breastfeeding. The health visitor did visit him at home, however, as he pointed out he missed the opportunity to talk to the other parents and this left him very isolated. A number of the men had been viewed with suspicion as to their underlying motives for wishing to be the primary carer of their child. Such prejudice came from all directions, other men, mothers and professionals. As paedophilia featured more and more in the media so the feelings against male primary carers became more widespread. The men interviewed in the programme expressed their sadness about this situation but were not deterred in continuing their role as primary carer.

There is more information on working with parents in a later chapter in this book.

Recent government initiatives

1 Child Health Promotion Programme (CHPP)

This document was published by the Department of Health in March 2008 and is aimed at the Chief Executives of Primary Care Trusts, NHS Trusts, etc. The document deals with the period from pregnancy through to five years of age. This is an updated version of the original document, the *National Service Framework for Children, Young People and Maternity Services*, which was published in 2004. There is a definite change in emphasis in this document from that of the 2004 document as a result of 'significant changes in parents' expectations, in our knowledge about neurological development, in our knowledge about what interventions work, and in the landscape of children's policy and services' (p. 8). The document has a very interesting section on the CHPP schedule that has advice for practitioners on the important points they should be promoting universally to parents, starting at the beginning of pregnancy and through the age groups birth to one week, one to six weeks, six weeks to six months, six months to one year, one year to three years and three years to five years. In addition to highlighting the main health promotional points, it also has progressive points that deal with the risk areas and how these might be addressed (www.dh.gov.publications).

2 Review of the Health Inequalities, Infant Mortality PSA Targets

This document, published in 2007 by the Health Inequalities Unit of the Department of Health, specifically looks at the inequalities in health that relate to the Infant Mortality Rates and the Public Service Agreement (PSA) targets. There is a target to reduce the infant mortality rate by 2010 by at least 10 per cent in the social group referred to as 'the routine and manual population as a whole'. They define this group as being workers in occupations such as porters, cleaners, bar staff, waiters/waitresses, sales assistants, catering assistants, train drivers. This is an interesting definition of a social group that does not seem to fit other social groupings in other areas, however, it does not explain why this group are at greater risk than others. The document itself is informative and one of its most useful areas is the appendix where it gives examples of good practice which can help prevent infant mortality (www.dh.gov.uk/publications).

3 Sure Start – an intervention initiative

Whilst this initiative is not new, it is still proving to be a very valuable initiative which is responsible for the development of Children's Centres and other provision that help parents.

A major aim of the Sure Start initiative is to prevent families spiralling into situations where they are unable to cope. The government has invested £452 million in setting up 250 Sure Start programmes over a three-year period. In 1999, the first 60 Sure Start programmes were started and they were designated as the 'trailblazers'.

Sure Start programmes must cover the physical, intellectual and social development of the 0–4 years age group. Sure Start programmes are locally devised so that they answer the needs of a particular area or group of people. Any Sure Start bid must demonstrate an integrated delivery of services across the following areas:

- outreach services and home visiting;
- support for families and parents;
- services to support good quality play, learning and childcare;
- primary and community health care;
- support for those with special needs.

Local programmes must ensure that stakeholders work together to improve the quality and accessibility of services for families; this includes parents, community volunteers, GPs, health visitors, midwives, education and child-care professionals, and others. Local programmes are able to provide services not already in the area, add value to existing services, provide new facilities, give parents clear information, train existing professionals and volunteers and improve joint working and coordination between existing service providers. Clear target objectives are laid down in order to evaluate local programmes.

In the initial stages there was some opposition from rural areas to the Sure Start initiative, as the requirement to bring the services to the people in need was clearly impossible in these areas. Schemes whereby local authorities in these areas had provided transport to bring the people to the services did not appear to fit in with the Sure Start requirements and were in danger of being marginalised or lost altogether. Clearly, rural areas needed to be consulted as to the best practice available to them, in order to ensure that the people in need got the services they required in the easiest and most cost-effective way.

Reflect upon …

1 On page 68 it states 'The quality of care that the child will get is very dependent upon the qualifications of the carer'. Compare this statement with the large number of early childhood qualifications that are available and their levels.

2 Heuristic play describes how children learn by exploration and discovery. Give some examples of the types of play that could be referred to as heuristic.

3 The Sure Start programme started in 1999 with 60 'trailblazers'; since then it has become a growing initiative across the UK. Look on your local authority website and identify the Sure Start initiatives in your area.

References

Albon, D. and Mukherji, P. (2008) *Food and Health in Early Childhood*, London: Sage Publications.

Bee, H. (1992) *The Developing Child*, sixth edition, New York: HarperCollins.

Bowlby, J. (1951) *Maternal Care and Mental Health*, Geneva: World Health Organisation.

Bowlby, J. (1979) *The Making and Breaking of Affectional Bonds*, London: Tavistock Publications.

Bruner, J.S. (1980) *Under Five in Britain, Oxford Pre-school Research Project 1*, London: Grant McIntyre.

Carnegie Task Force Report (1994) *Starting Points – Meeting the Needs of our Youngest Children*, New York: Carnegie Corporation.

DFEE (2000a) *Early Excellence Centres. First Findings Autumn 1999*, Suffolk: DFEE Publications.

DFEE (2000b) *Good Practice in Childcare No. 8, Providing a Wrap-Around Service in Early Years and Childcare*, Suffolk: DFEE Publications.

Department of Health (2007) *Review of the Inequalities in Health. Infant Mortality PSA Targets*, London: DH Publications.

Department of Health (2008) *The Child Health Promotion Programme. Pregnancy and the First Five Years of Life*, London: DH Publications.

Freedman D. (1979) in H. Bee (2000) *The Developing Child*, ninth edn, Needham Heights MA: Allyn and Bacon.

Goldschmeid, E. and Jackson, S. (1994) *People under Three*, London: Routledge.

Goldschmeid, E. and Selleck, D. (1996) *Communication between Babies in their First Year of Life*, London: National Children's Bureau.

Gopnik, A., Metzoff, A. and Kuhl, P. (1999) *How Babies Think*, London: Weidenfeld and Nicolson.

Hardyment, C. (1984) *Dream Babies – Child Care from Locke to Spock*, Oxford: Oxford University Press.

Healy, J. (1994) *Your Child's Growing Mind*, New York: Doubleday.

Holland, R. (1997) ' "What's it all about?": how introducing heuristic play has affected provision for the under-threes in one day nursery', in L. Abbott and H. Moylett (eds), *Working with the Under-3s: Responding to Children's Needs*, Buckingham: Open University Press.

Honig, A.S. (1994) 'Helping toddlers with peer group entry skills', *Journal Zero to Three* 14, 5 (ages 15–19).

Mayall, B. and Petrie, P. (1983) *Childminding and Day Nurseries: What Kind of Care*, London: Heinemann.

Piaget, J. (1952) *The Origins of Intelligence in Children*, New York: International Universities Press.

Priya, J.V. (1992) *Birth Traditions and Modern Pregnancy Care*, Shaftesbury: Element.

Rousseau, J.-J. (1762) *Emile, ou L'Education*, (English version) London: T. Bechet.

Siraj-Blatchford, I. and Clarke, P. (2000) *Supporting Identity, Diversity and Language in the Early Years*, Buckingham: Open University Press.

Trevarthan, C. (1995) 'The child's need to learn culture', *Children and Society* 9, 1: 5–19.

Whaley, K.L. and Rubenstein, T.S. (1994) 'How toddlers "do" friendship: a descriptive analysis of naturally occurring friendships in a group child cares setting', *Journal of Social and Personal Relationships* 11, 3: 383–400.

6   Feelings and relationships

This chapter explores the feelings and relationships between children and adults who are family members and those outside of the family. It also covers the relationships between children and other children. It explores different types of and reasons for children's behaviour and investigates a number of ways in which these can be dealt with.

First relationships are formed at birth within the family and slowly these are extended to encompass other adults and children. As we all know, not all relationships are happy ones, and throughout the chapter reference will be made to instances when things may go wrong and feelings may be hurt. An important aspect of feelings and relationships both for children and adults is the cultural dimension. Most people have heard of the English 'stiff upper lip', which is when it is not culturally acceptable for adults to show their emotions in public or to their children. Fortunately this attitude is changing, but there are still large numbers of English people who find it difficult to express their emotions or who view the expression of emotions by their children as weakness. Expressing one's emotions was viewed as a woman's thing but latterly the anonymity of doing this via mobile phones or email has enabled men to be more expressive about their feelings. At the opposite end of the scale we have people from other countries, for example, Mediterranean areas, who are very open in expressing emotions in public and whose everyday conversations are smattered with dramatic hand gestures and facial expressions. We need to remember that different cultures have different ways of establishing relationships with children. In addition to the cultural aspects, some people have been trained, because of the nature of their jobs, not to express their emotions; for example, doctors, nurses, police officers, armed-services personnel. These people may find it difficult to override this training when it comes to expressing emotions and feelings in their personal life and this can be very hard for their children. Children are very good at reading non-verbal communication from adults via body language and facial expression and adults are not always aware of this. This chapter will also explore how adults may interpret children's behaviour and how children's behaviour can best be managed.

The Early Years Foundation Stage (EYFS) area that deals with relationships can be found under Personal, Social and Emotional Development and defines what this means for children as follows:

- For children, being special to someone and well cared for is vital for their physical, social and emotional well being.
- Being acknowledged and affirmed by important people in their lives leads children to gaining confidence and inner strength through secure attachments with these people.
- Exploration within close relationships leads to the growth of self-assurance, promoting a sense of belonging which allows children to explore the world from a secure base.
- Children need adults to set a good example and to give them opportunities for interaction with others so that they can develop positive ideas about themselves and others.
- Children who are encouraged to feel free to express their ideas and feelings, such as joy, sadness, frustration, fear, can develop strategies to cope with new, challenging or stressful situations.

(*Practice Guide for Early Years Foundation Stage* 2007: 27)

First relationships and feelings

John Bowlby put forward his theories on attachment and loss in 1969, whereby he claimed that infants have an inborn drive to form stable attachments (or 'bonding') to their primary carer. At the time that Bowlby's book was published, the primary caregiver was interpreted as being the mother of the child. This led to a great deal of publicity being given to the idea that mothers returning to work following the birth of their child could do their child long-term damage by leaving its care to someone else. There were also beliefs that children who had failed to bond/make attachments would be more likely to become juvenile delinquents. However, the present-day interpretation of Bowlby's thesis, whilst not totally detracting from what he was advocating, makes it clear that the primary carer does not need to be the mother, though it does need to be someone who is consistently available and responsive to the needs of the child. Lindon (2007) defines attachment as 'feelings of emotional closeness and commitment between children and significant people in their daily life'. Such attachment or bonding is what makes the baby feel secure following birth. Studies have shown that an infant is able to have an attachment to more adults than just the mother, thus any consistent adult who deals with the child, answering its needs on a regular basis (for example, father, grandparent, older sibling) also become attachment figures in the baby's life. Research carried out in the kibbutzim (communal farms) in Israel found that the baby was equally attached to its mother, father and primary carer in the nursery. In agricultural societies, following the birth of a child the mother may return to the fields to work, leaving the baby with grandparents, aunts, older siblings or other close family members with no ill effects on the attachment relationship between mother and child.

A newborn baby is able to recognise the voice of its mother and the rhythm of her heartbeat. Later the baby will recognise the voices of other members of the family. The baby is able to identify those who are in regular contact with it by the way they hold it and touch it. From these early social interactions the child learns which behaviours will get which responses from the adult, for example crying usually results in the child being picked up and cuddled and talked to.

In recent years the role of the father has become more prominent in the attachment debate as more single-father families have come into existence, as have fathers who choose to stay at home to look after the children because the mother is the bigger income earner. Many fathers attend the birth of their child and are able to make attachments with the baby from the beginning. Sweden is a country that has encouraged the involvement of fathers since the 1960s, being one of the first European countries to legislate to allow paid paternity leave so that fathers could be with their child at the birth and in the weeks following.

Bowlby's theory of maternal deprivation (attachment and loss) relied heavily upon the thesis that there was a 'critical period' during which attachment took place. However, many critics of Bowlby have carried out research that shows that bonding can take place much later than Bowlby's 'critical period'. This is illustrated by relationships between adoptive parents and their children and instances when a mother and baby are separated soon after birth because of illness of the mother or baby or prematurity of the baby. Present-day research appears to discredit Bowlby's 'critical period' for attachment, particularly its link with juvenile delinquency and behaviour problems in children said to be caused by lack of bonding. Rutter (1999) (cited in Lindon 2007: 87) is undertaking a longitudinal study of Romanian children adopted from the impersonal orphanages of their birth country into UK families. The research has documented significant improvement in the serious cognitive delays of the children at adoption. However, the degree of

> cognitive catch-up was better for those children who had left the orphanages by six months of age. Children who left at between 12 and 18 months of age had experienced serious emotional deprivation and physical harm through malnutrition ... this study (and other studies) shows that serious psychological deprivation in the very early years affects children's emotional security and ability to make relationships.

Whilst it has to be accepted that the plight of Romanian children in the orphanages was extreme, this research does to some extent underpin Bowlby's theory of the 'critical period' for attachment. Factors previously related to the consequences of lack of bonding and attachment are now linked to poor parenting skills, inconsistency of care and the breakdown of the family and changes in family values. Pick (2001a) points out the importance of wider family relationships that enable other reliable attachments, such as grandparents and members of the extended family. Grandparents are often an extended source of reliable day-care for the family and often have more time to spend with the children than busy parents.

Once the mother's maternity-leave period is over the family will have to make decisions as to whether she will stay at home to look after her child or return to work and make alternative arrangements for the child's care. If that care is to pass to someone other than a family member then it may involve hiring a nanny or finding a suitable day-care setting for the child. This will also require the child to make relationships beyond the home. For very young children a small-scale day-care setting such as a childminder may be viewed as preferable to the larger setting of a day nursery. A childminder is able to offer the consistency of the same person caring for the child every day. However, research has shown that, providing the adult/child ratios are good, the care is of a high quality and there is low staff turnover, then there are likely to be no adverse effects in placing a young child in a nursery

(Melhuish 1990). There appears to be no research that shows that placing a child with a childminder or in a day-care setting has any detrimental effect upon the child's attachment to its mother or other family members. However, Richard Bowlby (2007) has criticised the Sure Start adult/baby ratios as there is no specification for the numbers of babies under one year of age that a carer in a Children's Centre may look after. As Bowlby points out, 'It specifies three children under 2 years and therefore does not address the need of babies to have individual time and attention in order to develop a secondary attachment to one carer.' However, Elfer *et al.* (2003) counteract Bowlby's argument by pointing out the importance of the Key Person Approach in the nursery in order to ensure that attachments and quality relationships are made between the children and staff. Once in the day-care setting, the child interacts and forges relationships not only with its carers but also with other children. Research carried out by Goldschmeid and Selleck (1996) produced a video film showing babies in their first year interacting with each other. This offers evidence to show peer-group relationships developing.

For good relationships to be made with young children, whether this be in the early days of life or later, it is important that there is interaction between the adult and the child. Whilst responding to the child's needs is an important part of this action, there is also a need for the adult to have physical contact with the child, talk to the child and play with the child. The child needs to be shown affection as cold, clinically delivered care does not lead to the forming of attachments. Therefore, in any relationship there must be feelings that are positive and make the child feel loved and secure. Bruner (1983) said that 'Babies are born endowed to interact with others and their principal "tools" for achieving their ends are other human beings.'

Relationships between children

As stated above, communication between children starts at a very early age. However, it is some time later before children start to form relationships with other children. The first children that a new member of the family will make a relationship with are its siblings. As children differ in their relationships with adults, so this will be the case with siblings. About 80 per cent of children have siblings, although this statistic may be a lot lower in countries where there are more one-child families, such as China and Germany. Judy Dunn (1993) points out: 'The striking differences between sibling pairs in their relationships are clear even to the most casual observer. Some brothers and sisters appear affectionate and concerned, real friends to one another. Others are constantly in conflict, even coming to blows.' Older siblings can be very caring and tolerant of younger siblings or they can be ambivalent and aggressive towards them. This latter reaction may be put down to sibling rivalry and, although researchers recognise this as an important dimension to the relationship, it is more complex than just straightforward rivalry.

Pick (2001b) points out that sibling rivalry is natural and normal, particularly when it involves an older child having a new baby appearing within the family. Dunn points out that some children are attached to each other very early in the sibling relationship and for some children this is a major aspect of their security. A longitudinal study carried out by Dunn and Kendrick (1982) showed that by the age of around one year, the younger sibling was imitating the older sibling and this continued for a number of years, sometimes into adulthood. However, it would appear that there has been little if any research carried out that examines the gender differ-ences or the age gap between siblings and how these may affect relationships. Changes in sibling relationships can occur when one sibling starts nursery or school and becomes more self-confident.

The child who has no siblings can sometimes be a very lonely child who spends more time with adults than with other children. What may appear as advantages over having siblings, such as the child not having to compete for their parents' atten-tion, not having to share or take turns, can in many ways prove to be disadvantages for the child when it is outside the home. Whilst these children may appear very confident in their dealings with adults, they may be socially inhibited when dealing with other children. Some of these children may appear mature for their age, enjoy being the centre of adult attention and can sometimes seem self-centred. It is very important that parents of only children recognise the need for them to spend time with other children. This should start at an early age and could be achieved by taking them to a mother-and-toddler club or attending a pre-school playgroup on a regular basis. In these situations they will learn to socialise with other children so that they gain an understanding of sharing, taking turns, working cooperatively and so on. The parents can also invite other children into the home to play on a regular basis so that their child is able to get used to sharing its own toys, sweets and other things.

Relationships with children from outside the family begin when a child meets with other children. Such meetings may start between two families who have chil-dren of a similar age. As previously mentioned, children in the first year of life will communicate (Goldschmeid and Selleck 1996) by touch and babbling. Between 14 and 18 months children may appear to be playing together but this is most likely to be parallel play, where the two are playing side by side. Eckerman (1993), cited in Lindon (2007: 152–3), observed very young children in contact with each other and noticed deliberate patterns of social play, for example:

- Mobile babies establish a joint focus of interest by making physical contact with an object that another child (or adult) is manipulating.
- In toddler interaction, imitative acts seem to open an exchange, because they often happen swiftly after the first contact.
- From two to three years of age words begin to be integrated into young chil-dren's play.

Around two-and-a-half years, there may be more coordinated play between two children involving imitation and chasing games. At the age of three children start to play more cooperatively with their peers and this is the first step in forming friend-ships. Such friendships make children sensitive to other children's feelings and enable them to develop social skills. Howes (1987) studied the friendships of pre-school children over a period of two years and found that these early relationships were not just passing occurrences but lasted for at least six months and many for much longer periods of time, such as a number of years. Other studies of pre-school friendships have found that the children who are friends are more tolerant, forgiving and supportive of each other and spend a lot of time interacting, whereas those chil-dren who are not friends are not treated in the same way. As children get older, so their friendships get stronger and more complex, as can be seen from observing children in the imaginative play areas. They discuss situations, decide on roles, take turns and so on. Sometimes they are capable of being 'cruel' to those who are not part of the friendship circle and who may be less confident in their interactions. The 'outsiders' may be given less-interesting roles or the 'friends' may be very bossy towards them or not let them join in the play. Early years workers need to be alert to these situations, as they can be very damaging for the child who is constantly the 'outsider'. Children who lack confidence and social skills may have difficulty in becoming part of the friendship circles, which leaves the child who is timid, shy or awkward very lonely and vulnerable. Early years workers also need to be aware of the dominant child making friends with one of the more vulnerable children as this may be a bullying situation that will need to be dealt with. The nature of friendships can change and friends will argue and become competitive, the latter being more common in boys (Hartup 1989). At this point one friendship may cease and new friendships start.

Ramsey (1991) puts forward what he describes as crude descriptors of four categories of children's social behaviour, as described below.

- Popular children are usually very capable and more intellectually, socially and emotionally mature than their peers. It is also a sad but evident truth that popular children are often more physically attractive and this is particularly noticeable with girls.
- Rejected children may show aggressive or withdrawn behaviour. They may angrily retaliate against others or avoid other children.
- Neglected children appear to take little part in the social life of the group and are often content with their own company.
- Controversial children are described as having a major impact on the social group, are socially and intellectually talented, but are often in trouble for aggressive behaviour and rule breaking. Although children in this group are often group leaders, some other children regard them with caution.

Many children who are socially well-adjusted may not fit into any of these groups.

Relationships with adults outside the family

Bee (2000) states that between six and 16 months of age children have a fear of strangers and between nine and 16 months they experience separation anxiety. Between these age groups children often become anxious, fearing strangers and crying and/or clinging to their mothers or primary carers when in the presence of strangers. Before they enter this stage of development they are quite happy to be picked up and cuddled by anyone, then suddenly they seem to develop a fear of strangers and separation anxiety. They become fearful to leave those they are familiar with. This type of behaviour begins to lessen around the age of two years. When children are going through the separation-anxiety phase it is not a good time to introduce them to new situations in which they will be left with people whom they do not know; people who appear to them as strangers. If the child has been looked after by a childminder or relative from an early age it will have formed attachments with this person and is likely to cling to him or her when strangers appear or experience separation anxiety if visiting unfamiliar places such as the mother-and-toddler club. Separation anxiety is very common when young children are first introduced to the pre-school playgroup or nursery setting around the age of two to two-and-a-half years. It is important that the early years workers understand this and have a programme for phasing in a child's admission. This entails the mother/primary carer staying with the child, and when leaving the child, this should be for a very short period of time in the first instance, gradually building up to longer periods of time spent away. The length of time the parent stays away from the child should be arranged in consultation with the staff who know how the child reacts when the parent leaves. With some children it can take a period of weeks before they are able to overcome their separation anxiety and settle down in the playgroup or nursery without signs of distress. It is important that in these early days of separation from the parent the staff in the setting give the child special attention and wherever possible assign one person to be the child's key worker. The child then only has one person to relate to and this can help encourage feelings of confidence and security. It can be too overwhelming for a young child in this situation to have to relate to lots of adults and children. For parents and children from diverse ethnic backgrounds the settling-in period may be particularly stressful. Pre-school playgroups and nurseries may be a new concept for the parents and they may be very concerned about leaving their child with other people. There may be language difficulties: even if the parents speak English they may have spoken to the child only in their heritage language. The clothes the staff wear, the routine and the food may all be unfamiliar to the child, which may only add to its initial anxiety. Siraj-Blatchford and Clarke (2000) offer the following settling-in strategies for children from diverse backgrounds, although many of the points on the list would be good practice for dealing with any new child who is settling in:

- encourage parents to visit with their children on several occasions before leaving them for the first time;
- encourage parents to explain the events of the day to their child in their own language;
- try to understand the parents' perspective and concerns for leaving their children for the first time;
- suggest to parents that they make the first few occasions when the children are left short;
- suggest the parents say goodbye, tell the child where they are going and when they will return, for example, after sleep;
- encourage the parents to leave something of their own for the child to care for in their absence;
- provide bilingual support for the child;
- allocate a particular staff member to remain with the child;
- make sure the parents leave a phone number on which they can be contacted during the day;
- provide play materials that are familiar;
- find out the routines of the child.

Once children have settled into playgroup/nursery they very quickly learn the routine of the establishment and what is expected of them. Routines are important to a child as they offer security – as they do to many adults! Children also learn what is acceptable behaviour within the setting and what is not. They also learn the consequences of unacceptable behaviour. Much of this comes to the child as it becomes familiar with the setting; however, with older children their peer group may be the ones to inform them of the 'house rules'.

Communication between adults and children is a two-way process and it is important that adults listen to children and take what they are saying seriously. Adults have an important role in developing and enhancing children's language development. Communication is not just talking and listening as messages can be transferred via body language, gestures, eye contact and so on. Children are very good at picking up non-verbal communication signals and many adults do not appreciate this fact. So whilst telling a child it should 'eat its greens', be careful that your own expression does not convey your distaste for 'greens'. Children aged between two and four years will often use gestures to help you understand the message they are sending. It is very easy for adults in their communications with children to make the children feel insecure. This usually happens when adults consistently start conversations with negative statements. Adults must respect children and accept that, like adults, children are also capable of making mistakes and we all learn by our mistakes.

Managing children's behaviour

All adults need to understand how they should react to children. Children need to be praised, trusted, encouraged, communicated with and empathised with in order for them to feel confident and happy. Managing children's behaviour is not just about dealing with behaviour problems but also about recognising and acknowledging when the child has achieved something or made great efforts to achieve something, however small that achievement may be. We all like to be praised for our efforts and children are no different from adults in this respect, as self-esteem and self-image are very important parts of the human psyche. A child's self-esteem and self-image build up slowly as part of the developmental process.

There are a number of stages in a child's development of a concept of self (Bee 2000). The first stage is called the 'subjective' self and occurs in the first year of life. During this period the baby is developing a sense of itself as an agent who can make things happen, and this is seen in the delight it gets from doing things such as moving a mobile, making a noise with a squeaky toy and communicating with adults. From this the child derives a sense of self. Piaget (1969) maintains that a critical element in the development of the subjective self is an understanding of object permanence that the child develops around nine to 12 months. As the child begins to understand that objects exist even when they are out of sight, so the child begins to understand that its parents exist and so does it exist.

The second stage in developing the concept of self (or 'objective' self) comes when the child understands that it is an object in the world. As a toddler, the child discovers that, as do the objects that surround it, it has a name, gender, size and personal qualities. A child of two-and-a-half to three years will know its own name, whether it is a boy or a girl, whether it is big or little and whether it has brothers and sisters, grandparents, aunts and other close relatives. Harter (1998) describes the pre-school child's self-concept as 'rather like a list: "I'm good at running"; "I don't like to play with dolls"; "I live in a big house"; "I have blue eyes".' Children's perceptions of themselves are at this age tied to specific settings and specific tasks.

As they get older, children will begin to compare themselves with other children in their peer group. From this the child is able to make a self-evaluation and judge its own strengths and weaknesses. The child's position in the family, the nursery or the class may reinforce its own evaluation of itself. By this time the child would also have mastered the different rules that govern its reactions and behaviour such as socio-cultural rules, moral rules and rules relating to expected behaviour in different settings. All of these things will be contributing towards the development of the child's personality. The following (adapted from Woolfson 1994) is a list of things that adults can do to improve a child's self-concept:

- take an interest in all the child does, the small things as well as the big things, and value what it does;
- respect the child for who it is not what it does;
- ensure the child has access to positive images that relate to its skin colour, gender, ability, disability and so on;
- emphasise the child's strong points, especially if the child feels less capable than its peers;
- even when the child misbehaves, do not repeatedly remind the child of how bad it is;
- take the child's feelings and wishes into account when making decisions about what it is allowed to do;
- act as a positive role model for the child, which requires the adult to have a positive self-image;
- provide experiences for the child in which it is likely to be successful and avoid those that you know the child is bound to fail at;
- have realistic expectations of the child's abilities and achievements.

Children with a poor self-image do not relate well to other children and may be social loners. They have high anxiety levels and are very critical of anything they do, never accepting that what they do may be of normal standards. They often feel guilty and ashamed and find it difficult to have honest, trusting relationships with other children and adults. It is important for child-care workers to recognise these behaviours so that they can work with the child towards helping it have a more positive self-image.

At some time all children will present challenging behaviour to their parents, carers or teachers. This is a natural way for children to find out about the world around them. Their behaviour will usually have a goal but they may operate on a trial-and-error basis. Behaviours that enable the child to reach its goal will be repeated; those that do not will be discarded. The child may be testing the adults by trying to find the answers to questions such as 'How far can I go with that adult before I am stopped?'; 'If I do that again tomorrow do you think that adult will notice or will I get away with it?'. The child may be trying to be recognised, to feel important or to belong. Kay (2006: 37) states that children's behaviour will be influenced by the following factors:

- family type and composition;
- the family's social and cultural background;

- home setting and environment;
- parenting styles and child-rearing practices;
- relationship with parents, siblings and other family members;
- the family's employment and financial situation;
- support for learning and other aspects of development;
- the child's own emotional needs and the extent to which these are met;
- the child's social skills and ability to relate to peers;
- factors influencing family behaviour, e.g. illness, bereavement, separation and divorce.

First behaviours are learned within the family and it is therefore important to involve the family when devising a way of dealing with children's challenging behaviour. In order to influence children's behaviour, the parents and the day-care/school staff need to work together. The Early Years Foundation Stage (EYFS) offers the following effective practice for dealing with children's behaviour and self-control from birth to 50 months:

- Find out as much as you can from parents about young babies before they join the setting, so that the routines you follow are familiar and comforting (birth–11 months)
- Demonstrate clear and consistent boundaries and reasonable yet challenging expectations (8–20 months)
- Reduce incidents of frustration and conflict by keeping routines flexible so that young children can pursue their interests (16–26 months)
- Help children understand their rights to be kept safe by others, and encourage them to talk about ways to avoid harming or hurting others (22–36 months)
- Share with parents the rationale of boundaries and expectations to maintain a joint approach (30–50 months).

(Practice Guidance for the Early Years Foundation Stage 2007: 37)

If children are persistently using challenging behaviour then the adults concerned with the child should be looking to see if there are deeper reasons for this than just the child going through a developmental stage. For example, there may be problems within the family that are having a detrimental effect upon the child's development. In these cases the parents need to be consulted and, where necessary, outside help offered. Much of children's challenging behaviour is based on the goals of wanting to seek attention from adults or other children, and/or wanting power over adults or other children.

Attention seeking is by far the most common form of challenging behaviour in children and it is a form of behaviour used by many adults in order to get their own way. Attention seeking can involve behaviours such as being a nuisance, being a clown, being a 'smart Alec', always asking questions, embarrassing people, unpredictable actions and mischief making. Unfortunately, some of the previously mentioned traits are viewed favourably by adults, such as clowning or being a smart Alec. Whilst adults should not give a lot of attention to this behaviour, they cannot totally ignore it. They need to explain to the child what they do not like about this behaviour and ask the child to stop it. Sadly, some children may lack attention at home and so deliberately seek it when they are outside the family.

Other types of attention-seeking behaviour may be more passive and include shyness, fearfulness, anxiety, tearfulness, eating problems, always wanting help and laziness. With this type of behaviour the child is gaining attention by not doing things. These behaviours are often of lesser concern to adults because the children that use this type of behaviour are usually very nice and do not disrupt the other children. However, these children are not interested in independence, as they want to rely on the adults to do everything for them, thus getting the attention they seek. With these children self-reliance needs to be encouraged, with the adult explaining to the child that it is possible to do things for themselves. For example, if a child is refusing to eat for no particular reason then the adult should not feed it but encourage the child to feed itself. If the child does not cooperate then the food can be taken away and no snacks given between meals. In this way the child has not had the attention it would have got by being coaxed and fed by the adult.

When children want power over adults and other children they may exhibit behaviours such as being rebellious, argumentative or defiant; contradicting; being disobedient; bullying; lying; being bossy; having temper tantrums (long after the age when it is normal development to have these); refusing to cooperate; or being stubborn and forgetful. These types of behaviours upset adults as they feel that their authority is being challenged. Most parents and adults want control over the children in their care and the instinctive reaction is to take on the challenge. However, adults entering the power struggle are just what the child wants. The best way to avoid this is to talk to the child, asking it to cooperate and encouraging it to participate with you in carrying out whatever is being asked, for example picking up toys. However, adults cannot make children do something they do not wish to do and they can only hope to be a role model that the child will follow.

There are other forms of challenging behaviour that would not be considered part of a child's normal developmental experience. These behaviours are likely to alert adults that there is a far deeper underlying problem that the child is trying to find ways of dealing with. Examples of these are when a child is deliberately cruel, inflicting pain on other children or animals; stealing; being withdrawn; refusing to mix with other children; behaving in babyish ways; or bedwetting. Children with special needs may exhibit difficult behaviour and they may be less receptive to the normal methods for dealing with that behaviour. Because of their disability these children may have low self-esteem and may not yet have learnt the social rules of behaviour. These children will need special attention, preferably through a key worker who can build a relationship with them as a secure base to work from.

Adults must look for positive ways to manage children's challenging behaviour. There need to be consistent ground rules that all children and staff understand but these must be based upon positive statements that are realistic and achievable. When dealing with children, the word 'realistic' means in relation to the child's understanding and developmental stage. If it is necessary to discipline children then physical punishment, such as smacking, must never be used. Neither should the adult use methods that threaten, humiliate or bribe children as these can damage a child's self-esteem and confidence and may not result in any behaviour change. When a child does conform to a request from the adult then this should be acknowledged through praise or by giving the child a reward such as reading a favourite story or playing a favourite game. If children are angry or upset about something they should be given the opportunity to tell the adult how they feel. With very young children the adult may need to distract their attention from the situation that is causing conflict and interest them in something else.

Most early years settings have a behaviour policy that has been written by the staff in conjunction with the parents. Such a policy enables staff and parents to understand what is acceptable and what is unacceptable behaviour in that setting. Behaviour policies should be regularly reviewed and always leave room for children to have choice within a defined framework. The policy should be written in positive terms and cover underlying principles such as not hurting others, not saying unkind things, not taking or damaging other people's property, not harming plants or animals. These underlying principles then need to be translated into a positive set of ground rules that the children understand, for example:

- we always try to be kind to others;
- we always try to speak kindly to each other;
- we look after our own and others' things;
- we put things back where they belong;
- we look after living things.

These positive statements will be understood by the children and form the basis of their behaviour management.

It is always difficult to know how to deal with the child who will not listen and who may present very challenging behaviour. The Save the Children website has a lot of useful information for parents on how to manage their child's behaviour. It offers the following advice for dealing with the child that will not listen:

- kneel or sit so that you are at the child's level;
- hold the child gently by the shoulders or hands while you make the request;
- look right into the eyes of the child;
- talk in a firm, clear, calm voice;
- look serious while you speak;
- make it clear you expect to be listened to as you would listen to the child;
- listen to the child's response and carefully consider its views;
- give children options wherever possible;
- try negotiation;
- give ample opportunity for children to complete the task;
- praise cooperation or explain the consequences of non-cooperation (without resorting to threats);
- give warnings and helpful reminders;
- encourage children's problem-solving skills.

As children get older they may repeat things that they have heard at home and this may lead to them making derogatory remarks about other children. Such remarks may be racist, sexist or refer to a child's disability and they always need to be challenged by the adult in a sensitive way. No name-calling may be one of the ground rules that have been established in the setting and this will need to be sensitively explained to the offending child. If the child is repeating what it has heard at home then it is important that the adult does not undermine the child's parents when dealing with the incident. The adult must explain that these remarks hurt and upset the child they are directed at and that they are not expressions that are used in the setting. The Persona Doll Project described in Chapter 1 has offered a very successful way of dealing with such incidents within the nursery. Persona dolls are able to give adults the opportunity to explore with young children issues that may otherwise be difficult such as racism, disability, being in a traveller family, being in a one-parent family, being fostered, and so on. Adults make persona dolls that represent children from these different backgrounds and tell the children the doll's story. Through the dolls the adults can explore with the children the feelings and concepts experienced by someone who may be different. However, an important aspect of persona dolls is that they come alive for the children and therefore need to be brought out at regular intervals and treated with care when not in use so that children do not worry about where they have gone. If they are not going to be used any more then their story must involve them moving away to another town so the children are able to accept why they have gone. Persona dolls are now being used successfully in the United States, Australia, Denmark, the Netherlands and Britain, where training to use the dolls is now an integral part of some early years care and education courses.

Reflect upon …

1   Bruner (1983) said that 'Babies are born endowed to interact with others and their principle "tools" for achieving their ends are other human beings.' Describe what this means for parents and early years workers with regard to their relationship with young children.

2   Richard Bowlby (2007) criticises the low staffing ratios required within the baby room of Sure Start centres. Elfer (2007) counteracts Bowlby's arguments by pointing out the importance of the role of the key worker. Which argument do you agree with and why?

3   Woolfson (1994), in his list of things adults can do to improve a child's self-concept, puts forward that the adult must have 'realistic expectations of the child's abilities and achievements'. What do you need to know in order to ensure that you have realistic expectations of a child?

4   Why is it necessary to involve parents/primary carers when you are trying to deal with a child's challenging behaviour?

References

Adler, A. (1957) *Understanding Human Behaviour*, New York: Fawcett.

Bee, K. (2000) *The Developing Child*, ninth edition, Needham Heights: Allyn & Bacon.

Bowlby, J. (1953) *Childcare and the Growth of Love*, Harmondsworth: Pelican Books.

Bowlby, J. (1969) *Attachment and Loss*, Vol. 1, London: Hogarth Press.

Bowlby, J. (1973) *Attachment and Loss*, Vol. 2, London: Hogarth Press.

Bowlby, R. (2006) 'The need for secondary attachment figures in childcare', paper sent to the *Daily Telegraph* (21 October 2006).

Bowlby, R. (2007) *Stress in Daycare*, available online: www.socialbaby.blogspot.com/2007/04/Richard-bowlby-stress-in-daycare.

Brown, B. (2001) *Combating Discrimination: Persona Dolls in Action*, Stoke-on-Trent: Trentham Books.

Bruner, J. (1983) *Child's Talk*, New York: Norton.

Dowling, M. (2001) *Young Children's Personal, Social and Emotional Development*, London: Paul Chapman.

Department for Education and Skills (2007) *The Early Years Foundation Stage*, Nottingham: DfES Publications.

Dunn, J. (1993) *Young Children's Close Relationships: Beyond Attachment*, London: Sage.

Dunn, J. and Kendrick, C. (1982) *Siblings: Love, Envy and Understanding*, Cambridge, MA: Harvard University Press.

Elfer, P., Goldschmeid, E. and Selleck, D. (2003) *Key Persons in the Nursery. Building Relationships for Quality Provision*, London: David Fulton.

Goldschmeid, E. and Selleck, D. (1996) *Communication between Babies in Their First Year of Life*, London: National Children's Bureau.

Harter, S. (1998) 'The development of self-representations', in W. Damon (ed.), *Handbook of Child Psychology*, Vol. 3: *Social, Emotional and Personality Development*, New York: Wiley.

Hartup, W.W. (1989) 'On relationships and development', in W.W. Hartup and Z. Rubin (eds), *Relationship and Development*, New Jersey: Lawrence Erlbaum.

Hennessy, E., Martin, S., Moss, P. and Melhuish, E. (1992) *Children in Day Care: Lessons from the Research*, London: Paul Chapman.

Howes, C. (1987) *Peer Interaction of Young Children*, monographs of the Society for Research in Child Development, 217, 153, 1.

Kay, J. (2006) *Managing Behaviour in the Early Years*: London: Continuum International Publishing.

Lindon, J. (2007) *Understanding Child Development. Linking Theory and Practice*, Abingdon: Hodder Arnold.

Melhuish, E. (1990) 'Research on day care for young children in the United Kingdom', in E. Melhuish and P. Moss (eds), *Day Care for Young Children International Perspectives*, London: Routledge.

Murray, L. and Andrews, L. (2000) *The Social Baby: Understanding Babies' Communication from Birth*, Richmond, Surrey: CP Publishing.

Petrie, P. (1989) *Communicating with Children and Adults*, London: Edward Arnold (Hodder & Stoughton).

Piaget, J. and Inhelder, B. (1969) *The Psychology of the Child*, New York: Basic Books.

Pick, R. (2001a) *Grandparents and the Extended Family. Understanding the Importance of Wider Family Relationships for Children and Their Parents*, London: Child Psychotherapy Trust.

Pick, R. (2001b) *Sibling Rivalry*, London: Child Psychotherapy Trust.

Ramsey, P.G. (1991) *Making Friends in School*, New York and London: Teachers College Press.

Save the Children website: www.savethechildren.org.uk/onlinepubs/workitout.

Siraj-Blatchford, I. and Clarke, P. (2000) *Supporting Identity, Diversity and Language in the Early Years*, Buckingham: Open University Press.

Sonstegard, M., Shuck, A. and Beattie, N. (1979) *Living in Harmony with Our Children*, Luton: Millford Reprographics.

Thompson, M. and O'Neill, C. with Cohen, L. (2001) *Best Friends Worst Enemies: Children's Friendships, Popularity and Social Cruelty*, London: Michael Joseph.

Woolfson, R. (1994) *Understanding Children: A Guide for Parents and Carers*, Glasgow: Caring Books.

7 Working in partnership with parents

> This chapter examines the differences between parental involvement and partnerships with parents. It also explores the different ways in which the child carer can work in partnership with parents and in particular the importance of involving fathers.

Parents[1] are the child's first carers and know their children; it is therefore imperative that early years workers establish good relationships with the parents of the children in their care. This chapter explores a number of concepts relating to working with parents, parental involvement and partnerships with parents. Whatever conclusions are drawn between these concepts, there is no doubt that parents have a right to know how their child is developing and to be given explanations of the activities that the child is involved in at the early years setting. It is important that the staff in early years settings make decisions about the role of parents within the setting. This will ensure that harmonious relationships are forged that are beneficial to the children and the setting. In addition, parents as partners is an integral part of the National Day Care Standards and the new Early Years Foundation Stage (EYFS), both of which are referred to later in this chapter.

Historical aspects of working with parents

Involving parents is not a new concept but one that has been advocated for many years, one of the earliest references coming from Margaret McMillan (1860–1931), who argued that mothers had a right to participate in and manage the nursery schools that their children attended (further detail is given in Chapter 10). Another advocate was J.W.B. Douglas (1964), who found that variation in parental attitudes could account for more of the variation in children's school achievement than either the variation in home circumstances or in schools. Following on from Douglas, the Plowden Report (1967) recommended that in order to achieve a closer partnership with parents there should be open evenings and reports that give more information to parents. The early 1960s saw the beginnings of the Pre-school Playgroup Association, an integral part of which required the involvement of the parents of the children in the group in order for the groups to operate. In 1988 the Education Act introduced parent-governors into the management of schools in the expectation that such involvement would encourage more parents to participate. As a result of the Children Act 1989, 'National Standards for Under 8's Day Care and Childminding' were drawn up and Standard 12 refers to 'Working in Partnership with Parents'. In 2005 there were amendments to the original standards, including Standard 12.

Between 2005 and 2007, a major project called 'Parents, Early Years and Learning' (PEAL) was initiated. The aim of this project was to support early years practitioners in involving parents and encouraging them to support their children's learning.

Partnership with parents or parental involvement?

In recent years the term 'parental involvement' seems to have become synonymous with the term 'partnership with parents'. In many cases it would appear that the two terms are interchangeable. The distinction between partnership and involvement does not always appear to be recognised by the user groups or higher authorities. Many textbooks have chapters entitled 'Partnership with parents', when the content of the chapter is actually on involvement of parents or parent participation. This confusion of terminology needs to be addressed, as it does not help the professionals or the parents to understand their roles. The following are some of the definitions of parental involvement and partnership with parents.

Smith (1980) has defined five categories of parental involvement: 'working with the children on educational activities, working in the group doing the chores, servicing the group but not actually working, involvement in management and the parent sharing in the child's experiences.'

Mittler and Mittler (1982, cited in Pugh and De'Ath 1989: 32) describe the elements of a partnership as: 'mutual respect and recognition of the essential equality between parents and professionals; sharing information and skills; sharing of feelings; sharing the process of decision making and recognition of the individuality of families.'

Likewise, Pugh and De'Ath (1989: 36) define a partnership as 'a working relationship that is characterised by a shared interest of purpose, mutual respect and the willingness to negotiate. This implies a sharing of information, responsibility, skills, decision-making and accountability.'

In 1990 the Department of Health published the document *Playgroups in a Changing World*. Part of this research into pre-school playgroups looked at the involvement of parents. The researchers found the word 'parents' misleading as involvement was predominantly that of mothers, and in non-rural areas less than half of the parents were involved in the actual sessions with the children in the playgroup. When there was involvement it was usually on a rota basis whereby parents agreed to one or two sessions every few weeks. One of the most important areas of parental involvement was as a member of the management committee. Some parents helped with the cleaning and maintenance in the playgroup.

These attitudes are reinforced by MacNaughton (2000: 189) when she states:

Parental involvement could mean one of the following:

- centre fundraising
- helping with snack times

- contributing to the management committee
- assisting with centre excursions
- distributing newsletters
- as visitors sharing a special skill or interest with the children

…Parents are also seen to benefit from involvement in their children's services, becoming empowered to make informed choices about their children's education and care.

The Early Years Foundation Stage (2007) refers to parents as partners and offers the following key messages:

- all parents can enhance their child's development and learning;
- parents have the right to play a central role in making decisions about their child's care and education at every level;
- successful relationships between parents and educators can have long-lasting and beneficial effects on children's learning and well-being;
- successful relationships become partnerships when there is two-way communication and parents and practitioners really listen to each other and value each other's views and support in achieving the best outcomes for each child.

Few of the above roles could be described as a partnership with parents as defined by Mittel and Mittel or Pugh and De'Ath.
Hughes and MacNaughton (2000) (cited in Dahlberg and Moss 2005: 164)

> conclude that most of the burgeoning literature places parents in a subordinate position to pre-school workers, especially with respect to knowledge … parental knowledge of the child is anecdotal, subjective, ad hoc, individualised and applicable only to specific children … parental knowledge is treated as unimportant, as inadequate or as supplementary.

This idea is reinforced by Dunlop and Fabian (2007), who point out that: 'Parents are always implicated in education, either as silent, passive partners or as vocal active partners.'

Developing partnerships with parents

The Early Years Foundation Stage has very clear statements on the way that partnerships can be developed with parents. There are six areas that the early years worker needs to understand and implement in order develop good working partnerships:

- communication;
- respecting diversity;
- learning together;
- effective practice;
- reflecting on practice;
- challenges and dilemmas.

There needs to be a welcoming atmosphere in the setting that makes parents feel comfortable to come inside and to talk to staff. Staff need to be approachable and there should be two-way communication between staff and parents.

Parents need clear answers to questions such as: Am I involved in my child's nursery or am I a partner? If I am involved in the nursery what is expected of me? If I am a partner in my child's education/care what is expected of me? If I am a partner and this is a true partnership am I able to participate in the decision-making process for my child or am I just here to wash the paint pots and be an extra adult on outings?

Professionals also need to understand their own role and need answers to questions such as: What am I able to share with Mrs Y about her child? Is it my role to discuss the behaviour of Mrs Y's child with her and together we work out a plan for dealing with the behaviour? Can I ask Mrs Y to accompany the group on outings and if she does come is she allowed to take responsibility for children other than her own?

It could be questioned as to whether any parent whose own child is a member of a playgroup or other early years setting is able to work in that group or setting with all the children. This would require a level of professionalism whereby the parent is able to put aside its own child's needs in order to satisfy the needs of the other children in the group. Most professionals prefer not to have their own child as a member of the group for which they are responsible and some may prefer to work in a totally different establishment to that attended by their own child. Howe *et al.* (1999) draw attention to the tensions that can arise when parents are participating in early years settings. Such tensions range from the parents wanting to remain involved because they wish to meet other parents to criticisms about the lack of confidentiality over how some children in the setting behaved. Many staff would have felt happier if they were able to select which parents could be involved with the setting rather than operating an 'open house' invitation.

Elfer *et al.* (2003: 18) advocate the role of the key person being an important aspect in developing partnerships with parents, particularly mothers, and states that:

> The key person approach ensures that parents have the opportunity to build a personal relationship with 'someone' rather than 'all of them' working in the nursery. The benefits are likely to be peace of mind and the possibility of building a partnership with professional staff who may share with them the pleasures and stresses of child rearing. It gives parents the chance to liaise with someone else who is fully committed and familiar with their baby or child.

There needs to be respect for parents regardless of their social class and ethnicity. Parental involvement, at one level, is linked with socio-economic factors. A parent who is in employment is not always able to participate in a parental-involvement scheme that requires attendance on a regular basis, although such a parent may be happy to take part in fund-raising activities. However, this may not preclude the parent being in partnership with the setting as this enables discussion of the child's progress and the sharing of information at the end of the session or at open evenings. Provided the setting respects that this is a working parent and makes the required arrangements, there is no reason why a successful partnership cannot exist. However, this parent would never be able to fulfil the roles required by involvement other than participating in the odd fundraising event such as buying raffle tickets and going to the summer fair.

Cultural factors may prevent a parent's involvement. A parent who has English as an additional language may not feel confident in being in a totally English-speaking environment. In some cultures, including some members of the white working-class culture, the tradition may be to deliver one's child to the school or playgroup and leave the rest to the professionals who work there.

A home visit before the child joins the nursery or playgroup can help cement initial relationships with reluctant parents. The parent/s may feel more confident on home territory. However, the home visitor must be mindful not to draw stereotypes from a person's home or label the child and its family on the strength of a snapshot picture. Those embarking on home visiting should first undergo training so that they are aware of how these sensitive situations should be approached.

The new Children's Centres have a number of facilities on site that encourage parents to come into the centre. These may be local projects that could be based on their site, such as adult-education classes and language classes that enable the parents to visit on a regular basis in order to gain new skills. There may also be other facilities available such as health visitors, social workers, special needs advisers and advice for job seekers. As the parents' confidence grows so will the parents' involvement with the establishment, based on mutual respect and trust.

The Child Care Bureau of the United States Department of Health and Human Sciences has funded the Child Care Partnership Project. The project provides a series of technical assistant resources and materials to support the development and strengthening of partnerships with parents. The project offers the following tips for success:

- teach parents and partnership leaders how to work together;
- give parents meaningful roles;
- facilitate parent involvement;
- draw linkages between parents.

Cullingford and Morrison (1999) examined the complexities of involving parents in the school. They claim that official attitudes towards parents are ambiguous: for example, on the one hand parents are made accountable for the truancy of their children and on the other hand they are given greater power over schools. This ambiguity can lead to mistrust and recrimination on the parts of parents and the establishment.

As David (1999) points out, one of the Blair government's major projects was to get more women, especially mothers, back into the workforce when their children start school, thus moving the balance away from parental involvement in school and into the workplace.

The DfEE publication *Good Practice in Childcare No. 12* (2000) devotes a whole chapter to children and parents. The opening paragraph, entitled 'Building a partnership with parents', states:

> Parents need to be sure that while they are at work or studying, their children are safe, well looked after and enjoying themselves. When parents bring their children to your scheme, they are asking you to become closely involved with

their family and will want to work in partnership with you. You need to be accessible to parents and should encourage and welcome their ideas. Parents can offer a lot of support to a scheme; help with fundraising, useful contacts, involvement on the management committee and so on.

Parents as customers

In more recent years, with the rise of the private child-care sector and more women returning to work following child birth, parents are being seen and treated as customers. Now parents have choice within the 'market place' of early years settings to decide where they will leave their child. The OFSTED Inspection regime makes it possible for parents to use the Internet to find the inspection report of any child-care establishment they may be thinking of using. Martin and Vincent (1999) put forward a theory about consumerism and customer choice based on Hirschman's work *Exit, Voice and Loyalty* (1970). 'Voice' is when the customer is able to make known its opinions and criticisms, which in turn leads the provider to become more accountable and change its practices and policies. This aspect of consumerism is applauded within the public sector as it promotes better services. Citizens' Charters were the early attempts to give the clients of the public sector a voice. The Citizens' Charter for Parents lays down the citizen's responsibilities in the form of parents' involvement in their children's education, in addition to their rights to receive certain standards of service. This led to more accountability on the part of the producers, publicised in the form of league tables for education, hospital death rates for health, and so on. These act as quasi prices; for example, where school league tables are poor or hospital death rates are high, consumers are expected to vote with their feet and go elsewhere (what Hirschman refers to as 'Exit'). However, the parents/clients are not in control of the league tables or hospital death rates and therefore in reality they are not able to exert their opinions on them; thus they do not really have a choice. Where would they go? The private sector is the only alternative and is beyond the means of the majority of families. Martin and Vincent do not explore the 'Exit' and 'Loyalty' aspects of Hirschman's theory.

There are ambiguities raised in extrapolating a consumerist theory and applying it to education, as Martin and Vincent point out. For instance, having the opportunity to choose a school for one's child does not necessarily lead to corresponding opportunities for a voice within that school. The school normally determines the home–school relationship on its own terms. Martin and Vincent researched six schools, three of which were primary schools and all of which were described as having high levels of parental involvement. One of the highest levels of parental involvement was in the area of what the authors term 'Volunteerism', where the school involves the parents as active volunteers/parent helpers. In one school, despite its population being multicultural, the majority of mothers who volunteered were white, monolingual women who had time available.

Easen *et al.* (1992) explored the views of parents working together with educators and found they were grounded in two main opinions:

- some parents ought to be worked with in order to compensate their lack of skills and inadequate lifestyles;

- all parents as taxpayers and consumers of education have a *right* to be worked with.

The main assumption of the first viewpoint is that parents will be able to bring up their children better if professional workers tell or show them how to do it. More recently this compensatory approach has been questioned and thinking about partnerships has become more refined. A more effective way for parents and educators working together to promote children's development may be possible when a shared relationship is established and information exchanged.

The partnership relationship is complex and is fraught with problems in practice. The 'equal but different' definition does not take into account the very real inequalities of power between professional workers and parents. There are also inequalities in what people think is important for them to know and what other people think is important to tell them. This argument is taken up by Frank Furedi (2001), who maintains that no parent can be an equal partner with the child-care expert as the terms of any such unequal 'partnership' will be set by the party that has the professional expertise. The parent has to listen and defer to outside opinion because to ignore such expertise is to risk the accusation of being an irresponsible parent. Parents are unlikely to have a strong sense of control if they constantly feel the need to prove themselves. Furedi views this solution as the disempowering of parents by undermining their confidence and promoting the authority of the professional. The writers and deliverers of parenting programmes and 'working together' philosophies appear to be insensitive to their potential in undermining and deskilling parents. Professionals are not concerned with the negative impact they may have on parental confidence as they believe that their crusade is far too important for them to worry about what upset they may cause to the odd mother or father. Furedi believes that the professionals have vastly inflated the complexity of the child-rearing task, thus viewing their own role as indispensable. According to Furedi, a responsible parent today is someone who is prepared to solicit the indispensable advice and support offered by the professional. However, he points out that the very concept of a parenting 'skill' obscures the essence of a child–parent relationship. Children do not benefit from the erosion of their parents' authority. He does acknowledge that there is a need for professional support for families but says that that support should be unobtrusive and targeted towards the small minority of parents who have genuinely failed to establish their authority over their children.

From all of the above research there is one very clear message, which is that settings must be very clear about whether they are advocating parental involvement or partnership with parents. The two concepts are not the same or inter-changeable. Having decided which of these positions the setting is going to take, clear definitions of roles and expectations for parents and professionals need to be drawn up. There also needs to be training for the professionals in order to bridge any gaps in their knowledge and skills associated with working with parents.

Empowering and engaging parents

Whilst there are references in the literature of the UK to empowering and engaging parents, the most detailed ideas and research appear in the literature of the United

States. This is probably because the United States has been involved in implementing these concepts for a great deal longer, starting in the 1960s with Project Head Start.

Dean (1991) defines empowerment as a process through which people and communities move towards more equitable, respectful inter-relationships with themselves and their environment. Dean claims that for lasting change to occur, it needs to have both personal and policy components. In order for empowerment to happen, the balance of power needs to change from 'power over' to 'power with'. Empowerment emphasises family members' strengths. Goldring and Hausman (1997) state that parental empowerment goes beyond simple involvement as it also requires the mind-set, attitude and beliefs of parents in their own abilities to be involved in education and to influence decisions. However, the researchers point out that the emphasis on power sharing in the empowerment equation makes the professionals reluctant to empower parents as they do not wish to share their own power. Low-income parents have more difficulty accessing a power-sharing relationship than do affluent parents. Goldring and Hausman believe that empowerment comes as a result of the parents' motivation to want to change things. Empowered parents feel more ownership of their children's education whilst enlightened professionals view empowered parents as an asset to the setting. Parents are able to bring a valuable perspective to the setting, as they understand their children's needs and are aware of the community's perceptions, values and beliefs.

One important group of people who need to be empowered and encouraged into parental partnerships are fathers. Barrows (2001: 102) points out that:

> Fathers (and father figures) make a vital contribution to their children's development. What fathers have to offer their children is different from what mothers offer, but it is just as important to the child … The vital message is:
>
> - Whether and how fathers get involved can make a big difference to their children's lives
> - Not getting involved means missing the opportunity of an enjoyable and rewarding relationship for both children and fathers.

How then can fathers be encouraged to participate in their child's early years provision? One way is for more males to be encouraged to work in the early years settings. In Scandinavian countries this has not been a problem but in the UK there are still stigmas attached to men who work in the early years field. In one children's centre in a multi-ethnic area of London, the two centre deputies are both male, one is Afro-Caribbean and the other of Scandinavian background. From the time these men were appointed there has been a rise in the number of fathers who have become involved in the centre. At weekends there are activities at the centre that encourage male participation such as fathers-and-sons football sessions, fathers-and-children outings to museums and visits to local activity centres, the cinema and theatre. These activities not only encourage fathers' participation but also empowers them in their role within the family. For fathers who may no longer live with their children, these weekend centre facilities give them the opportunities not only to undertake interesting activities with their children but also to gain confidence and support from their partnership with the centre staff.

Once a setting has decided that it is going to implement a real partnership with parents in which there will be changes in the balance of power, it needs to look at ways in which it can engage parents in order to encourage them to become involved. Swick (1991) puts forward the following ideas for engaging parents and professionals in joint-learning activities:

- support each other in joint-learning activities;
- support each other in the respective roles of parent and professional;
- carry out classroom- and school-improvement activities;
- conduct collaborative curriculum projects in the classroom;
- participate together in various decision-making activities;
- be advocates for children.

In addition to these, Swick points out that an integral part of success in these areas is the various parent and teacher roles and behaviours that make for a successful partnership.

The DfES (2002) has drawn up the following points for consideration as the medium for engaging parents when producing a home–school agreement:

- Have you asked parents what they expect from the school?
- What do you expect from the parents?
- Have you asked parents what they think of the school?
- How do you involve parents?
- Why do some parents not get involved?
- What can you do to establish an effective working relationship with the 'missing' parents?
- What can you do to help parents help their child?
- What priority do teachers give to working parents?
- What does your school do to listen to the views of pupils?

The document then goes on to list practical methods that might underpin better and more effective relationships with parents. In the Early Years Foundation Stage these issues come under the heading of 'Respecting diversity and valuing all families'. One of the ideas put forward relates to inter-agency collaboration with services that share an interest in parents and their children such as health workers, Travellers' Service, adult education, English for Speakers of other Languages (ESOL) workers and voluntary-sector workers. We are now able to see this idea coming to fruition within the new Children's Centres where these and other services may be available to parents.

Research carried out by Rosado (1994) in the United States looked at ways of promoting partnership with minority parents. A number of findings from this research could be used to inform professionals in the UK when they are designing their implementation strategy for parental partnerships. Researchers worked with Hispanic parents, who are the second-largest ethnic minority and the largest linguistic minority in the United States. The results of the study suggested that cultural, socio-economic, linguistic and educational differences affected the participation of Hispanic parents in the education system. The Hispanic parents in general perceived the teachers as being distant and impersonal as they did not speak to these parents or give them attention equal to that given to other parents. Parents viewed a lack of respect for them from the school staff as a major barrier. Particularly for Hispanics, respect is seen as the foundation for any professional relationship. Once respect is lost it is virtually impossible to resume the interaction. Parents also cited language- and work-related problems as reasons for not being able to visit the school more frequently. The educational background of Hispanic parents also discouraged their participation in school activities (57 per cent of parents in the study had either never been to school themselves or had had less than five years of schooling). As a result of their own poor schooling, these parents found it difficult to be role models and to perform their educational duties as parents.

Settings need to ensure that their staff are behaving towards parents in a way that does not embarrass, humiliate or disrespect the parents. Where additional languages might present communication problems, the setting must ensure that there are interpreters available when the parents visit. It is not respectful to the parents to expect their children to act as interpreters, and it could also be embarrassing if the child is asked to interpret things about itself or confidential information about the family situation. Settings also need to give consideration to the difficulty that parents may have attending meetings and functions when they are in poorly paid jobs that only pay the worker for the hours spent at work. In these cases it means that a time slot convenient to the parents needs to be found in order to ensure that they can attend.

Finally, given below is a useful list of positive things that need to be remembered when setting out to establish effective partnerships with parents:

- All families have strengths.
- Parents can learn new techniques.
- Parents have important perspectives about their children.
- Most parents really care about their children.
- Cultural differences are both valid and valuable.
- Many family forms exist and are legitimate.

All parents want the best for their children and want to have positive relationships with all staff.

It is also important to remember that when forming relationships with parents, special skills are required on the part of the professional. These include good listening techniques, tact, kindness, consideration, empathy, enthusiasm and an understanding of parent–child relationships.

Reflect upon …

1 Discuss the differences/similarities between 'partnership with parents' and 'parental involvement'. Which description do you think is the most useful?

2 Parents are now also customers of early years settings. What does this mean for the staff in terms of the way they treat and respond to parents?

3 The head of your children's centre has asked you to draw up a programme aimed at involving fathers as partners in their child's care and education. What would you put into this programme and how would you organise it so that fathers were able to participate? Give your reasons for including each activity.

Note

1 'Parents' in this chapter means anyone who is the primary carer of a child.

References

Barrows, P. (2001) *Fathers – Understanding the Vital Role that Fathers, and Father Figures, Play in Children's Emotional Development*, London: Child Psychotherapy Trust.

Central Advisory Council for Education (1967) *Children and Their Primary Schools* (Plowden Report), London: HMSO.

Cullingford, C. and Morrison, M. (1999) 'Relationships between parents and schools: a case study', *Educational Review* 51, 3: 253–62.

Dahlberg, G. and Moss, P. (2005) *Ethics and Politics in Early Childhood Education*, London: Routledge Falmer.

David, M. (1999) 'Home, work, families and children: New Labour, new directions and new dilemmas', *International Studies in Sociology of Education* 9, 2: 111–32.

Dean, C. (1991) 'Empowering partnerships with families', in *Innovations in Community and Rural Development*, New York: Cornell Community and Rural Development Institute, Cornell University.

Department of Health (1990) *Playgroups in a Changing World*, London: HMSO.

DfEE (2000) 'The childcare start up guide', *Good Practice in Childcare* 12, Nottingham: DfEE Publications.

DfES (2002) 'Parental Involvement: partnership with parents', available online: www.standards.dfcc.gov.uk/parentalinvolvement.

DfES (2007) *The Early Years Foundation Stage*, Nottingham: DfES Publications.

Douglas, J.W.B. (1964) *The Home and School*, London: MacGibbon and Kee.

Dunlop, A.-W. and Fabian, H. (2007) *Informing Transitions in the Early Years*, Maidenhead: Open University Press.

Easen, P., Kendal, P. and Shaw, J. (1992) 'Parents and educators: dialogue and development through partnership', *Children and Society* 6, 4: 282–96.

Elfer, P., Goldschmied, E. and Selleck, D. (2003) *Key Persons in the Nursery*, London: David Fulton.

Furedi, F. (2001) *Paranoid Parenting*, London: Allen Lane, The Penguin Press.

Goldring, E. and Hausman, C. (1997) 'Empower parents for productive partnerships', *The Education Digest* 62, 6: 25–8.

Howe, C., Foot, H. and Cheyne, B. (1999) 'Moving towards real partnership', *Research in Education* 64, Spring 1999, Edinburgh: Scottish Council for Research in Education.

MacNaughton, G. (2000) *Rethinking Gender in Early Childhood Education*, London: Paul Chapman Publishing.

Martin, J. and Vincent, C. (1999) 'Parental voice: an exploration', *International Studies in Sociology of Education* 9, 2: 133–54.

Mittler, P. and Mittler, H. (1982) *Partnership with Parents*, London: National Council for Special Education.

Moss, P., Brophy, J. and Statham, J. (1992) 'Parental involvement in play-groups', *Children and Society* 6, 4: 297–316.

Pugh, G. and De'Ath, E. (1989) *Working towards Partnership in the Early Years*, London: National Children's Bureau.

Rosado, L.A. (1994) 'Promoting partnerships with minority parents: a revolution in today's restructuring efforts', *The Journal of Educational Issues of Language Minority Students* 14: 241–54.

Smith, T. (1980) *Parents and Preschool*, London: Grant McIntyre.

Swick, K. (1991) *Teacher-Parent Partnerships to Enhance School Success in Early Childhood Education*, Washington, DC: National Education Association.

8 Play

All work and no play ...

This chapter deals with the value of play in children's learning and discusses ways in which the adult can support and extend play activities. Cultural and gender differences are explored as well as a consideration of how computers may affect the play behaviours of children.

From time immemorial children and adults have played. Early writings and paintings have described activities that are seen as the opposite of work, a form of time wasting when people were engaged in trifling activities as a break from their normal routines. However, the old adage 'all work and no play makes Jack a dull boy' recognises that play has some value and since the middle of the nineteenth century philosophers and psychologists have realised that 'play' has an important role in the lives of adults and children, and young children in particular.

But what is play? Many people have spent long hours debating the meaning of the activities that we term play. To date there has been little success in finding an exact definition, as it is a word that means different things to different people in different settings. The *Concise Oxford Dictionary* has 24 definitions of the verb 'to play' and ten interpretations of the noun. The first definition of the verb is 'to move about in a lively or capricious manner'. However, when we think about some situations in which the word is used it is apparent that play does not always involve 'moving about in a lively manner'.

Let us consider the following very ordinary settings in which the verb is used:

1   The baby is lying in the pram 'playing' with her fingers.
2   Two adults are sitting at a table, with intent expressions, playing a game of chess.
3   The girls are building a castle. They have been playing with the Lego for hours.
4   The teacher told the children at the back of the class to stop playing around and get on with their work.
5   The organist was playing a difficult piece of music.
6   The boy is in his bedroom playing with his Nintendo.

Does 'play' mean the same thing in each of those situations? I suspect that most readers would think that playing the organ or a game of chess was different from the baby playing with her fingers or the children being disruptive in class. It is not surprising that there are numerous definitions of play when the word is used in such a wide range of settings. Furthermore, as Sutton-Smith (1995) has pointed out, any definition reflects the discipline, ideology and cultural preferences of the author.

Even if scholars cannot agree over a definition, it is universally agreed that we engage in playful activities throughout life, although play is mainly associated with childhood and early childhood, in particular from birth to eight years. Throughout the world whenever we observe children in natural settings we see that play is the unique, single central activity of childhood. All children, unless they are sick or severely mentally disturbed, will play if given the opportunity, since it is through play that they learn to make sense of their world and to come to terms with their environment. However, social and cultural preferences affect the development of play and will also affect whether or not it is acceptable to play in certain settings. For example, children soon learn that in some societies it is unacceptable to play in the presence of elders. However, even though its value is widely accepted in many Western societies, including our own, play is being undermined by the pressures of formal learning at too early an age.

The characteristics of play

Although we cannot define play precisely, authors agree that there are certain characteristics associated with play and playful activities. The most generally accepted are those associated with Garvey (1977), Rubin *et al.* (1983) and Fromberg (1997), who argue that play can be defined in terms of dispositions and characteristics.

For them, play is:

- *symbolic* in that it represents an 'as if' and 'what if' attitude. 'As if' behaviour involves the play itself which enables children to experience particular feelings and attributes, whereas the 'what if' behaviour is the activity of the mind that promotes further thinking of ideas through play;
- *meaningful* in that it connects or relates experiences;
- *active* because individuals are doing things. The playing of children is always an active process and it is also essential for adult thinking;
- *pleasurable* even when the activity is serious, e.g. playing a game of chess;
- *voluntary and intrinsically motivating*. The motive may be curiosity, or mastery;
- *rule-governed*, whether implicitly or explicitly expressed. Children's play is often highly rule-governed although the child usually imposes the rules;
- *episodic* in that there is evidence of emerging and shifting goals that develop through experience. As children play, their goals alter and develop in various ways;
- *flexible*. For Garvey, flexibility is a hallmark of play.

I think readers will see that if play is defined in terms of these dispositions and characteristics then it will cover all the situations described earlier.

Tina Bruce (1991) has argued that these characteristics and dispositions are not sufficient to describe the play of children and has focused on what she terms 'free-flow' play. She developed a view of play derived from the principles of Gleick's chaos theory (1988). This theory is based on the view that the relationship between the process and the product in all systems is non-linear. In play situations the observer is never entirely sure how the child is involved and what she or he is getting out of it. As a result there is chaos and controversy with regard to the adults' interpretation of the play and its value. According to Bruce 'free-flow' play helps the child to integrate, adapt and apply their knowledge and understanding in a play environment without adult direction.

Bruce characterised 'free-flow' play under 12 headings, many of which have much in common with the dispositions of Rubin *et al.* (1983).

For Bruce, 'free-flow' play:

1　is an active process without a product;
2　is intrinsically motivated;
3　exerts no eternal pressure to conform to rules, pressures, goals, tasks or definite direction;
4　is about possible alternative worlds, which involve supposing and 'as if'. This involves being imaginative, creative, original and innovative;
5　is about participants wallowing in ideas, feelings and relationships and involves reflecting upon and becoming aware of what we know (metacognition);
6　uses previous first-hand experience, including struggle, manipulation, exploration, discovery and practice;
7　is sustained and, when in full flow, helps us to function in advance of what we can actually do in our real lives;
8　during 'free-flow' play, we use the technical prowess, mastery and competence we have previously developed and so can be in control;
9　can be initiated by a child or an adult, but if by an adult he/she must pay attention to features 3, 5, and 11;
10　can be solitary;
11　can be in partnerships or groups of adults and/or children who will be sensitive to each other;
12　is an integrating mechanism, which brings together everything we learn, know, feel and understand.

Bruce summarises the 12 features by stating that: '"Free flow' play = wallowing in ideas, feelings and relationships + application of developed competence' (Bruce 1991: 59–60).

Theories of play

In this section we shall look at some of the major play theorists and consider their contribution to the argument that play has a crucial role in children's learning.

Friedrich Froebel (1782–1852)

Froebel, whose influence was widespread in both Europe and Britain, postulated his views on play in *The Education of Man*, which was published posthumously in 1896. In this he wrote that 'play truly recognised and rightly fostered, unites the germinating life of the child attentively with the ripe life of experiences of the adult and thus fosters the one through the other'. Froebel believed that play is developed from within the child, but that the presence of the adult and the provision of appropriate materials nurture it. He produced a set of structured toys and playthings, materials that, although not used today, were at the turn of the twentieth century seen as an important part of education for play. He wrote 'at this age play is never trivial, it is serious and deeply significant' (para. 30). Froebel is discussed in more detail in Chapter 10.

Herbert Spencer (1820–1903)

Spencer put forward a surplus-energy theory. He believed that the higher animals, including man, often had periods of excess energy and play is an acceptable way to use up this excess energy. For him, play had no value other than this and it is totally separated from work. In his book *The Principles of Psychology* (1855), he argued that play is carried out 'for the sake of the immediate gratifications involved, without reference to ulterior benefits'. The origins of the 'surplus-energy theory' can be traced back to the writings of the eighteenth-century philosopher Schiller.

Karl Groos (1861–1946)

Groos published two important books, *The Play of Animals* (1898) and *The Play of Man* (1901), where he criticised Spencer's theory, arguing that surplus energy may provide a favourable condition for play but was not essential. He argued that play was the means of helping children prepare for life as it provided opportunities for the practice of skills and the possibility of exploring and learning what they will need to know as adults. This view is held by modern theorists, such as Bruner, whose ideas are discussed later in this chapter.

G. Stanley Hall (1844–1923)

Stanley Hall disagreed with the views of Karl Groos, whom he said saw play simply as practice and in its place he proposed the 'recapitulation theory' of play. Stanley Hall argued that through play the child acts out all man's primitive behaviours of our evolutionary past. For example, rough-and-tumble play is reminiscent of the wrestling and fighting of the past.

Freudian theorists

Most Freudian theorists have referred to play, but I have selected those who I believe have had some impact upon our understanding of play with young children.

Sigmund Freud (1856–1939)

Although Freud did not write a great deal about play, it has nevertheless become an important part of psychoanalytic theory. Freud believed that play was a cathartic experience for children. According to psychoanalytic theory, play takes the form of wish fulfilment and enables the child to master traumatic experiences. Freud wrote: 'every child at play behaves like an imaginative writer, in that he … creates a world of his own or, more truly, he arranges the things of this world and orders it in a new way that pleases him better' (1958: 45). Play enables children to express themselves completely, without reservation or reprisal, because children at play feel safe. Children will use toys and other materials to express the feelings and ideas that they are unable to verbalise. Likewise, during play they will do things that they know they would be otherwise reprimanded for doing. For example, the arrival of a new baby in the family may produce anti-social behaviour in the older child as she comes to terms with the existence of her sibling. She is perfectly aware that she must not hurt the baby, but there is nothing to stop her giving vent to her feelings of jealousy and hatred by drowning her doll. Another way of expressing her distress could be to engage in an imaginary play situation and walk around sucking a 'bottle' in an attempt to draw attention to the fact that she too needs to be fussed over.

Eric Erikson (1903–94)

Erikson postulated eight stages of development from birth to adulthood, arguing that for each stage there is a certain optimal time. He argued that there was no point in trying to rush children through the stages to make them grow up quicker, a notion that many people would do well to consider. The first stage, from birth to around two years of age, is one of basic trust versus mistrust when the well-loved child develops feelings of trust and security and a basic optimism in life. In the next stage, from two years to around three-and-a-half, termed by Erikson 'autonomy versus shame', the well-parented child emerges as one who has developed a sense of self-control and proud of herself. Erikson refers to his third stage of development, from four to six years, as the 'play age'. During this period children need to engage in both solitary and cooperative play as it helps them to develop their initiative and deal with their disappointments and failures. Like Freud, Erikson sees 'as-if play' to be important during childhood.

Donald Winicott (1894–1971)

Winicott argued that there are three stages in development. The first, 'undifferentiated unity', where the child imagines she is connected with, not separated from, the mother. This is followed by 'transition', when the child experiences the disconnection from the mother and disillusionment takes place when she realises that others sometimes take precedence over her and that the feelings of others need to be considered. The child comes to understand its dependence and learns about loss. An important part of the child's transition towards independence is the transitional object that is substituted for the mother and used to develop a sense of self. If the transition is effective, then the child will develop a healthy false self that they can present to the world and with which they are comfortable. Otherwise, the child remains uncomfortable with itself. Winicott considered that total independence is seldom fully attained as we always have some dependence on the presence of others. He stresses the importance of the transitional object in the development of play, for many children this is a blanket or piece of material that accompanies them everywhere. Winicott argues that play allows children the possibility of suspending reality and exploring potentially threatening experiences in the 'safe' environment of their fantasy world, helping them towards independence. A child takes a big step towards independence when she finally discards the transitional object.

Susan Isaacs (1885–1948)

Isaacs advocated the importance of play in both the emotional and cognitive growth of children. As a psychoanalyst she believed in the emotional benefits of play, arguing that play has a positive effect upon children's social and cognitive development. She wrote

> play is indeed the child's work, and the means whereby he grows and develops. Active play can be looked upon as a sign of mental health; and its absence, an indication of either some inborn defect, or of mental illness.
>
> (1929)

For her, it was through play that children can tell us about their emotional states and we can begin to understand their personalities and behaviours. Isaacs derived her ideas from the many observations she made of children at the Malting House School at Cambridge. Her influence on the early education curriculum is described in detail in Chapter 10.

Cognitive theorists

Jean Piaget (1896–1980)

Piaget based his theory on observations of his own and other children in schools in Geneva. He argued that children are active learners and that two activities, play and imitation, are important for the development of infants and young children. Piaget considered that play was a product of assimilation, whereas imitation resulted from accommodation. During play, children act out their already established behaviours and adapt reality to fit them in an enjoyable manner. By contrast, during imitation, the child is trying to copy another person's actions in order to understand the world around them.

Piaget argued (1962) that children's play evolves in three stages which could be linked to his four stages of intellectual development. There are three different forms of cognitive play which emerge during the early years: 'practice games' or mastery play, symbolic games, and games with rules'. The mastery stage is predominantly associated with his sensori-motor stage of cognitive development, while the symbolic stage is closely linked to the pre-operational stage of behaviour. For him, it is not until the phase of concrete operations that children are able to engage in games with rules. He argued that the symbolic play stage was crucial for the development of symbolic representation, which he believed is necessary before children can engage in co-operative play. True co-operative play is impossible until children can develop social perspective taking skills, which are a pre-requisite to playing games with rules. Piaget has argued that at the pre-operational stage children's thinking is egocentric and therefore they cannot engage in true game play. More recently theorists have argued that children are capable of playing co-operatively at an earlier age and have disputed the point of view that children are unable to see another person's point of view. (See Chapter 3 on 'How Children Learn'.)

Jerome Bruner (1915–)

Bruner sees play as beneficial to cognitive development as for him it is a preparation for the 'technical social life that constitutes human culture'. He argues that play serves both as practice for mastery in skills, and as an opportunity to try out new combinations of behaviour in a safe setting. Exploratory play in which children experiment with materials and social play, which encourages children to acquire the rules and rituals of the society in which they live, are beneficial to the child. Bruner believes that all play has rules, but unlike Piaget, does not think they come with increasing age, rather the rules are there from the start. In his now-famous Peek-a-Boo experiment he demonstrated that even a very young child understands the rules of turn taking that are the basis of this game. However, Bruner does not see all play of equal value. For example, he sees rough and tumble play, as less intellectually challenging than 'high yield' activities like construction or drawing activities that are more goal orientated. (Sylva *et al.* 1980).

Lev Vygotsky (1896–1934)

Although his ideas were known in Russia earlier, Vygotsky's views on play did not become well known in the West until the second half of the last century. For Vygotsky play is a vehicle for social interaction and is the leading source of development in the pre-school years. He argues that a 'zone of proximal development' is created by play, and therefore in play children are learning how to function beyond their present capabilities. Like Piaget, Vygotsky sees play developing into games with rules but, for him just as the imaginary situation has to contain rules of behaviour, so every game with rules contains an imaginary situation. For example, when children are playing at 'hospitals', each child within the group will have taken on a role and be acting it out according to his or her own interpretation. He or she will be governed by the rules laid down by the group. Vygotsky, as Bruner and Piaget, believes that from about eight years of age games with rules are more important than free play.

Play develops symbolic thinking by facilitating the separation of thought from objects and actions. A special feature of the Vygotskian approach to play is that he believes that in play the child is not truly free, as the play situation actually sets the limits on behaviour. Through language and symbolic thought, play involves self-regulatory behaviour that involves children developing the ability to plan, monitor and reflect upon their own behaviour. Vygotsky argues that children who are unable to practise these skills in their play will be unable to use these processes when they are engaged in other non-play activities.

Maria Montessori (1870–1952)

By contrast with some of the more recent theorists and early childhood educators who advocate the value of play in children's learning, Montessori considered that children learn through real-life activities. For her, play 'in the life of the child ... is perhaps something of little importance which he undertakes for the lack of something better to do' (Montessori 1956). Montessori is discussed in depth in Chapter 10.

What are the functions of play and how does it contribute to young children's learning?

Since the end of the nineteenth century, the writings of Rousseau and Froebel were influential in promoting a tradition in Western Europe and the United States that regarded play as essential to learning and development. One of the leading early childhood educators of the time, Susan Isaacs (1929), wrote that 'play indeed is the child's work and the means by which he or she develops'. This point of view is still held today by many early childhood educators who aim to provide young children with ample opportunity to practise and develop skills and competences in play settings.

Before we consider the contribution of play to children's learning, it is important to look at the various stages of play and how they develop throughout childhood. One of the earliest studies to look at the development of children's play is that of Mildred Parten (1933), who observed children between the ages of two and five years playing in nursery school without any adult intervention. She identified four categories of social participation among these children:

1   solitary independent play – the child plays alone independently and with her own toys without reference to others;
2   parallel activity – the child plays independently but the chosen activity encourages the child to play beside others, although she is not influenced by the activities of the other children. She plays *beside* rather than *with* other children;
3   associative play – the child plays with other children. There is a sharing and borrowing of materials but the play is not organised; each child behaves as she wishes without reference to a group;
4   cooperative play – generally around four to five years of age the child plays in a group that is organised for a purpose. For example, socio-dramatic play, or playing a formal game.

Although the younger children normally prefer solitary or parallel play, there are also occasions when older children choose to play alone. The level of solitary play may be lower when engaged in by the youngest children, but as Rubin *et al.* (1983) have pointed out, when older children are involved in solitary play it can be cognitively very complex, for example when an older child is playing with construction material.

Sarah Smilansky's (1990) research into children's play behaviours has shown how play develops as a complex adaptive system as children grow older. She argues that there are five basic forms of play:

1   functional or exploratory play – the child uses his sensory motor abilities to learn about his surroundings; much of the motor and object play in the early years is at this level;
2   constructive play – the child combines objects or articles, such as building with blocks;
3   dramatic play – the child pretends to be someone else, imitating a person's actions and speech, role taking and using either real or imaginary props;
4   socio-dramatic play – this involves cooperation between at least two children around a theme that evolves over a period of time;

5   games with rules – these include cooperative players, often winners and losers. The rules are normally child-controlled rules and are therefore different from the competitive games or sports that have adult-regulated rules.

Socio-dramatic play is the most complex, combining as it does elements or combinations of other types of play. It is this form of play that is valued most highly by early childhood educators as they believe that in these play bouts children learn a great deal about the world in which they live.

Fantasy/socio-dramatic play

Piaget saw fantasy play in terms of assimilation and accommodation, arguing that during fantasy play children create pretend new situations and assimilate the fantasy elements into existing schema. In this way they come to make sense of their world. Several writers have emphasised the importance of fantasy play in children's learning. Erikson (1965) stressed the importance of the life-rehearsal element in fantasy play, suggesting that it helps children come to terms with social issues like loneliness, failure and disappointment. Bruner, on the other hand, saw fantasy play as the precursor of social rules. Cognitive, social-interactionist and psychoanalytical theorists all appear to agree that fantasy play has value for children's development. Singer and Singer wrote: 'Imaginative play is fun, but in the midst of the joys of making believe, children may also be preparing for the reality of more effective lives' (1990: 152).

Pretend play becomes evident around 12 months of age, as children use a brush or comb on their hair or a cup to pretend to drink. However, this early pretending is a solitary activity and it is not until around two years of age that activities like taking the baby doll for a walk in parallel with another toddler occur. Even though a pair of two-year-old children play at going shopping, they are not yet aware of the social roles involved. By the time the children are aged three or older they can engage in complicated dramatic play sequences that become more and more involved with increasing age. Role play develops and it is not uncommon for children to take on a whole range of characters, both real and fictional. Socio-dramatic play involves high levels of both verbal and physical interaction with other children.

What do we mean by socio-dramatic play or fantasy play? Smilansky and Shefataya (1990: 22) consider the following elements should be present. These are:

- imitative role play – the child undertakes a make-believe role and expresses it in imitative action and/or verbalisation;
- make-believe with regard to toys – movements or verbal declarations and/or materials or toys that are not replicas of the object itself are substituted for actions or situations;
- verbal make-believe with regard to actions and situations – verbal descriptions or declarations are substituted for actions or situations;
- persistence in role play – the child continues within a role or play theme for a period of at least ten minutes;
- interaction – at least two players interact within the context of the play episode;
- verbal communication – there is some verbal interaction related to the play episode.

The first four of these relate to fantasy play, but to be defined as socio-dramatic play there must be all six elements.

Smilansky observed children aged three to five at play and proposed a number of ways in which she thought socio-dramatic play was beneficial in the development of the creativity, intellectual and social skills of children.

In socio-dramatic play children can be seen carrying out some or all of the following:

1 creating new combinations out of experiences;
2 selectivity and intellectual discipline;
3 discrimination of the central features of a role sequence;
4 heightened concentration;
5 enhanced self-awareness and self-control;
6 self-discipline within the role context (e.g. the child within a game might inhibit shouting out because it was not in keeping with the behaviour of the character);
7 the acquisition of flexibility and empathy towards others;
8 the development of an intrinsic set of standards;
9 acquisition of a sense of creativity and empathy towards others;
10 development of cooperative skills, since make-believe games in groups require effective give and take;
11 awareness of the potential use of the environment for planning and other play situations;
12 increased sensitivity to alternative possibilities so that the notion of father need not be one's own father but may include many kinds of behaviour associated within the broader concept of fathering;
13 increase capacity for the development of abstract thought by learning first to substitute the image for the overt action and then later a verbal coding for both the action and the image;
14 heightened capacity for generalisations;
15 a set towards vicarious learning and a greater use of modelling.

(Smilansky in Singer 1973: 224)

Other writers like Johnson (1990) have argued that it is during socio-dramatic play, when children formulate their own goals and engage in cooperation and reciprocity, that they develop the ability to build the conceptual frameworks necessary to help them understand and integrate different areas and levels of experience.

Case study: a group of four children aged 4 years

The following is a description of a socio-dramatic play episode that took place in a nursery after two of the children had visited local dentists.

The teacher, who was aware that the children had recently visited the dentist, had arranged a play area as a dental surgery. This group of four children wandered into the area and spontaneously decided to 'play at dentists'. One girl took on the role of the dentist and two boys were patient and dental nurse respectively, while the youngest child was given the role of the receptionist.

During the play, which lasted for more than 20 minutes, the children acted out their roles with a considerable degree of accuracy using the language and behaviours of the adults they were imitating. The play was complex and as the children acted out their roles, they recalled their previous experiences at the dentist showing clearly that they had an understanding of the various adult roles. One of the liveliest language exchanges took place when the two children who had been seen in two different surgeries discussed the 'differences' between the two practices. As the play progressed so they moved away from the rules that govern 'dentist play' and adopted another theme that had been triggered by the discussions. All the time they were reformulating and elaborating their plans and renegotiating their roles. To the onlooker it was apparent that the new theme was as absorbing as the original one.

Throughout the play bout all the children had displayed a high level of social and emotional competence and had demonstrated their ability to transform past experiences into new settings. Both perceptual and motor skills were used as they acted out their interpretation of the roles of dentist, patient, nurse and receptionist. To the adult onlooker during this particular play episode there was evidence to uphold Smilansky's thesis on the value of socio-dramatic play in developing of intellectual and social skills.

What other evidence is there to suggest that children learn through play? One of the few controlled studies to test this was carried out by Hutt (1966). She suggested that there are two forms of play: exploratory and ludic. During exploratory play children are involved in a range of activities that are conducive to learning, as opposed to ludic play that she considered to be trivial and purposeless.

Hutt set out to see how a group of children reacted to a novel object (a toy box that had flashing lights and made different noises) and whether the exploratory behaviour changed as they became more familiar with the toy. From her observations of 30 children aged from three to five years, Hutt argued that children explored first and then played. In the beginning, when the children explored the toy box 'to find out what it could do', their behaviour was serious and focused. Once they had satisfied their curiosity their behaviour became more relaxed and play changed to 'what can I do with this object?'. In 1972, Hutt and Bhavnani followed up the children who had been involved in the original study. They found that those children who had played in many imaginative ways with the toy after a thorough exploration scored significantly higher on tests of creativity than those who had not played much with the novel object.

A study of children with learning difficulties has linked physical play to learning and in a study carried out in a Frankfurt kindergarten it was found that 'increased accidents in the playground were directly linked to lack of movement and body control' (Blythe 2001).

Value of play in children's emotional development

Children possess the capacity for experiencing deep emotions. When the child hurts it hurts all over. You have only to observe a three-year-old child who has momentarily lost her mother to see the intensity of feeling as the child calls out 'Mummy, Mummy' and sobs and sobs, the whole body shaking. Equally, when children are happy they are intensely happy. Their mood swings are rapid and to the adult unpredictable. At this early age they are unable to manage their emotions, and the feelings of frustration, anger and sadness they experience can be very frightening. Young children do not possess the verbal language to express the depth or range of their feelings; for them the most natural language of communication is through play. Play is a form of self-expression and symbolic play in particular is an important vehicle for expressing feelings. When children are offered a safe and non-threatening environment they will communicate the depth of their feelings through play. Children do not talk about their concerns and problems, they play them out.

Bettelheim suggests that during play

> objects such as dolls and toy animals are used to embody various aspects of the child's personality which are too complex, unacceptable, and contradictory for him to handle. This permits the child's ego to gain some mastery over these elements, which he cannot do when asked or forced by circumstances to recognize these as projections of his own inner processes.
>
> (1978: 55)

As discussed in Chapter 3, more recently writers like Goleman (1995) have argued the case for 'emotionally literacy' as an important part of children's later learning and development. See the list on page 40 for a reminder of the key components of emotional literacy.

All the skills and competencies of emotional literacy can be learned most effectively in play settings. Socio-dramatic play is especially valuable for helping children to develop 'emotional literacy', as during their play children can have feelings of power over the environment, emotional awareness and sensitivity. Above all, in many role-play situations young children can develop emotional strength and stability, humour and positive feelings about themselves.

Empathy and understanding of the feelings of others develops from an early age. One has only to see the concern on the face of the two- or three-year-old when another child falls over and cuts her knee to realise that children are certainly not totally egocentric. During role play in pre-school and primary-school settings, children are able to interact through language. As they interact with assumed roles, children are able to experience emotional responses to each role and can decide whether to continue in that role, change roles or select an entirely different role. This type of activity is not only supporting children's emotional development but helps in problem-solving situations.

Strong emotions such as aggression, frustration and fear can all be controlled during play sessions. Susan Isaacs believed that it was crucial for educators to understand the inner world of the child, a world that adults did not necessarily share. She realised that early capacities for emotional expression and recognition are the foundation of social learning and communication.

A study by Kelly-Bryne (1989) showed how one child's play revealed themes of fear, aggression and violence as she played out battles of good and evil, beauty and ugliness, sense and stupidity. The little girl was displaying powerful feelings and behaviours that some children can only learn to control and understand in pro-social ways if they are given the opportunity to articulate these feelings in a supportive context. The result may be behavioural problems that lead further into a negative cycle of difficulties that then affect peer and adults alike.

It is through their subjective, emotional world that young children learn to make sense of their relationships and eventually their place in the wider world. All this can be learned in play situations.

Children and computers

Children are exposed to technology from a very early age. The child of 15 months is well able to press the on/off button on the TV or DVD player and in a relatively short time will be sitting at the computer or playing with a Nintendo or other similar equipment. No aspect of children's play is more controversial. There are those who would ban computers from all pre-school classrooms, while others believe that it is the answer to many educational problems. A wealth of literature has arisen on the subject

When three- and four-year-old children are sitting at the PC are they learning skills and gaining knowledge or simply giving the adults some peace and quiet?

Let us analyse what skills they may be acquiring.

Case study: a four-year-old child sitting at the computer screen

Mary is staring at the screen with concentration as she manipulates the controls, with dexterity. She is using a programme that involves driving a car. An adult asks why she is moving the mouse in a particular way. Her reply is 'That's what you have to do to make it go.' Further adult probing indicates that she has no cognitive understanding as to how or why the car moves in a certain way when she moves the mouse.

There are a number of studies that support the view that children learn both gross and fine motor skills from use of the mouse and the keyboard but unless children can read the instructions and interpret them, which most cannot at an early age, then they are usually pressing buttons by trial and error and have little or no understanding of real cause and effect.

A major problem of playing with a computer compared with ordinary play materials like blocks or Lego is that the child always believes that the computer must be right as opposed to other materials where they can challenge and become autonomous. If the child does not have control over their learning and fully understand cause and effect, the spatial skills learned on the computer may not transfer to later mathematical and scientific skills.

There have been very few controlled studies on the use of computers in the pre-school classroom, but Plowman and Stephens (2005) collected evidence from seven pre-school settings that found that some of the problems encountered resulted from the fact that the practitioners regarded the children as 'playing with the computer' in a nursery with emphasis upon free play and gave the children no adult guidance. As a result, interaction with the computer was a limited experience. Guided interaction with an adult could produce more positive results.

A number of studies have drawn attention to the effect of computer use at a young age on social and emotional relationships. Children who play with computers to excess could risk over-stimulation to the right hemisphere of the brain and under-stimulation of the left hemisphere. Fox *et al.* (1995), in a highly provocative study, found that four-year-old children with greater amounts of left-frontal activation displayed more social competence while children with right-frontal activation displayed social withdrawal. We know from various research studies that personal and language interaction is primarily dependent upon effective adult interaction, therefore, if this study is replicated, then children with high levels of exposure to computers that over-stimulate the right frontal lobe are at risk.

I think maybe, when we consider the use of computers in the nursery, we should remember the warnings of Healey (2003), who argues that children will be enthusiastic about anything novel, but generally uncritical. It is the adult who must be able to discriminate and select what is valuable. There is no doubt that limited, controlled use of the computer is beneficial to children from the age of three upwards, but they should not be used as babysitters nor should there be sustained use without any adult interaction. There is excellent software that stimulates children, but we must not ignore findings that suggest that social development may suffer and that the children may become physically inactive and, as a result, unable to sleep.

Parents have an important role to play in both controlling their children's use of the computer and helping them to use it advantageously. Computers have been introduced into most pre-school settings, but educators must ensure that there is a limit to their use and ample opportunity for pretend play.

There is no space in this section to discuss the many research papers available but there are many websites like ERIC and www.nwrel.org/request/june01/child.html where the interested reader may follow up the research.

Cultural and gender differences in children's play

In a review of play in different cultures, Curtis (1994) found that play was the dominant culture of children in all cultures. Although writers like Brazelton (1977) have argued that among some cultures where swaddling is practised infants are not able to play because they are on their mothers' backs all day, others have observed these children finding opportunities for playing with objects, even if it is only the jewellery worn by their mothers. Imaginative play is another area where writers have observed differences between the cultures. Feitelson (1977) argued that children from some traditional cultures are deficient in imaginative-play abilities, but others, including myself, would argue that if children are observed for long enough it is possible to see the emergence of imaginative play even though there is a paucity of toys and equipment. I have watched young children in South America playing with tins and stones and although I could not understand what they were saying it was very obvious that some form of imaginative play was taking place.

There are interesting cultural differences on the value of toys. In most Western societies, adults value toys that are designed to teach skills and develop cognitive understanding, whereas in most traditional African societies, parents give their children toys just to play with, the learning comes later. Children need not only time and space to play, but they also need adults to help them develop their skills. Parental attitudes towards their children's play varies across cultures, but the evidence suggests that where the attitudes are positive children are likely to become involved in high levels of imaginative and creative play.

There are few studies that look in detail at children's play in different cultural settings and, as has been pointed out by Roopnarine *et al.* (1998), these have been mainly with North American or European families and may be culturally biased. From the review of the literature, they found that when traditional and non-traditional families were compared, the following differences could be noted:

- children's play is more likely to reflect rituals and customs in traditional societies;

- one-to-one play occurs more often in non-traditional families;
- gender differentiation has been observed in child–parent play in non-traditional families but not consistently observed in traditional societies;
- variations in games such as Peek-a-Boo and Pat-a-Cake between adult and child occurs in both types of societies;
- group participation, interdependence and community values are transmitted through play in traditional cultures, whereas self-reliance, independence and competition are encouraged by non-traditional cultures.

(Roopnarine *et al.* in Sayeed and Guerin 2000: 20)

There has been a great deal of discussion about whether there are gender differences in children's play. Until about three years of age children of either sex play in a similar way, but by the age of three it seems that play preferences emerge. Some researchers suggest that by the time girls are three they will focus upon play with dolls and household items, art activities and dressing up, while boys play with cars and blocks and engage in more large group and aggressive play. It has been suggested that during fantasy play boys will tend to act out fighting and more aggressive activities while girls will act out real-life situations based on their immediate culture. As early as 1933, Parten had found that during free play children elected to play with same-sex playmates, a finding that is supported by many early years workers of today.

In a review of the literature of children under school age, Nepply and Murray (1997) looked at sex-stereotypical behaviour and found that imaginative play tended to occur most frequently when children were in same-sex pairs. They found that boys are more likely to engage in large-group aggressive play, whereas girls play in smaller quiet groups. Interestingly, Thorne (1993) also found that the play of girls was generally more collaborative as opposed to the hierarchical nature of the play of boys. Serbin *et al.* (1982) found that girls, possibly due to their greater linguistic ability, were more likely to use polite requests and persuasion to get their own way, whereas boys were more likely to use force and aggressive comments. Whether this is true of the play of all children is questionable and it may reflect the approach both of the parents and of the school and the personality of the child.

A cross-cultural study carried out by Lindsey *et al.* (1997) suggests that parents may contribute to children's gender-specific styles of play by treating their daughters and sons differently.

They found that:

- girls were more likely to engage in pretend play;
- boys engaged more in physical play;
- fathers of boys engaged in physical play more with their children than mothers or fathers of girls;
- mothers' presence encouraged both sexes to engage in pretend play.

In a study in Tower Hamlets, London, Sayeed and Guerin (1997) found that although teachers found few differences in children's play across cultures, there were distinctly identifiable gender differences.

Even though parents believe that they are providing their children with equal opportunities within the play setting, many are horrified when they realise that their children still adopt sex-stereotypical behaviours that they cannot believe they have learnt from home. Dixon (1990) has argued strongly that toys and play materials are important in shaping the outlook of young children. Television and the media have been criticised for the gender images they convey, but research has suggested that children are not just passive consumers who accept the stereotypes shown, but do in fact, work out for themselves what is appropriate. Hislam (1996) has pointed out that there are powerful influences upon children to behave in socially sexually appropriate ways and that by exploring the roles in their socio-dramatic play, they come to terms with 'who they are' and see themselves as individuals.

Role of other children in play

During the early years of life, both adults and other children act as play partners, each providing different kinds of play experiences. Many would argue that the prime reason for sending children to early-childhood settings is to help the children socialise and learn to play with others. There has been a great deal of research on the role of siblings and peers supporting development which is discussed in Chapter 3, but overall it appears that during play siblings and peers provide opportunities for children to:

- learn about different cultural and family backgrounds;
- broaden their experiences with a diversity of peers;
- develop friendships and other peer relationships;
- develop individuality apart from siblings and family;
- engage in different social roles in various play activities.

Role of the adult in children's play

There is no doubt that children can learn a great deal during free-play activities but, as most of the theorists have suggested, adults have an important influence upon children's play, both directly and indirectly. The adult may provide the stimulus by structuring the environment, as in our example of the 'dental practice corner', or by taking children on an outing like a visit to the shops. Vygotsky believed that the adult is needed to model and show the child how to play with materials and how to take turns. It is the adult who leads the child through the zone of proximal development helping them to progress to higher levels of play. Bruner has a similar approach, arguing that the adult provides the scaffolding for the child. This does not necessarily mean that the adult should be involved in the play, but should make the suggestions or organise the activities so that more mature behaviour occurs.

Smilansky (1968), working with disadvantaged children, believed that they seldom engaged in complex socio-dramatic play compared with children from more advantaged backgrounds. She suggested that educators work with these children to initiate role play and help them to sustain and develop their roles. In her programme early years workers were trained to engage in 'play tutoring', using four main approaches:

1 modelling: the teacher participates in the play and acts out a role, demonstrating how it can be carried out;
2 verbal guidance: the teacher does not necessarily join in but comments and offers suggestions to the children on how to develop the role;

3   thematic-fantasy training: the children are encouraged to act out familiar story dramas. This type of more structured approach is often found in nurseries in Eastern Europe;

4   imaginative play training: the teacher encourages the children to use finger puppets and practise making facial expressions to represent different emotions.

From her studies, Smilansky and others argued that as a result of play tutoring, children from socially disadvantaged backgrounds engaged in more sophisticated play and used more language. Smith *et al.* (1998) carried out a similar experiment in nursery settings with children mainly from economically disadvantaged backgrounds and found that after play tutoring the children engaged in greater fantasy play. Their sample was small but it is one of the few controlled studies in this country that points to the value of play tutoring.

Not everyone agrees that adults should intervene in children's play, particularly imaginative play as it can have an adverse effect upon the children. There is no doubt that intervention must be sensitive and unobtrusive otherwise that particular play bout will end abruptly. Most educators and parents can remember occasions when they have offered what they thought was a useful resource only to find it rejected by the children, who immediately ceased playing. Educators need to be skilled in knowing when and how to intervene and the strategies required to empower children as learners. Jones and Reynolds (1992) looked at the role of the educator in children's play and found that teachers used a variety of strategies to support and promote quality play. They acted as a planner, stage manager, scribe, mediator, role model, player and assessor and communicator. In each of these situations the adult was helping the children to find their own solutions but at the same time accepting the ideas and interests of the children.

Conclusion

Article 31 of the UN Convention on the Rights of the Child states: 'Parties recognise the right of the child to rest and leisure, to engage in play and recreational activities appropriate to the age of the child and to participate freely in cultural life and the arts.' The importance of this right is recognised by most adults but many still consider play as a time-wasting activity and not as an activity that is the main vehicle for learning in the early years of life. Throughout this chapter we have seen evidence that play, and socio-dramatic play in particular, is of value in promoting children's social and emotional development. However, there is little hard evidence to show that free play is essential for cognitive growth. Most early childhood educators will accept that there are certain skills and competences that cannot be learnt during free-play settings, for example, learning to cut with scissors. Nevertheless, they would argue that children are more likely to be successful in cognitive tasks in school if they have had the opportunity to explore and try out varying strategies in play settings before being presented with formal instruction. If play is to be seen as a process that will promote learning and development, it must be of high quality. Educators should not only provide an environment that offers high-quality resources, but also guide children so that they can develop their confidence as successful players and learners. No one would argue that play is the only way children learn, but the child who has been given ample opportunities for quality play of all types –

physical, social and cognitive – is more likely to be an eager, enthusiastic and successful learner.

Finally, all who work with children and young people should recognise the *Play Charter* published in 2007, which listed the following eight principles:

- children have the right to play;
- every child needs time and space to play;
- adults should let children play;
- children should be able to play freely in their local areas;
- children value and benefit from staff play provision;
- children's play is enriched by skilled play workers;
- children need time and space to play at school;
- children sometimes need extra support to enjoy their right to play.

Reflect upon …

1   Observe a group of children engaged in socio-dramatic play and analyse your observations using Smilansky's criteria on page 111.
2   Is there a role for the computer in the nursery and if so what is that role?
3   Educators argue about whether or not adults should intervene in children's play. Give your arguments for and against intervention.

References

Bettelheim, B. (1978) *The Uses of Enchantment*, Harmondsworth: Penguin Books.

Blythe, C. (2001) *Play Time Not Optional*, TES, 12 January 2001.

Brazelton, T. (1977) 'Implications of infant development among Mayan Indians of Mexico', in P. Leiderman, S.R. Tulkin and E. Rosenfeld (eds), *Culture and Infancy: Variations in the Human Experience*, New York: Academic Press.

Bretherton, I. (ed.) (1984) *Symbolic Play: The Development of Social Understanding*, New York: Academic Press.

Bruce, T. (1991) *Time to Play in Early Childhood Education*, London: Hodder & Stoughton.

Bruner, J. (1971) *The Relevance of Education*, New York: Norton.

Bruner, J. (1972) 'Nature and uses of immaturity', *American Psychologist* 27, 8: 687–708.

Curtis, A. (1994) 'Play in different cultures and different childhoods', in J. Moyles (ed.), *The Excellence of Play*, Buckingham: Open University Press.

Dixon, B. (1990) *Playing Them False: A Study of Children's Toys, Games and Puzzles*, Stoke on Trent: Trentham Books.

Erikson, E. (1965) *Childhood and Society*, London: Routledge & Kegan Paul.

Fein, G.G. (1981) 'Pretend play in childhood: an integrative review', *Child Development* 52: 1095–118.

Feitelson, N. (1977) 'Developing imaginative play in pre-school children as a possible approach to fostering creativity', *Early Child Development and Care* 1: 181–95.

Fogel, A. (1979) 'Peers vs mother-directed behaviour in 1–3 month old infants', *Infant Behaviour and Development* 2: 215–26.

Fox, N., Rubin, K.H., Calkins, S.D., Marshall, T.R., Coplan, R.J., Porges, S.W., Long, J.M. and Stewart, S. (1995) 'Frontal activation as memory and social competence at four years of age', *Child Development* 66, 6: 1770–84.

Freud, A. (1958) *Normality and Pathology in Childhood: Assessments of Development*, New York: International.

Froebel, F.W. (1896) *The Education of Man*, New York: Appleton.

Fromberg, D. (1997) 'A review of research on play', in C. Seefeldt (ed.), *The Early Childhood Curriculum*, second edition, New York: Teachers' College Press.

Garvey, C. (1977) *Play*, first edition, London: Fontana Press.

Gleick, J. (1988) *Chaology*, London and New York: Heinemann.

Goleman, D. (1995) *Emotional Intelligence*, New York: Bantam.

Groos, K. (1898) *The Play of Animals*, New York: Appleton.

Groos, K. (1901) *The Play of Man*, New York: Heinemann.

Hislam, J. (1996) 'Sex-differentiated play and children's choices', in J. Moyles (ed.), *The Excellence of Play*, Buckingham: Open University Press.

Howes, C. and Matheson, C.C. (1992) 'Sequences in the development of competent play with peers: social and pretend play', *Developmental Psychology* 28: 961–74.

Hutt, C. (1966) 'Exploration and play in young children', *Symposia of the Zoological Society of London* 18: 61–87.

Hutt, C. and Bhavnani, R. (1972) 'Predictions from play', *Nature* 237: 171–2.

Isaacs, S. (1929) *The Nursery Years*, London: Routledge & Kegan Paul.

Johnson, J.E. (1990) 'The role of play in children's cognitive development', in E. Klugman and S. Smilansky (eds), *Children's Play and Learning: Perspectives and Policy Implications*, New York: Teachers' College Press.

Jones, E. and Reynolds, G. (1992) *The Play's the Thing: Teachers' Roles in Children's Play*, New York: Teachers' College Press.

Kelly-Bryne, D. (1989) *A Child's Play Life: An Ethnographic Study*, New York: Teachers' College Press.

Klugman, E. and Smilansky, S. (1969) *Children's Play and Learning: Perspectives and Policy Implications*, New York: Teachers' College Press.

Lindsey, E., Mize, J. and Gregory, S. (1997) 'Differential play patterns of mothers and fathers of sons and daughters: implications for children's gender role development', *Sex Roles: A Journal of Research* 37, 9–10: 643–62.

Montessori, M. (1956) *The Child in the Family*, New York: Avon. (First published 1936.)

Nepply, T. and Murray, A. (1997) 'Social dominance and play patterns among preschoolers: gender comparisons', *Sex Roles: A Journal of Research* 36 (5–6).

O'Connor, E. (1991) *The Play Therapy Primer*, New York: John Wiley.

Olfman, S. (ed.) (2003) *All Work and No Play*, Westport: Praeger.

Parten, M. (1933) 'Social play amongst pre-school children', in *Journal of Abnormal and Social Psychology* 28: 136–47.

Piaget, J. (1952) *The Origins of Intelligence in Children*, New York: Norton.

Piaget, J. (1962) *Play, Dreams and Imitation in Childhood*, New York: Norton.

Play England (2007) *The Play Charter*, available online: www.playengland.org.uk.

Plowman, L. and Stephens, C. (2005) 'Children, play and computers in pre-school education', *British Journal of Educational Technology* 36, 2: 145–57.

Roopnarine, S., Lasker, J., Sacks, M. and Stores, M. (1998) 'The cultural contexts and children's play', in O. Saracho and B. Spodek (eds), *Multiple Perspectives on Play in Early Childhood Education*, Albany, NY: Steele University/New York Press.

Rubin, K., Fein, G. and Vandenberg, B. (1983) 'Play', in P. Mussen (ed.), *Manual of Child Psychology* 4: 693–774, New York: Wiley.

Sayeed, Z. and Guerin, E. (1997) 'Play, assessment and culture', in S. Wolfendale (ed.), *Meeting Special Needs in the Early Years*, London: David Fulton Publishers.

Schwartzmann, H.B. (1978) *Transformations: The Anthropology of Children's Play*, New York: Plenum.

Serbin, L., Spratkin, A., Elmin, M. and Doyle, M. (1982) 'The early development of sex-differentiated patterns of social influence', *Canadian Journal of Social Science* 14: 350–63.

Singer, J.L. (ed.) (1973) *The Child's World of Make Believe: Experimental Studies of Imaginative Play*, New York: Academic Press.

Singer, J. and Singer, D. (1990) *The House of Make Believe: Children's play and developing imagination*, Cambridge, MA: Harvard University Press.

Smilansky, S. (1968) *Effects of Socio-dramatic Play on Disadvantaged Pre-school Children*, New York: John Wiley.

Smilansky, S. (1990) 'Socio-dramatic play: its relevance to behaviour and achievement in school', in E. Klugman and S. Smilansky (eds), *Children's Play and Learning: Perspectives and Policy Implications*, New York: Teachers' College Press.

Smilansky, S. and Shefataya, L. (1990) *Facilitating Play: A Medium for Promoting Cognitive, Socioemotional and Academic Development in Young Children*, Gaitherrsburg, MD: Psychological and Educational Publications.

Smith, P., Cowie, H. and Blades, M. (1998) *Understanding Children's Development*, third edition, Oxford: Blackwell.

Spencer, H. (1898) *The Principles of Psychology*, New York: Appleton.

Sutton-Smith, B. (1995) 'The persuasive rhetorics of play', in A. Pellegrini (ed.), *The Future of Play Theory: Essays in Honor of Brian Sutton-Smith*, Albany: State University of New York Press.

Sylva, K., Roy, C. and Painter, M. (1980) 'Child-watching at playgroup and nursery school', *Oxford Pre-school Research Project*, Oxford: Grant McIntyre.

Thorne, B. (1993) *Gender Play: Boys and Girls in School*, Milton Keynes: Open University Press.

Vygotsky, L.S. (1967) 'Play and its role in the mental development of the child', *Soviet Psychology* 12, 6: 62–76.

Winicott, D.W. (1964) *The Child, the Family, and the Outside World*, London: Penguin Books.

9 Management and leadership issues in the early years

This chapter explores the different types of leadership and management roles that occur within early years settings. It looks at the role of the Early Years Professional. It includes different ways of managing and leading teams, including managing conflict. It investigates the types of staff, policies, customer awareness, etc., that the provision needs in order to offer a quality service.

In recent years, due to the changes in early years provision, there has been a strong emphasis on management and leadership. Since the introduction of the Early Years Professional Status (EYPS) in 2007 there is a distinct difference between the role of the manager and the role of the curriculum leader. In order to clarify the situation, the words 'manager' and 'leadership' in this chapter will be interchangeable, whereas 'curriculum leadership' will be confined to the EYPS role. There is more about the EYPS role later in this chapter.

The Early Years Professional is responsible for leading the curriculum, particularly in the new Early Years Foundation Stage which is required to be implemented from September 2008 in all provision that caters for children from birth to five years of age. From that date it is the legal responsibility of the providers to make sure their provision meets Section 40 of the Childcare Act 2006. It is therefore necessary for all managers to ensure that the provision meets the requirements of the Act that cover the learning and development requirements of the children and the welfare regulations that cover the area of safeguarding and promoting children's welfare, suitable people, suitable premises, environment and equipment, organisation and documents (DfES 2007). Thus the role of the early years provision manager is now one of great importance, which requires them to have the relevant qualifications to do the job efficiently and effectively. As Firestone and Riehl 2005 (cited in Aubrey 2007: 9) suggest:

> New leaders are increasingly being held accountable for the actual performance of those in their charge with a growing expectation that leaders can and should influence learning. Hence it is important to understand how leadership, learning and equity are linked.

There have also been changes in the way managers and leaders have to work as more and more centres are offering year-round provision, extended hours (wrap-around care) and are a 'one-stop shop' for parents and carers where they can access support and additional services such as IT training. This type of provision brings together professionals from different outside agencies such as health visitors, social workers, child psychologists, play therapists and further education teachers. Therefore managers will not only be integrating and working alongside their own staff but they will also need to build 'partnerships between professionals, parents and the wider community' (Bottle 2007: 155). The government expects that early years provision, like any other provision, will place an emphasis upon inter-agency working. This will require managers and staff, who in the past have only been used to working with internal staff and parents, to develop good relationships and communication skills in order to communicate effectively across a wide audience.

As Bottle (2007: 156) states:

> The task of any potential leader of an early years centre, then, is a complex and difficult one. This unique situation will require a distinct and special type of leadership. He or she will need to have drive and enthusiasm committed to the development of centres of excellence for children's services and be passionately committed not only to the centre staff but to developing and serving the local community as a whole, for without the backing and partnership of the community the centre will not develop its full potential.

Thus early years management and leadership in both the present and the future will have a large number of challenges to face.

Recent years have seen the publication of a number of books on management/ leadership that are specific to early years settings, thus acknowledging that not only is this an important topic but it is probably quite different from other management situations. Managing an early years setting requires effective communication skills with parents, children and staff. It also requires a level of communication between other professionals that may also require an understanding of their specific job roles. It is the acknowledgement of this that has led to new courses and qualifications that overlap the general management role and the specific early years management role, legitimised by the introduction of the Early Years Care and Education National Vocational Qualification (NVQ) Level 4 Management strand. The performance criteria for the NVQ Level 4 clarify what the management role entails and what the requirements are in order to be an effective manager of an early years setting.

Sadek and Sadek (1996) define the role of the manager as follows:

- ensure that the children are given a quality of service of care;
- support and supervise staff who deliver this service;
- consult and respect wishes of the children's parents/carers;
- provide adequate resources in the nursery to enable the service to function;
- set up a rich and stimulating environment in which the service can be delivered;
- undertake external liaison and fulfil an ambassadorial function;
- be a role model for the staff and children.

This chapter will look at specific aspects of management and the issue involved.

Managing the provision

When we talk about managing children we quite often look at the effectiveness of ensuring that there are parameters laid down within which the children can function. Such parameters offer the child a secure environment in which to explore and learn. It is no different for adults, who, like children, want to know the boundaries within which they can safely operate. In managing a nursery, these boundaries consist of a mission statement and a number of policies and procedures within which staff have to work.

The idea of a 'mission statement' originated in America among the big corporations and quickly spread to smaller establishments such as schools and welfare services. The UK has happily adopted the mission-statement concept and it has now become an integral part of most provisions' day-to-day working. A mission statement is best drawn up by all the staff so that there is a feeling of ownership and commitment to its aims. It is important that all workers, from the cleaners to senior managers, are in agreement with the philosophy of the setting as laid down in the mission statement. Sadek and Sadek (1996) state that an effective mission statement will:

- State clearly the purpose or intention of the organisation
- Indicate an underlying value system
- Be written in good plain English
- Be no less than 30 and no more than 100 words
- Be translated into the first language of all the users.

In addition to the mission statement, there are a series of policy and procedure documents that the setting needs to have in place. Some of these will be required by law, i.e. Health and Safety Policy; some may be required by the Children Act 1989 registration regulations, i.e. Child Protection Policy; and others may be there in order to ensure good practice, i.e. Financial Procedures.

Examples of policy statements are as follows:

- Equal Opportunities Policy;
- Behaviour Management Policy;
- Health and Safety Policy;
- Inclusion of Children with Special Needs/Disabilities Policy.

Examples of Procedures are as follows:

- Complaints Procedures;
- Accident procedures;
- Financial Procedures.

Whilst it might appear overly prescriptive to have such a large number of policies and procedures it does add to the security of the staff as they know that if something untoward happens, there is a definite way it should be dealt with. Policies and procedures prevent haphazard thinking in times of stress and enables staff to feel reassured that by following the policy/procedure they have taken the correct action in a moment of crisis. In terms of equal opportunities, policies and procedures ensure that all incidents are dealt with in exactly the same way regardless of who is involved.

Parents are also reassured by policies/procedures, as they know that the setting has thought through what it is doing and how situations will be handled in the event of their child being badly behaved or having an accident.

Sadek and Sadek (1996) put forward the following list of roles a manager needs to undertake in order to manage staff:

- Manager as leader
- Manager as motivator
- Manager as support
- Manager as empowerer
- Manager as controller

However, as Adirondack (1998) has pointed out, no one person can be good at all aspects of management; however, they can use their own strengths and skills to best advantage in order to become a 'good enough' manager.

Managing people (human resource management)

All nursery establishments have a range of staff such as qualified child-care workers, teachers, unqualified child-care assistants, cook, laundress, caretaker, kitchen staff and gardener. Each occupational area will have its own conditions of service, pay scales, working hours and trade union or professional association. The person in charge of human resources and/or delivery of the service in the setting will need to be aware of the situation as it affects each occupational area and will need to work within these in order to get the best quality of service, for example, ensuring that the staff are trained and appropriately qualified to a standard that enables them to provide the establishment with the best possible service. Some staff may require additional training in order to achieve the establishment's mission-statement aims.

Being a human resources manager, according to Adirondack, involves:

- ensuring the organisation has clear appropriate and workable policies and procedures for all aspects of employment;
- ensuring all staff, whether paid or voluntary, are properly recruited, inducted, supervised, trained and supported;
- ensuring all workers are valued and feel they are part of a team and the organisation;
- involving workers in discussions and decisions that affect their work or working environment;
- ensuring workers know what they are supposed to be doing, how to do it and how it fits into the organisation's overall work;
- helping workers plan their work and assess priorities;
- setting deadlines and informing workers about them;
- setting standards of performance and monitoring them and dealing with poor performance;
- dealing with workers concerns and grievances.

(adapted from Adirondack 1998)

Managing quality of service delivery

There are three steps to ensuring quality of service delivery within early years settings. First, there is the need to identify the customers' requirements: what do parents want/expect from your setting? Susan Hay (1997) suggests a list of questions that parents focus on when they first visit the setting. These questions fall under four headings: first impressions; what about the staff?; day-to-day operations; and hygiene and safety. An example of these may be:

- First impressions – Am I and my child made to feel welcome; do the children look happy; do the children talk with the adults?
- What about staff? – Are there enough adults working with the children; are they trained for the job, do they seem to enjoy being with the children?
- Day to day – Do the activities take into account my child's age, cultural background, special needs; are both boys and girls encouraged to use the equipment; is the food good and varied?
- Hygiene and safety – Are the premises clean, maintained and safe; are gates and fences secure; do they have adequate fire appliances?

Only when an establishment has ascertained what the customer wants and expects can it then move towards providing quality service delivery.

It is essential that the establishment has a method for researching and identifying parents' needs and expectations on an ongoing basis. The results of the research then need to be analysed and evaluated. Following the evaluation there may be a need to change methods of delivery or ensure that all staff are aware of the establishment's quality indicators.

In the field of early years care and education there is a second customer who is the direct recipient of most of the service offered: the child. One difficulty in viewing children as customers is that it is hard to get feedback on what they think of the service if they are very young. However, there are mechanisms for ensuring that the interests of the children are satisfied and these come via the inspections and registration carried out by OFSTED. In order for a setting to be operating within the law it must be registered with OFSTED under Part X of the Children Act 1989. The OFSTED-Registered Inspectors will not just look at the premises and health and safety issues but also at the early years curriculum to ensure that the Early Learning Goals are being met. At the time of writing this text, the government is in the process of finalising the National Standards for the Regulation of Day Care and Childminding in England. The 14 standards put forward are defined according to five settings: childminding; crèches; full day-care; out-of-school care; and sessional care. The 14 standards are:

- suitable person;
- organisation;
- care and learning;
- physical environment;
- equipment;
- safety;
- health;

- food and drink;
- equal opportunities;
- special needs (including special educational needs and disabilities);
- behaviour management;
- working in partnership with parents and carers;
- child protection;
- documentation.

These standards will form the baseline on which establishments will be measured in order to gain registration under the Children Act 1989, Part X regulations. Many establishments may wish to enhance these baseline standards so that they can offer parents and children a 'value-added' quality of service.

Management styles

Styles of management result from the dynamics between the culture of the organisation and each individual's approach to management issues. The majority of managers adopt a different style of management depending upon the task. The following are definitions of well-known styles of management as cited in numerous management textbooks.

Authoritative: This is when decisions are made 'at the top' of an organisation and passed down to the workers to implement. Such decisions may be made by a Board of Management, the most senior manager or the senior management team. This form of management is necessary when the senior management is responsible for implementing decisions that have been made by a Board of Trustees, local councillors' sub-committee or other outside body which has a management role for the establishment. It is more likely to be seen in voluntary sector early years establishments such as play groups and voluntary-body family centres, although it could apply to any setting.

Participative: This is when decisions are made based upon consultation with experts, advisers or those who will be affected by the decision. It is a useful way of working although the final decision is likely to rest with the senior manager or board of management.

Democratic: This form of decision making involves everyone in the establishment and can result in a vote or a consensus. It is a useful way of making decisions as it means that everyone is 'signed up' to the outcome and therefore has a responsibility for implementation of the decision.

Authoritarian: Note that this is not the same as authoritative management. Authoritarian management is repressive, dominating and requires staff to obey orders without question. It is a management style that can produce rebellion or poor working output from staff. It does not result in a happy establishment and can therefore lead to a high staff turnover.

Individualistic: This is when managers may make decisions that they do not have the authority to make. It might happen when no one appears to be managing or making decisions and this leaves the field open to others to take individual action.

Laissez-faire: This is when the senior manager or senior management team choose to ignore issues that require decisions. Instead they adopt the 'ostrich position' of burying their heads in the sand. This can lead to those who shout the loudest becoming the decision makers.

Chaotic: This is where there is a lack of consistency in management decisions and workers are unsure as to who is responsible. There is a lack of authority and so ordinary decisions are not made and situations develop into crises. So often we read about crisis management when something has gone dreadfully wrong and is featured in the media. However, if there is solution it may come from an authoritarian person stepping into the role.

A manager needs to balance all the arguments and decide which is the best style of management to adopt in order to ensure that all the staff are behind the decision. However, ultimately the manager is accountable as that is where the lines of accountability stop (as they say, 'the buck stops here'). There are also lines of accountability to outside bodies such as the Charities Commission and the Registrar of Companies. In early years establishments, additional accountability comes in the form of parents, local authority social services department, Children Act 1989 and OFSTED.

As a manager it is useful to also know something about yourself. Jung (1971) came up with what is referred to as the 'four functions', outlined below.

Thinker: enjoys tackling problems with logic; is strong on analysis but weak on implementation solutions; is a methodical worker; is sceptical of projects unless backed up with sound, rational arguments. *At work*: good with facts and figures, researching, systems analysis, accounting, the financial side of business.

Sensor: is good at getting things done; often impatient with the planning stage; feels at home with routine work; has a lot of common sense and is practical; works hard and is usually well-organised, energetic and single-minded. *At work*: good at initiating projects, setting up deals, negotiating, troubleshooting and converting ideas into action.

Intuitor: enjoys playing with ideas and theories; is good at seeing the 'overview' but misses the detail; is creative and has strong imaginative sense; will often get hunches about things that turn out correctly. *At work*: good at long-term planning, creative writing, lateral thinking and brainstorming.

Feeler: enjoys company; assesses on personal values not technical merit; is warm and sympathetic; is perceptive about people's moods, feelings and reactions; may overlook blatant facts in favour of 'gut feelings'. *At work*: good at cementing team relationships, counselling, arbitrating, public relations, will talk as easily with clerk as with executive.

Belbin (1981) carried out a long study concerning the best mix of characteristics in a management team. His first finding was that a team made up of the brightest people did not turn out as the best working team. From his work Belbin came up with eight roles that are needed for an effective management team, as outlined below.

The chairman: the team coordinator who is disciplined, focused and balanced. Talks and listens well, is a good judge of people and things and works through others.

The shaper: the task leader, and in the absence of the chairman would leap into the role, even though they may not do it well! This person's strengths lie in their drive and passion for the task but can be over-sensitive, irritable and impatient. They are needed in order to spur the team into action.

The plant: this person is the source of original ideas and proposals and is often the most intelligent and imaginative member of the team. They may be careless in details and may resent criticism.

The monitor-evaluator: this team member is analytical and has the ability to dissect ideas and see the flaws in arguments. Often less involved with other team members but is a good quality checker.

The resource-investigator: a popular team member, being extrovert, sociable and relaxed. They are able to bring in new contacts, ideas and developments. They are the salesperson, diplomat or liaison officers.

The company worker: the practical organiser who turns ideas into manageable tasks. Schedules and charts are their thing and they are methodical, trustworthy and efficient.

The team worker: this member holds the team together by being supportive to others, listening and encouraging. They are likeable but uncompetitive.

The finisher: without the finisher the team may never meet its deadlines. This is the person who checks detail, worries about schedules and chivvies the others with a sense of urgency.

(adapted from Belbin 1981)

A management team needs a balance of all of the above and in small team situations one person may have to adopt more than one role. As Adirondack points out, the best use of Belbin's categories in a small organisation is to identify and build upon the strengths of the individuals involved and fill gaps by bringing new people or by developing those strengths within the existing staff.

Leadership

Jillian Rodd (1994) has devoted a whole book to examining leadership in early childhood. She begins by looking at the differences between leadership and management. Using Hodgkinson (1991) she defines leadership as:

- an art rather than a science;
- focused on policy rather than execution;
- concerned with values rather than facts;
- to do with generalism rather than specialism;
- the use of broad strategies rather than specific tactics;
- reflective rather than active;
- concerned with human as opposed to material resources;
- focused on deliberation rather than detail.

Rodd states that the above statements point out that successful leaders are more than just efficient managers. However, it could be argued that in order to be a good leader you do also need some management skills; the two roles are not divorced. A leader is good at delegating tasks to the people who are most able to carry them out. This requires the leader to have a good knowledge of the staff and understand their strengths, weaknesses and the targets that they have been set at their appraisal. Sergio-vanni (1990) defines these essential tasks of an efficient leader as being empowerment, enablement and enhancement. Neugebauer (1985) offers four types of leadership:

- *task master*: places heavy emphasis on the task or the results and little emphasis on relationships or morale;
- *comrade*: places heavy emphasis on relationships and morale but little emphasis on the task or results;
- *motivator*: places strong emphasis on both the task and relationships;
- *unleader*: places little emphasis on either results or relationships.

From this list it would appear that the 'motivator' style of leadership would best suit early years establishments as it is a mixture of the 'task master' and the 'comrade', neither of which, on their own, is likely to fulfil Sergiovanni's qualities of a good leader. Also, one of the main driving forces of early years workers is to motivate the children in their care to develop and learn so it therefore may seem appropriate that the motivator style of leadership could have the same effect upon the staff.

Leadership involves influencing the behaviour of others, supervision of staff, planning and implementing change and administering the day-to-day service of the establishment. In carrying out these leadership tasks there is a need to remember the other aspects required of the leadership role so that all the staff are motivated to complete the tasks at hand. Although leadership and management complement each other, it is the leadership aspect that is responsible for inspiring staff and initiating change.

Rodd (1994) draws attention to the differences between women as leaders and men as leaders. There has been a great deal of research that shows that even when men and women perform the same leadership tasks there is a marked difference in their approaches. Men's leadership styles are concerned with authority and power whereas women are acting more as facilitators. Therefore women need to understand the male approach to leadership and ensure that they are able to cope with this by developing assertion and communication skills that give them confidence in a variety of situations. Whilst there are at present few men in early years it is not uncommon for child care and education workers to find themselves with men from other disciplines such as social work, medicine and police working alongside them as members of a multi-agency team.

Assertion and communication skills

Alberti and Emmons (1970) describe assertiveness as a straightforward statement that conveys opinions, beliefs, feelings, etc., in a way that does not have an impact on the self-esteem of the other person. Assertiveness is not aggression, which is demanding, blaming, threatening, interrupting, attacking, putting others down, etc. Assertiveness is stating clearly what you want, making brief but to-the-point statements, saying 'no' when you want to, making decisions, standing up for yourself, acknowledging another person's standpoint, etc. Assertion is the position of balance between avoiding conflict and winning at all costs. In addition to behaving in an assertive manner it is also useful to think assertively. Thinking assertively ensures that your own and others' needs are met and individual rights are maintained. In order to act assertively you have to believe that you have the right to do so. There are nine rights that refer to the work situation:

- to know what is expected of me;
- to have regular feedback on performance;

- to make mistakes sometimes without having to constantly be blamed for them;
- to be consulted about decisions that affect me;
- to take decisions that are within my area of work;
- to refuse unreasonable requests;
- to expect a certain standard of work from my staff;
- to ask for information when I need it;
- to be able, when appropriate, to constructively criticise the performance of my staff.

However, as Rodd (1994) states, most people have some difficulty in communicating assertively in certain situations or with certain people. Few people have the level of confidence and skill to be consistently assertive. Being assertive is one aspect of good communications within the work place. An effective communication system is based upon the following:

- knowing your purpose, strategy and message;
- identifying your target audience;
- overcoming the physical and psychological barriers;
- selecting the appropriate type and style of communication;
- transmitting the message;
- obtaining feedback.

Knowing your purpose, strategy and message: before communicating anything it is important that you are aware of what you want to achieve. You can then decide on the outcome you hope to obtain and what is the best way to word the message.

Identifying your target audience: this is the need to consider who you are speaking to and what language is best suited to the delivery of the message. How will the message be received by the target audience? There is a need to know the culture and values of the people you will be delivering the message to.

Overcoming the physical and psychological barriers: the temperature of the room, the comfort/discomfort of the seating, the time of day that the meeting is taking place are all physical conditions that may prove a barrier. The psychological barriers may be the gender, age or cultural/religious/social values of the audience. The status of the speaker in relation to the audience may also be a barrier.

Selecting the appropriate type and style of communication: is the message best communicated face to face, in a written form, via email, etc?

Transmitting the message: this is the most important part of the communication process and all the previously thought-out strategies may need to be abandoned in favour of another strategy if the message is not being received.

Obtaining feedback: this is the process whereby the communicator checks that the message has been received in the form that was planned. It is very easy for those receiving a message to get muddled, misinterpret the message or get a wrong message, therefore feedback is important to avoid this.

Communication may be verbal or non-verbal. Non-verbal communication usually refers to body language but at work we now have an additional area of non-verbal communication in the form of email. A person's body language may be giving the totally opposite message to the verbal message they are transmitting. There are times when people wish to hide their feelings for reasons best known to them. Some people are very good at this, for example, actors, politicians and salespersons. By and large, most people are not good at this and so you get the situation where they are verbally giving one answer whilst signals from their body will offer another. There is an important rider to consider when interpreting a person's body language and this is the cultural aspect associated with the way people may behave. We live in a pluralistic society and a person's cultural behaviour may lead them to behave in a way that is easily misinterpreted by the viewer. For example, many Asian women do not make eye contact with strangers for reasons of modesty rather than dishonesty. In some cultures it is accepted that it is not polite to have too great a physical distance between yourself and the person you are communicating with. This is the opposite to the Anglicised version of events where invasion of personal space is not welcomed and where others are best kept at arm's length. It is therefore a dangerous exercise to base interpretations upon body language alone.

Facial expression is a common way in which true feelings may be revealed. A raised eyebrow might denote scepticism at what is being said, whilst wearing a continuous smile can belie anger and annoyance. Eye contact is another telling signal. When a person refuses to make eye contact there can be value judgements made, for example, the person is not telling the truth or does not like the other person. Physical proximity is another area that can send out conflicting messages. Moving too close to a person may indicate intimidation or admiration, however, it could also indicate that the person cannot hear very well. There are lots of human resources textbooks that explore the different areas of non-verbal communication in depth.

Email is a modern method of communication between people that transfers words without being able to see the sender. It is used as a tool for improving and speeding up communications within companies as well as enabling easy contact with colleagues outside the company. Problems have resulted when people have not made themselves clear in an email and the recipient has become angry or upset. Emails are dashed off as a quick response mechanism and no thought may have gone into the reply. Email may not leave any room for negotiation in the same way that a face-to-face meeting will be able to do. The language used in an email might be interpreted as bullying/intimidating and can start a complicated situation within the workplace. Whilst email has a place in modern society and is a quick mechanism for transferring important messages and files around a company or outside a company it is not a useful medium for resolving conflict, motivating people or enabling people to be part of a greater whole. Fortunately, most early years establishments are very small and there is no necessity for introducing internal email in order to improve communication.

Managing conflict and dealing with difficult people

Conflict may arise within the team or from outside the team. In some situations managers may find the conflict arising from outside the early years setting, i.e. from parents, social services departments, inspectors, etc.

Taylor (1999) gives three definitions of conflict:

- conflict occurs when two or more parties believe that what each wants is incompatible with what the other wants;
- conflict arises when differences cannot be satisfactorily dealt with;

- the Chinese characters for conflict are 'opportunity-danger' (this covers the idea of positive as well as negative potentials of conflict).

Handy (1993) puts forward the following causes of conflict:

- formal objectives diverge;
- role definitions diverge;
- the contractual relationship is unclear;
- roles are simultaneous;
- there are concealed objectives.

Handy's work directly relates to large companies but there is no reason to suppose that the information cannot be extrapolated in order to fit a small-scale setting. It is interesting that Handy refers more to the control of conflict rather than the resolution. In a small-scale setting a speedy resolution to conflict is important as the consequences of a conflict continuing will affect everyone very quickly. According to Taylor, the main aspects relating to conflict resolution are each individual's personal response to their conflict and their skills in handling it, any external environmental or organisational factors that might be contributing and a manager's responsibility for providing a framework for handling team conflicts. In addition to these, how people react in difficult situations also depends on their personality, past history, etc. Conflict may arise as individual differences, factors within a team situation, factors within the organisation or as a result of the management culture. As mentioned earlier, management styles are important and certain styles of management may lead to conflict, particularly those that appear to others as intimidating. The senior management styles will often define the culture of an organisation which may lead to conflict such as a blame culture.

Examples of the types of behaviour that can lead to conflict or are used in response to conflict are outlined below.

Aggression can be active or passive, the latter often being overlooked or not viewed as aggression. A passive-aggressive person will always agree to undertake a request but rarely carry it out on time or at all. These are the people who agree to meet dates and times but may be late or not turn up at all; agree to do a certain piece of work but forget or overlook doing it. These people are probably one of the most difficult types to deal with. Active aggressors are often hostile (but not always), dominating, antagonistic, arrogant and want to steamroller through their ideas or resolutions. They use tactics that terrorise or humiliate the other members of their team.

Defeatists and pessimists are those people that respond to every suggestion with a negative response and believe that only luck can produce a good outcome. These people have a destructive influence on the other team members and/or staff, as negative attitudes can become contagious.

People who stay silent or offer only a mumbled acknowledgement. These people can be soul-destroying, particularly if you have put a great deal of effort into a project you are discussing with them or want the opinions of all the members of your team. Sometimes their silence is a protection; they may be naturally shy or unable to indulge in small talk. In other situations their silence may appear as rejection, silence being used to denote resentment. Silence can also denote suppression, a prolonged silent period whilst a person is trying to control their true feelings of anger or other emotions (what in the past may have been referred to as gritting their teeth and bearing it). Finally, silence may denote boredom either with the topic being discussed or with the other people involved. Sometimes people just do not have anything to say or do not understand what is being discussed but do not wish to have matters clarified. Dealing with each of the above personality types can prove challenging and may not always be successful as some of these personality traits may be too entrenched to expect any noticeable changes, however, in order to resolve conflict it is important to understand people's behaviour. Handy (1993) sees conflict as being a normal part of team development and gives the following definitions of the stages of a group growth cycle:

- *forming*: the group is not yet a group but a set of individuals. This stage involves defining the purpose of the group, its composition and leadership pattern;
- *storming*: most groups go through a conflict stage when a lot of personal agendas are revealed and a certain amount of interpersonal hostility is generated. This is an important stage for testing norms in the group;
- *norming*: the group needs to establish norms and practices, when and how it should work, how it should take decisions, what type of behaviour, what degree of openness, etc. At this stage there will be a lot of experimentation to test the level of commitment of the members;
- *performing*: this is the final stage at which the group reaches maturity and is able to be productive.

Once a conflict has arisen the manager must take steps to resolve the situation. First, it is necessary to find out what has happened and what the reasons for the conflict are. The reasons for the differences may be related to roles, information or a person's perceptions or values. In addition to these, other factors may be involved such as personality, attitude, communication style and culture. If the differences involve bullying, harassment, prejudice or equal-opportunity issues then the manager may have to implement the disciplinary process or the victim may choose to use the company's grievance procedure. If necessary, the manager can arrange for the services of a neutral mediator from within the company or an outside facilitator. The manager may need to negotiate with the people concerned or, alternatively, attempt to solve the problem that is causing the conflict. Negotiation requires all parties involved to have a positive action towards resolving the issues. If taking the problem-solving route, the manager will need to ascertain what the real issues are, gather the evidence, evaluate and decide alternatives/solutions. If the solutions are not acceptable to the people involved in the conflict, more stringent action may need to be taken.

Early Years Professional Status (EYPS)

The new category of early child care worker has a specific role as the provision leader for the implementation and ongoing monitoring of the Early Years Foundation Stage (EYFS). The EYP role will be found in many settings across the private, voluntary, independent and maintained provision. The major role of the EYP is to be the agents of change in improving practice within the setting. The present government's policy is to have an EYP in all children's centres by 2010 and in every full day-care setting by 2015.

The EYPS is graduate status with courses based within universities. There are three pathways candidates can go through in order to get the EYPS depending on the qualifications they are entering the pathway with. One of these pathways enables candidates to gain the EYPS alongside their Early Childhood Degree, however, in order to get the EYPS they must pass the degree. (For more information on this aspect, go to the Children's Workforce Development Council website: www.cwd-council.org.uk.)

Funding for the EYPS was originally via the Transformation Fund but in March 2008 the government introduced a Graduate Leader Fund specifically targeting graduate early years professionals. In order to meet the Childcare Act 2000, which has targets for improving the outcomes for all young children, the government has introduced the Graduate Leader Fund in order to upgrade the quality of the early years workforce. Nurse (2007) raises the question of the relationship between the EYPS and the Qualified Teacher Status (QTS) and how these two roles, which complement each other, will work together to provide a cohesive workforce. As Nurse (2007: 5–6) states:

> the DFEE proposed a foundation degree in early years to raise the level of qualification in the sector, introducing the Senior Practitioner status, and thus aimed to improve the quality of practice in early years provision. What this actually meant in reality was never defined and now the EYPS has superseded this, applying to full graduates (Level 6) rather than the foundation degree graduates (level 5).

Reflect upon …

1   Management and leadership are to do with being able to motivate staff in order to ensure that they produce high-quality outcomes in the tasks they are allocated. Think of a task you have recently been given and describe what factors motivated you to produce high-level outcomes.
2   Check the list of requirements on page 124 for a mission statement as laid down by Sadek and Sadek. Check this list with a mission statement from an early years setting you are familiar with and see how it fits.
3   Look at the list of Jung's four functions (1971) on page 128 and decide which of these refers to you.

References

Adirondack, S. (1998) *Just About Managing? Effective Management for Voluntary Organisations and Community Groups*, London: London Voluntary Service Council.

Alberti, R.E. and Emmons, M.I. (1970) *Your Perfect Right: A Guide to Assertive Behaviour*, San Luis Obispo: Impact.

Aubrey, C. (2007) *Leading and Managing in the Early Years*, London: Sage Publications.

Belbin, R.M. (1981) *Management Teams: Why they Succeed or Fail*, Guildford: Butterworth-Heinemann.

Berne, E. (1964) *The Games People Play*, Harmondsworth: Penguin.

Bottle, G. (2007) 'Leadership in the early years', in A. Nurse (ed.), *The New Early Years Professional. Dilemmas and Debates*, London: Routledge.

Boutall, T. (1996) *The Good Quality Managers Guide*, London: Management Charter Initiative.

Denny, R. (1997) *Succeed for Yourself*, London: Kogan Page.

DFEE (2000) *National Standards for the Regulation of Day Care and Childminding in England* (consultation document), London: DFEE.

DfES (2007) *Early Years Foundation Stage Statutory Framework*, Nottingham: DfES Publications.

Dickson, A. (1984) *A Woman in Your Own Right: Assertiveness and You*, London: Quartet Books.

Handy, C. (1993) *Understanding Organizations*, Harmondsworth: Penguin.

Hay, S. (1997) *Essential Nursery Management*, London: Baillière Tindall.

Jung, C.G. (1971) *Psychological Types*, London: Routledge.

Neugebauer, R. (1985) 'Are you an effective leader', *Child Care Information Exchange* 46: 18–26.

Nurse, A. (ed.) (2007) *The New Early Years Professional. Dilemmas and Debates*, London: Routledge.

Peters, T. and Waterman, R. (1982) *In Search of Excellence*, New York: Harper and Row.

Peters, T. (1987) *Thriving on Chaos*, London: Pan Books.

Rodd, J. (1994) *Leadership in Early Childhood*, Buckingham: Open University Press.

Sergiovanni, T.J. (1990) *Value-Added Leadership: How to Get Extraordinary Performance in Schools*, Florida: Harcourt Brace and Jovanovitch.

Sadek, E. and Sadek, J. (1996) *Good Practice in Nursery Management*, Cheltenham: Stanley Thornes.

Smith, A. and Langston, A. (1999) *Managing Staff in Early Years Settings*, London: Routledge.

Taylor, G. (1999) *Managing Conflict*, London: Directory of Social Change.

10 Early years education

This chapter looks at the Early Years Foundation Stage programme for children from birth to five years and reviews current research evidence on the value of early childhood education. Early influences on the curriculum are also considered and a final section provides examples of some international early childhood curricula.

There is an increasing amount of national and international evidence to show that quality early childhood education has a positive long-term effect upon children's later development. Governments worldwide have at last begun to recognise that early childhood education matters. In the UK, since the first edition of this book was published, early childhood education has undergone a number of major changes culminating in 2008 in the introduction of the Early Years Foundation Stage that sets the standards for learning, development and care from birth to five years of age. This chapter will discuss some of the more important research underpinning these changes as well as looking closely at the Early Years Foundation Stage (EYFS) and other curricula approaches that affect early childhood education and care.

Early influences on the curriculum

Early childhood education has a long history in the UK and much of what is termed 'good practice' today can be found in the writings of the pioneers of the nineteenth and early twentieth century.

Friedrich Froebel (1782–1852)

One of the first theorists to influence the early years curriculum in the UK was Friedrich Froebel, whose ideas on childhood pioneered a new approach to our understanding of children's activities and ways of learning. He saw children's development as a whole and argued that children need to develop and integrate all their activities through play. Froebel was the first to introduce play as a major medium for instruction in the school curriculum. However, he did not believe that play should be unstructured as it was too important to be left to chance. Froebel wrote:

Just because he learns through play, a child learns willingly and he learns much. So play, like learning and activity, has its own definite period of time and it must not be left out of the elementary curriculum. The educator must not only guide the play, since it is very important, but he must also teach this sort of play in the first instance.

(Lilley 1967: 167)

Froebel believed that children should have real experiences that involved them being physically active both indoors and outdoors. He used the name *kindergarten* for his nursery school as it signified for him both a place for children, where they can interact and observe nature, and a garden of children where they could grow and develop. In his kindergartens children were introduced to a carefully sequenced set of materials known as 'gifts', six sets of playthings that formed a sequence, beginning with a number of soft balls and leading on to wooden spheres, cubes and cylinders. He also expected children to carry out a set of creative activities such as drawing and modelling that he termed 'occupations'. The gifts and occupations, together with singing, games, dancing, stories and talk, made up the curriculum. Froebel thought that teachers should maintain a flow of talk in the classroom by coaching, prompting, making suggestions and by asking questions. His emphasis on the importance of the teacher–child relationship has continued to be an important part of the philosophy of early childhood education to this day.

One of Froebel's many legacies to young children was his notion of treating the school day as a complete unit in which activities continue for varying lengths of time according to the needs and interests of the children. This practice, which exists today in the majority of nurseries, was in complete contrast to the infant schools of the time, in which all the children sat in rows and everything was governed by the bell.

Maria Montessori (1870–1952)

Maria Montessori was an Italian doctor who worked among the socially and intellectually handicapped children in Rome at the beginning of the twentieth century. From close observation of the children in her Children's House (the name she gave to her nursery schools), she concluded that children pass through sensitive periods of development when certain skills and competences are learned more easily. This is supported by research referred to in Chapter 3. Montessori's stages covered the ages from zero to six years, six to 12 years and 12 to 18 years. For her, the purpose of education was to aid young children to develop their fullest potential through their own efforts. The young child learns through observation, movement and exploration and for this reason must not be educated in the same way as the older child. Montessori also believed that children have an intrinsic love of order and expected each one to take responsibility for taking and replacing materials and equipment in good order.

Montessori's didactic materials were highly structured and designed to move from the simple to the complex. The child must always wait to be shown how to use new equipment correctly by the teacher and, if unable to use it properly, it is taken away and produced again later when the time is felt to be appropriate. Montessori believed that the child needs love, security and affection and a protected environment. The teacher, whom Montessori called a directress, was not there to direct the child but, where possible, the direction and correction for the young child should be inherent in the structure of the self-correcting exercises and apparatus. The role of the directress is:

- to prepare herself (or himself);
- to prepare the environment and provide a stimulating and challenging environment that will help children by creating a spontaneous learning situation;
- to act as a link between the child and the materials. This is done by demonstration and example;
- to observe each child and note its interests and how the child works. These observations are used to decide what next should be represented to the child, how it is presented and when.

For Montessori, the prepared environment was both in and out of doors, and included the organisation of space and resources. The Montessori classroom is organised into areas of learning and, on the shelves, which are all low enough for children to access easily whatever material they require, is equipment to help develop all the senses of the children. Everything the child requires for a particular activity is to be found in one particular area of the classroom, and this is always in the same space in order to provide security for the children.

The curriculum was developed based on Montessori's beliefs that the child has two 'creative sensibilities': an 'absorbent mind' and 'sensitive periods', which are aids to help the child adapt to the environment. In the Montessori Method, Montessori referred to freedom within a structured environment, but that does not mean a licence to do whatever one wants. Montessori argued that we cannot be absolutely free or we would not be able to live in society.

Montessori argued that the child needs freedom to explore and interact with the environment and so construct a cognitive understanding of the world around it. The child makes choices from a variety of materials, appropriate to its stage of development, that will lead to greater understanding. However, it is the directress who controls and limits the freedom of the child within the educational environment.

Unlike Froebel, Maria Montessori did not stress the importance of relationships or of being part of the community, but stressed that children must work alone as in this way they become independent learners. It has often been said that Montessori did not agree with play. In reality she did not ban play but believed that children should work through the learning sequences before being allowed free choice of creative activities. In this respect, her philosophy is very different from that of her fellow educationalists in the first half of the twentieth century, who considered that children learned about materials by playing with them, whereas Montessori only allowed children to experiment with materials after they had learnt to use them appropriately.

There are an increasing number of Montessori nursery schools in the private sector as many parents believe that their children will learn better in a structured environment and are impressed by the calm atmosphere and sense of order that almost always prevails in a Montessori nursery setting.

Rudolph Steiner (1861–1925)

Steiner based his view of education upon a specific view of child development. He believed that children go through three stages: the will, zero to seven years; the heart, seven to 14 years; and the head, from 14 years upwards; and that the education offered must be appropriate to these stages. Steiner was concerned primarily with the development of the whole child and believed that through understanding the nature of children their individuality will come to fruition. The child who is offered a creative and balanced curriculum will grow into a flexible and creative adult. The curriculum aimed to provide children with balanced experiences of the arts and sciences as well as opportunities to develop processes of thinking, feeling and willing. Steiner believed that it is essential to provide children with open rather than limited options.

The organisation of the day is important. The teacher organises a routine for each morning with singing and circle games that provide plenty of opportunity for movement before the children are guided, sometimes through a story, into their play. The children may play alone or with others. They can play, draw or sew. The teacher is always ready to help them if required but the children are not offered any instructional material and no attempt is made to introduce them to numerical or reading skills until the age of seven, and then writing will be taught before reading. In Steiner's approach, during the period from zero to seven years children should be allowed to develop the full play of their imagination at an age when imaginative play is so important in their lives.

He thought that children should have the same teacher for seven years, who should personally greet each child on arrival at school. The teacher's role is to help children learn to do things as well as possible. An important feature of the environment is the design of the classroom, which is a room painted in a warm colour with soft materials and few hard angular corners. The materials in the room are natural and always at the child's own level. All materials are stored in aesthetic containers such as wooden baskets that can be incorporated into the children's play. There are no plastic toys, but there are wooden blocks of every dimension and texture as well as natural materials. There are small felt dolls and puppets and a workbench is available with miniature but real tools, where children can make their own toys. The home corner is filled with cots and home-made soft dolls, and there are simple cookers and ironing boards for children to use in their play. Everything that is in the room is multi-purpose and encourages children's play and imagination.

Outside, play equipment is minimal, but there are plenty of natural playthings: for example, trunks and logs for children to scramble over. It is argued that the lack of equipment encourages children to become more creative and imaginative.

At the end of the morning the teacher gathers the children together in a special part of the nursery where there are seasonal decorations. A child is asked to light the 'story candle' and the children wait quietly for the teacher to tell them a story. The story is always told, never read, as it is felt that books come between the children and the storyteller; also the children will be better able to imagine the situation and not have pictures in a book to destroy their own images. The morning closes with a farewell song before the children leave.

The influence of Steiner is not strong in the UK, although there are now over 800 Rudolph Steiner or Waldorf schools throughout the world, and as educators maybe we should look again at some of his more radical beliefs.

Margaret McMillan (1860–1931)

Margaret McMillan was a pioneer educator who believed in the importance of first-hand experiences and active learning. Like her sister, Rachel McMillan, she was concerned with both the health and home conditions of the children with whom she worked, arguing that children who are sick and undernourished cannot learn. In order to help these children and their families, McMillan set up medical centres to help improve their general health and provided baths and washing facilities for children that needed them. She also provided meals for all the children before the introduction of the School Meals Service.

McMillan saw her nursery schools as extensions of the home and encouraged her teachers to forge close links with parents, as she believed that the family played an important role in the education of children. Aware that many of the mothers had received little or no education, Margaret McMillan encouraged mothers to come into the nursery and learn alongside their children.

She was a firm believer in the value of play and ensured that there was ample material available to stimulate children's imagination. During play children were able to develop feelings and relationships as well as physical and cognitive skills, and through story, rhyme, talk and song, children were encouraged to develop their language abilities and musical appreciation. McMillan's nursery schools had gardens in which children could find plenty of fresh air. They were encouraged to play freely outside as it was here, she argued, that children learned the rudiments of science and geography. Both inside and outside, Margaret McMillan provided an environment in which learning was inevitable.

Her views on nursery education, to be found in *The Nursery School* (1919), had a profound influence upon nursery education in the UK for several decades. In 1937, P. Ballard, a nursery inspector, wrote that 'the modern nursery school is the product of Miss McMillan's genius'. Her views on the need for the nursery school to be part of the community and to work closely with parents are still valid and are included in the current practice guidelines for the Early Years Foundation Stage.

Susan Isaacs (1885–1948)

As mentioned in Chapter 8, Susan Isaacs contributed a great deal to our understanding of the social and intellectual development of children. At a time when very little was understood about the inner feelings of young children, Susan Isaacs, influenced by the psychoanalytic theories of Melanie Klein, made every effort to ensure that children had freedom of action and expression. At Malting House School in Cambridge, children were encouraged to express openly their feelings of hostility, anger, fear and aggression, as Isaacs believed that their suppression would be harmful to the child.

Susan Isaacs valued play and in particular make-believe play, which she thought gave children the freedom to think and reason and to relate to others. She also advocated that children should be free to move about as much as they needed and disliked classrooms that were very restrictive. Isaacs believed that young children could solve problems and disagreed with Piaget's view that young children were egocentric and unable to reason. Her detailed observations of the children at Malting House School demonstrate clearly that children can understand complex ideas if they fully understand the language used and are working with adults who pose meaningful and challenging questions. Like Margaret McMillan, Susan Isaacs valued the role of parents in their children's education and saw the nursery school as an extension of the home. Her links with parents were maintained through contributing regularly in a magazine for parents under the pseudonym Ursula Wyse, in which she wrote numerous articles including ones on the 'normal fears and anxieties of children'.

Probably her greatest contribution to early childhood education were the detailed observations she kept over a number of years and used in her in-service training courses for teachers at the London Institute of Education. Her books *Intellectual Growth in Young Children* (1930) and *Social Development in Young Children* (1933) are full of astute observations that are as relevant today as they were at the time they were written. Through her lectures, Isaacs was to have a powerful influence upon nursery and primary education in the post-war years, particularly in creating an awareness of the need to appreciate the social and emotional inner life of children.

Does early childhood education have any value?

Most of the longitudinal research indicating the effectiveness of early education has been carried out in the United States, the best-known being the Perry Pre-school Programme (Schweinhart *et al.* 2005). In this study, begun in the 1970s, Weikart demonstrated the lasting effects of high-quality early intervention. Other studies in the United States included research on the Early Headstart project (Love *et al.* 2002). The international review by Melhuish (2004) on the impact of early years provision on young children found that high-quality care and education was beneficial for young children from three years of age, particularly for those from disadvantaged backgrounds. However, there is some evidence to suggest that negative effects on development can occur for younger children, from birth to three years, although there may be other factors that affected these results. This issue is discussed fully in Melhuish's review.

In the UK there has been little large-scale research into the effects of early childhood education. The 'Start Right' Enquiry (Ball 1994; Sylva 1994) reviewed the evidence of British research and recommended that more rigorous longitudinal studies be carried out. The Effective Pre-school Education Project (EPPE), funded by the DfES, was a direct outcome of these recommendations. This was the first British longitudinal study (1997–2004) that attempted to answer the following questions:

1   What is the impact of pre-school on children's intellectual and social/behavioural development?
2   Are some pre-schools more effective than others in promoting children's development?
3   What are the characteristics of an effective pre-school setting?
4   What is the impact of the home and childcare history on children's development?
5   Do the effects of pre-school continue through Key Stage 1 (ages six and seven)?

(Sylva *et al.* 2004)

Some key findings from the study at the pre-school stage:

- attendance at pre-school, compared to none, improves the all-round development in children;
- length of time attending is important; an earlier start (under the age of three) is related to better intellectual development;
- full-time attendance led to no better gains for children than part-time provision;
- good-quality pre-school experiences were of significant benefit to disadvantaged children;
- disadvantaged children attended pre-school for shorter periods of time than those from more advantaged groups (around four to six months less);
- there are significant differences between individual pre-school settings and their impact on children;
- quality care and education can be found across all types of early years settings, although quality was higher overall in settings integrating care and education and in nursery schools;
- high-quality pre-schooling is linked to better intellectual and social/behavioural development for children;
- children make more progress in settings with staff with higher qualifications;
- where settings view educational and social development as complementary and equal in importance, children make better all-round progress;
- the quality of the home learning environment is more important for intellectual and social development than parental occupation, education or income;
- what parents do is more important than who parents are.

(adapted from Sylva et al. 2004)

This research has underpinned much of the thinking for the Early Years programme implemented in September 2008

Early childhood curriculum

Every society has its own expectations of its children, and the curriculum, both in content and method of delivery, reflects these expectations. In some societies children are seen as 'empty vessels' that need to be filled with facts and figures. This seems a deficit model in which emphasis is placed upon what the child cannot do rather than what the child is able to do, the implication being that only the educator/adult can supply the knowledge and skills required for a child to become a competent person. The child is expected to be a passive recipient of knowledge and there is no recognition of the role played by the child itself. In other societies the approach is very different. Children are seen as active learners and it is accepted that they enter school with certain knowledge and abilities, the role of the educator being to build upon these strengths. A society that really respects children is one in which there is true communication between children and adults. The voice of the child is heard and listened to, and the child is involved in decision making from an early age.

Among early years educators in the UK, the term 'curriculum' is associated with the image of the 'whole child' who is an active learner and brings skills and competences into the school. Learning cannot be compartmentalised. The cognitive, emotional, social and physical domains are integrated and learning in any of these areas must necessarily involve all the others. However, it is necessary for the educator to plan all the content areas of the curriculum to ensure that children receive as broad a set of learning experiences as possible.

Provision for young children from birth to five years

Unlike many countries, children in the UK can be found in a number of educational settings during the first five years of life. All are the responsibility of the Department for Children, Schools and Families and must be registered with OFSTED or CISW, but as the research has shown (see Table 10.1) there are differences in the quality of provision.

Table 10.1 Child-care provision for children from 0–5 years

Type of provision	Age of children
Childminders Self-employed carers who provide care and education in their own home. Must be registered with nurseries inspectorate. OFSTED or CISW-inspected annually	From 0–teenage Registration regulations only apply to care of children under eight Children maybe full or part time
Children's centres Offer early education services combined with care from 8.00a.m. to 6.00p.m. five days a week, 48 weeks a year. Provide a base for a childminder network, child and family health services, support for children and parents with special needs. Have links with training providers. Registered and inspected by OFSTED or CISW	From 0–5 years
Day nurseries Usually open all day, but not evenings and weekends. Different types of nurseries, including private, community, council and workplace nurseries. Normally between 25 and 40 children, usually grouped by age. All nurseries registered and inspected by OFSTED or CISW	From six weeks to five years
Out of school kids' clubs Offer play and care to school children. Include breakfast and after-school clubs. Open during school holidays	From three years and over Clubs for under-eights registered with OFSTED or CISW
Playgroups Provide play and education for children for 3–4 hours a day, although some offer extended or full-day care. Groups are registered with OFSTED or CISW	From 2–5 years

Table 10.1 continued

Type of provision	Age of children
Nursery schools and classes A nursery school is independent of any school for older children. Open during school hours, during term time. A nursery class is a pre-school class attached to an infant or primary school and is part of the state education system. There are also nursery schools in the independent sector	From 3–4 years
Reception classes First class in the primary school for children who are five or will be five during the school year	From four years
Nannies Employed by parents to care for children in the home. They do not need qualifications although many have nursery or childcare training. No central registration of nannies	From birth and over
Sure Start Sure Start programmes bring together health workers and play workers to provide a variety of services and activities for children and their parents. Activities include toy libraries and swimming lessons as well as support groups for mothers. Caters mainly for deprived children and families	From birth to four years

What is a curriculum?

There are many definitions of the term 'curriculum', which traditionally has been interpreted as a 'course of study'. Readers may find the following definitions of interest. The curriculum for young children includes:

- all the activities and experiences provided for them by adults;
- all the activities they devise for themselves;
- the language that adults use to them and that they use to each other;
- all that they see and hear in the environment around them.

(Drummond *et al.* 1989)

- the concepts, knowledge, understanding, attitudes and skills that a child needs to develop.

(DES 1990)

- an organised framework that delineates the content that children are to learn, the processes through which children achieve curricular goals, what teachers do to help teachers achieve these goals and the context in which teaching and learning occurs.

(National Association for the Education of Young Children 1991)

- a consideration of the process of learning (how a child learns), the learning progression (when a child learns) and the learning context (where and why a child learns).

(Ball 1994)

- everything that affects the child in the learning environment, overt and covert. It covers not only the activities, both indoors and outdoors, offered to young children, but also the attitudes of the staff towards not only the children but to each other, to parents and anyone who visits the setting.

(Curtis 1998)

- The term curriculum is used to describe everything children do, see hear or feel in their setting, both planned and unplanned.

(DfEE 2000)

The last definition is the one given in the Curriculum Guidance for the Foundation Stage.

Early Years Foundation Stage

Every Child Matters (2003), a document that underpins the Children Act 2004, introduced the five outcomes that are believed to be the key to well-being in childhood and later life:

- to be healthy;
- stay safe;
- enjoy and achieve;
- make a positive contribution;
- achieve economic well being.

(See Appendix 1 for a full description of the outcomes.)

The new Early Years Foundation Stage (EYFS), introduced in 2008, aims to bring together a framework for all carers and educators of children from birth to five years, merging three documents, *Birth to Three Matters*, the *Early Years Framework* and the *National Standards in Childcare*. It covers all aspects of learning and care and is intended for all children in whatever setting they may be (state, private or voluntary sectors). In order to provide a framework that will integrate care and education, the government has removed the Foundation Stage from the National Curriculum as it is believed that this will offer the best possible outcomes for children. The EYFS is more than a curriculum. The document looks at all aspects of what should characterise effective early years provision:

- relations with parents;
- partnerships;
- creating a good learning environment;
- health and safety issues;

- equality;
- the importance of planning based on observations; and above all
- the importance of understanding how children learn.

The welfare requirements of the EYFS replace the National Standards for Day Care introduced in 2001. The document combines the principles that come from *Birth to Three Matters* and the Foundation Stage and these have been grouped into four complementary themes, each broken down into four commitments:

- *A Unique Child* recognises that every child is a competent learner from birth who can be capable, confident and self-assured. The commitments are focused around development, inclusion, safety, health and well-being;
- *Positive relationships* describe how children learn to become independent as a result of a loving and secure relationship with parents and/or key person. The commitments are focused around respect, partnership with parents, supporting learning and the role of the key person;
- *Enabling environment* explains the importance of the environment in supporting and extending children's learning and development. The commitments are focused around observation, assessment and planning, support for every child, the environment;
- *Learning and development* recognises that children learn and develop in different ways and at different rates; all areas of learning and development are equally important and interconnected.

(DfES 2007)

It is believed that this approach will meet the desired outcomes set out in *Every Child Matters*.

Principles into practice

These principles have to be put into practice by early childhood educators. Children need to be offered an appropriate curriculum in a secure and stimulating setting and in order to do this, educators must have a sound understanding of how children develop and learn. Each child is different and will bring into school its previous experiences and expectations. Meeting the diverse needs of children means more than being aware of their previous experiences, interests, skills and knowledge. It also involves being aware of the requirements of equal opportunities that cover race, gender and disability as well as the Code of Practice relating to the identification and assessment of children with special educational needs.

Children with special educational needs include the more able, children from diverse linguistic backgrounds, those with disabilities and children from different ethnic and cultural groups including travellers, refugees and asylum seekers. Each of these groups of children will need to be offered planned opportunities that build on and extend their existing knowledge.

Providing a differentiated curriculum to meet the needs of individual children who learn at different rates and in different ways requires much skill and knowledge from the educator. In planning the daily programme, a wide range of teaching strategies will be necessary that involve individual and large and small group activities.

Not only should the provision offer children opportunities for a wide range of creative and imaginative play activities, but there should be sufficient time and space to allow children to develop and extend their play, sometimes alone and sometimes in the company of other children or an adult. The Childcare Act of 2006 requires the EYFS learning and development programme to comprise three elements, outlined below.

1   The early learning goals:

- personal, social and emotional development;
- communication, language and literacy;
- problem solving, reasoning and numeracy;
- knowledge and understanding of the world;
- physical development;
- creative development.

2   The educational programmes – skills, processes and knowledge that must be taught to young children.
3   Observation and assessment of young children to evaluate their progress.

Probably the most important part of this section of the document is Point 2.5 in Section 2:

> None of these areas of Learning and Development can be delivered in isolation from the others. They are all equally important and depend upon each other to support a rounded approach to child development. All the areas must be delivered through planned purposeful play, with balance of adult-led and child-initiated activities.
>
> (DfES 2007)

Critics of the document argue that the programme in the hands of untrained or poorly qualified staff could result in young children being given an inappropriate formal curriculum. However, the practical guidance that is offered not only stresses that play underpins all the development and learning for young children but argues that practitioners should provide well-planned experiences based on the children's spontaneous play, both indoors and outdoors. The introduction of the EYFS professional is designed to ensure that the early years educators are highly qualified and skilled at observation and assessment. This programme became mandatory from September 2008 for all children in registered settings.

The Montessori Schools Association has published a helpful document demonstrating how the principles of the EYFS can be put into practice within a Montessori perspective (*Guide to the Early Years Foundation Stage in Montessori Settings* 2008).

In the *Practice Guidance for the Foundation Stage* (DfES 2007), the early learning goals have been separated into six steps, ranging from birth to 11 months; eight to 20 months; 16 to 26 months; 22 to 36 months; 30 to 50 months; and 40 to 60 months. The overlap in the age ranges is designed to remind educators that some children develop more quickly than others and may progress beyond the goals in some areas, while others may still not have achieved by the age of five. In this respect the new guidance is more proscriptive than the previous Foundation Stage where the stepping stones were colour-coded, but not age-related. However, it is anticipated that the majority of children will achieve most of the goals by the end of the Foundation Stage.

Although the guidelines stress the value of well-planned play, both indoors and outdoors, this aspect may be overlooked, particularly for children who enter reception classes when they are only just four years of age. These children are frequently expected to sit at tables for long stretches of the day. Research from Sylva (2001) has shown that children who are encouraged to learn through play are likely to achieve better exam results than those who receive a formal nursery education. She has warned the government of the possible detrimental effects of placing too great an emphasis upon more disciplined forms of early education.

Early learning goals

Personal, social and emotional development

Early childhood educators all over the world stress the importance of children's social and emotional development during the early years of education. Unless children learn to establish positive relationships with other children and with adults, they are unlikely to achieve their full potential in later life. The learning goals in this area of development focus on helping children to become independent and autonomous. Young children are naturally curious and it is important to ensure that they have a positive approach to new experiences.

Throughout the Early Years Foundation Stage, educators help children to develop self-confidence and self-esteem and to become aware that people have different needs, views, cultures and beliefs. This is a natural process for children growing up in a multicultural classroom but more difficult for those whose environment is less culturally mixed, although in every group of people there will always be differences of opinion and belief. Understanding about 'right and wrong' and being responsible for the consequences of one's actions is something that many children find difficult and may take a long time to appreciate. Nevertheless, self-discipline and self-control are crucial aspects of being able to deal with one's feelings and relationships with others.

Practitioners are well-aware of the importance of supporting children in their personal, social and emotional development and most work closely with parents or carers, but it is often an area of the programme that is less well-planned than others. Although much of this learning is incidental and occurs during play and other activities, there are times when planned intervention can be highly effective.

Communication, language and literacy

One of the main aims of these goals is to encourage children to have the confidence to speak and listen in different situations. Talk is an important part of our lives and learning how to engage in dialogue is a gradual process. It has already been mentioned that babies from an early age learn to 'turn-take' and communicate non-verbally long before they can express themselves in spoken language. Children need to have opportunities to speak and listen to others and to use language to represent their ideas, thoughts and feelings. For some children when they enter the nursery, for example those for whom English is a second language, their communication may be mainly non-verbal, with gestures, eye contact and facial expressions taking the place of words. Shy, non-confident children may also use non-verbal communication when they start but, as their confidence grows, language will come, first as a whisper, and then as an audible voice for all to hear. Even though children have the confidence to engage in conversations with others, few will initiate conversations with adults unless they have something meaningful to say and feel very secure in the company of the adult. When children and adults engage in conversation it is essential that the adult listens to the child and responds appropriately. Adult–child conversation is often dominated by questions and answers, with the adult asking a lot of 'closed questions' – those that have definite answers. Discussion needs to be open-ended and structured so that the child can respond in a variety of ways.

By the end of the Foundation Stage it is expected that children's language skills will have developed so that they can interact with others and negotiate activities and plans with other children. Children will also be learning how to use language to organise their thinking and express their feelings and ideas. The guidance for this stage gives educators some useful ideas on extending children's skills in this area.

The literacy content of these early learning goals involves talking about and listening to stories, poems and nursery rhymes. Those children who have shared books and stories with adults from babyhood soon become aware that the 'marks' on the paper can be deciphered into words, while others may enter the nursery with no knowledge of stories or nursery rhymes and may not even know how to turn the page of a book. Reading begins with listening to stories and as the children listen they extend their vocabulary and gradually come to understand that written language is different from spoken language. Children need to hear stories told as well as seeing them in books with pictures and written text.

During this period some children will be developing an awareness of sounds and the letters of the alphabet; others may have started to read. At the same time that children are developing as readers, so they are beginning to emerge as writers. Their first scribble patterns will gradually turn into recognisable letter shapes and finally into words. By the end of the Foundation Stage most children will be able to use a pencil and hold it correctly but they should not be pressured into 'writing' at too early a stage.

In the next chapter we shall be looking at the emergence of literacy in greater detail and the role of the adult in that development.

Problem solving, reasoning and numeracy

In a world in which so many adults are 'frightened' of anything to do with mathematics, it is imperative that children become confident in learning the skills associated with this area of the curriculum. Young children enjoy using and experimenting with numbers, particularly large ones, in their play and much early mathematical understanding is developed through imaginative play, stories, rhymes and games. This area of learning includes counting, sorting, matching, recognising shapes and patterns, understanding relationships and working with numbers, space, shapes and measures. Mathematics is about making connections and solving problems and there are many practical activities in the nursery that can help develop these abilities, beginning with the early explorations of babies.

As children begin to learn to use numbers in appropriate ways they not only need practice in counting, but they also have to learn the language of mathematics – 'more' and 'less', 'addition' and 'subtraction' – before they can begin to understand the concepts.

During this stage children learn about topological concepts such as on/off; over/under; up/down; across; in/out. To understand these properly, children need lots of practical experiences so that they can feel their bodies going 'over' or 'under' the chair or 'across' the room. These mathematical concepts are constantly being reinforced during physical activities. Children will be learning from a very young age about shape and size from handling and playing with objects. Some shapes will be geometric ones, such as square, circle and triangle; others will be more amorphous and children will need to use their imagination to describe what they see.

Talking about objects of different sizes requires knowing the relevant adjectives for size and shape and comparisons such as 'bigger than' and 'smaller than'. These expressions have to be learned in context.

Cookery sessions offer endless opportunities for children to estimate and predict what will happen. They will be weighing and measuring using scales and balances, but it is also useful if the adult asks them to guess whether one amount is heavier or lighter than the other. Children need to become familiar with terms such as 'the same as', 'more than', 'less than', 'full' and 'empty', as these are fundamental to their later understanding of mathematics. The language of mathematics cuts across all areas of learning and for children to use it accurately it is essential that they have as much practice as possible.

Many of the mathematical concepts that children develop during the foundation years will arise during a variety of activities. The educator can develop these by talking 'mathematically' with children during their play and other activities.

Knowledge and understanding of the world

Children are striving to make sense of the world from a very early age and will have brought to the pre-school setting a vast range of experiences and knowledge. Young children are constantly exploring, observing, problem solving and making decisions about what they see, hear, feel, touch and taste. The setting will continue to provide activities that extend this knowledge and understanding. This area of learning will lay the foundation for later work in science, design and technology, history, geography and information and communication technology.

Children need a wide variety of practical activities, mainly using the basic provision in the outdoor and indoor areas available in every nursery. There are endless opportunities for educators to introduce science to children in the Foundation Stage. For example, children like to experiment with sand and water – how and why does the material change? Experiments with water, magnets, pulleys and torches are common activities in many nurseries. Cooking is an activity that can help in learning about temperature, transforming materials from one state to another, as well as helping with mathematical concepts.

In the natural world of plants, trees and animals there are many opportunities for extending children's understanding and knowledge. Where possible, take children out to see real-life examples; even in a dense urban area there is usually some vegetation nearby. Books can be used to follow up and extend the experience.

Children learn skills through the use of a wide range of tools, for example scissors, rulers, computers, magnifiers and gardening tools. However, most of the skills we need in science come from observation, exploration, prediction and forming hypotheses. Children enjoy the challenge of being asked questions such as 'What will happen if...?' or 'Which do you think will go the fastest?'. It is the role of the adult to encourage children to ask 'what', 'why', 'when', 'where' and 'how' questions and to help them think logically. Children also need help to extend their vocabulary so that they have the language to be able to make predictions and hypothesise.

Both boys and girls are interested in finding out how things work and rapidly learn how to perform simple programmes on the computer. By the time they reach the end of this stage most children can use CD-ROMs, videos, tapes and other media competently.

The foundations of history are laid down as children begin to develop a concept of time and to think about past and present events in their families and their own lives. At this stage children become interested in absent members of the family and what has happened to them. For example, if a grandparent has died before the child was born, questions are asked about that person.

During this period children become more interested in the environment and the role of those around them. They begin to develop a sense of place and will ask about their own cultures and beliefs and those of other people. Open discussions and stories and songs from cultures and languages help encourage positive attitudes towards others, irrespective of race, religion, gender or disability. There is evidence that many children enter school with negative stereotypes about certain groups of people and this programme is designed to help overcome this. Much of this learning will take place through well-structured play, but even more will occur as a result of positive adult involvement.

Physical development

Babies and young children need to move about and get as much fresh air as possible. The importance of fresh air to our brain development has already been mentioned earlier in the book. This is a period when children are learning many large and fine motor skills and they require the time and space to practise them repeatedly before they are perfected. Young children are naturally curious and this leads them to be constantly on the move, much to the chagrin of many adults. Many educators feel that as the children come to the end of the nursery years they should be sitting at a table and carrying out paper and pencil tasks – 'getting ready for proper school'. The result is frequently a group of bored, inattentive children, who sit and stare or, more often, get up and walk around and may become generally disruptive. Educators complain that these children lack the ability to concentrate. This may be so, but it is more likely that the task is inappropriate. If the children are involved in an activity of their own choice they are much more likely to display good attention skills.

The opportunity to move around freely and explore enables babies and young children to gain control and confidence in the use of their bodies. As they move around the classroom or the outdoor areas they are developing an awareness of space, of themselves and of others.

It is to be regretted, but once most children enter primary school there are limited opportunities for physical exercise during the school hours. Furthermore, changes in society mean that children are less likely to play in the streets after school but will probably go home to sit in front of the small screen. There is official awareness of this problem and, with luck, changes may be made in the school curriculum in the future. In the meantime it is essential that children at the Foundation Stage get as many opportunities as possible for physical exercise as it is vital for their later academic development.

The recognition of the importance of being healthy is an aspect of this programme that was not present in the previous Foundation Stage. From a very early age children are encouraged to have an awareness of their healthy practices with regard to sleeping, eating and exercise so that by the end of this stage they understand the importance of eating healthily and taking regular exercise.

Creative development

For children to develop creative and aesthetic awareness, as many opportunities as possible should be made available to explore and experiment with a wide variety of materials and tools and to try out ideas alone or with others. This requires time and space.

Children should be exposed to both two-dimensional and three-dimensional activities and learn to explore colour, texture, shape and form in both dimensions. The guidelines point out that children must be able to express themselves freely and that the role of the adult is to support them where necessary.

Music is an important part of the early years curriculum and children should be encouraged not only to sing traditional songs from different cultures but also to listen to and make music for themselves. Children of this age will often break into spontaneous dance or act out a song to music. In European nurseries a large part of the curriculum is devoted to music and dance and I am always impressed by the high standards achieved by children as young as three or four years of age.

By the end of the foundation period it is hoped that most children will be able to use their imagination in art, design, music, dance, stories and imaginative play. Many children will enjoy seeing and talking about pictures and beautiful shapes and objects. Discussions with an adult, or other children, will help to foster language development and encourage children to express their feelings about what they see, hear, smell and taste.

Although this is the last learning goal, it is nevertheless fundamental to learning. Imaginative play and role play are extremely important in learning as, during their play, children cross the boundaries of various areas of learning. Earlier in the book the value of imaginative play was discussed and it is crucial that this aspect of the life of the child is not sacrificed in favour of a programme dominated by endless worksheets. It may be more difficult to assess the child's progress on learning targets during play but good observations by a skilled observer will reveal a wealth of learning across several areas of the curriculum.

The Principles into Practice cards have some excellent suggestions for practitioners to follow. The EYFS places high emphasis upon meeting diverse and special educational needs, on play and observing children and using these experiences to further their development. A welcome new approach is the emphasis on starting with what children can do and including children in planning their own learning. Researchers have found that many educators find it difficult to implement play-based learning, because of pressures, particularly from parents, to meet the early learning goals. It is to be hoped that the new highly trained Early Years Professional will be able to resist these pressures and offer play-based learning that has been shown to be so beneficial to children.

Children with special educational needs

Children with special needs may require individual learning programmes for part of the session, but it is important for their development and that of the other children in the setting that they participate as fully as possible in the normal routines. However, some children with disabilities will need extra guidance and support from an adult to gain from the normal learning opportunities that occur throughout the day. It may be appropriate to adapt the environment or an activity for a particular child.

Children with behavioural difficulties are a challenge to most educators and they require a well-structured programme to help them learn how to work effectively either alone or in a group. Strategies such as setting reasonable expectations in discussion with the child and its parents, establishing clear boundaries and giving positive feedback are all useful in helping the children to manage their own behaviour.

Children with English as an additional language

In many parts of the UK there are children for whom English is an additional language. Many of these children are bilingual from birth but there are others who come into the nursery from households in which there is no knowledge of English. These children will have developed concepts, vocabulary and linguistic skills in the language of the home and can communicate their needs and interests. It is important that we do not ignore this prior knowledge. The educator needs to be particularly sensitive to this as many parents from non-English-speaking backgrounds are anxious about the possible distress that their children will experience when they enter the early childhood institution, especially since they themselves are probably facing difficulties in the community.

Children will learn English just as they learned their first language, through hearing it and being encouraged to use it in situations that are meaningful to them. Many children who are new to English will use gestures to communicate, point to things they want, and/or lead staff by the hand to show them. This period of non-verbal communication is frequently accompanied by the 'silent period', when the child is listening but does not speak at all. Although a normal part of second-language learning, it can be most perplexing for both adults and other children. During this period the children are acquiring knowledge of English and will begin to speak when they are ready. The role of the educator is to continue talking even when there is no response, in the same way as we hold conversations with very young children, as there is understanding long before there is talk. Children need to hear English and it is important that adults speak clearly and precisely to them as it is only in this way that children can learn the stress and intonation of our language.

As children begin to speak English they use spontaneous expressions that they hear, generally from other children, such as 'hello', 'it's mine', 'my go'. These phrases help to maintain a conversation and enable them to join in with their peers. Naturally the children make mistakes but gradually they become confident as users of English and are able to participate in all the nursery activities.

Having children in a nursery who are non-English speakers can be quite daunting to educators and where possible bilingual support should be available. Children should be given opportunities to see books in and hear their home language as well as English. Naturally if there are several children in the nursery who have the same mother tongue they will use that language, particularly during imaginative-play bouts. However, normally as children begin to develop some facility in English they will also begin to play with native English speakers. Workers in nursery settings in which there is a large number of children with English as an additional language are always amazed at the speed with which these children learn a second language when given the appropriate support.

Evaluating children's progress

Educators need to monitor children's progress all the time in order to plan for the next stage of development and to identify any area of concern so that they can take action to provide support and seek additional help if necessary either within the nursery or from other agencies.

Practitioners also want to know whether the teaching programme is effective in helping children to achieve the desired learning outcomes. What benefits are there to children from attending the programme? If the benefits have not been as great as was hoped for, what must be done to amend the programme so that the learning goals can be achieved?

Another reason for assessing children's performance is to find out whether a particular teaching strategy has been more effective than others. The reflective practitioner may devise a variety of teaching approaches to support the children's learning and needs to know which is the most successful. For example, the practitioner may decide to change from a structured approach to one in which the children are allowed the freedom to select their own activities and wish to know whether this change has been beneficial.

Early years practitioners have traditionally based their assessment of children upon detailed observations supported by examples of the 'children's work' to provide evidence of progress over time. The guidelines in the EYFS document state that there should be 'ongoing assessment as an integral part of the learning and development process'. Observational evidence from a range of learning experiences should involve all who are concerned with the child in their pre-school setting as well as information given by parents. The partnership between parents and educators should be ongoing throughout the time the child is in the pre-school setting.

There is now a new profile at the end of the Foundation Stage: the Early Years Foundation Stage Profile which sums up the child's learning and development at the end of the final term of the year in which the child reaches the age of five. Parents must be provided with a copy of the completed profile. The new scheme will involve ongoing observation and assessment of each child's progress towards all six of the early learning goals. Like the previous profile, this national approach to assessment places emphasis upon observation, the traditional form of assessment in the early years of education, and will help identify children with special educational needs. The profile provides a useful tool to both educators and parents, but as with all assessment schemes for young children, there is a danger that it will be interpreted as a test to be passed rather than an assessment of children's progress to help teachers plan appropriately to support their learning. Parents are naturally anxious about their children's progress and, as a result, this could lead to unwelcome pressures on children unless the scheme is adequately explained. There is also the possibility that some early years practitioners will see the assessments as a test of their teaching during the Foundation Stage and they too will place too great an emphasis upon formal learning.

The new EYFS is currently operating in England only. Other documentation is being produced in Scotland, Wales and Northern Ireland.

The role of the adult

The adult has an important role to play in supporting children's learning. Both Bruner and Vygotsky place emphasis upon the importance of the adult in facilitating children's learning. In this country the Effective Early Learning Project, led by Pascal and Bertram, has identified three main ways in which adults can help support children to learn. They termed this the 'Engagement Scale'. It considers:

- how the adult encourages the child to achieve independence;
- the sensitivity of the adult to the child;
- how the adult offers stimulating and challenging experiences.

Although a didactic approach is inappropriate in most instances, there are occasions when direct teaching is necessary, for example when a child is making a model and is having difficulties in joining two materials together. Adult intervention at that time is highly appropriate and will help the child to succeed and so feel in control of its own learning. This is a very different situation from a child being told to sit at a table and stick tissue paper onto a prepared shape or draw round templates. Over the years I have heard many reasons why these sorts of activity are of value to children, but no one can convince me that they have any intrinsic value. There are other, more effective, ways of encouraging the development of fine motor skills.

There is an increasing body of research to show that children can learn from each other as well as from adults, particularly when the children are of mixed ages. This type of grouping, which is a characteristic of our nurseries, is a legacy from our early childhood educators who were well aware of the value of child–child learning.

Partnership with parents is an essential part of early childhood education. All the research has indicated that where parents are actively involved in their children's education the children will benefit most from their time in the nursery. When partnership with parents is built on mutual trust and respect, children feel secure and safe within the early childhood setting. Parental cooperation is particularly important at times of stress for the child, for example during the transition from home to school or from nursery to primary school.

Some international examples of curriculum for children from three to six years

In this section are included several examples of curricula for young children that have influenced the ideas and thinking of educationalists in the UK.

High Scope Curriculum

The High Scope Curriculum, originally called the Pre-school Perry Project, a programme for disadvantaged children in Ypsilanti in the 1960s, has been subjected to careful evaluation over a period of more than 30 years. Its consistently positive results have been used by many to support the argument for the cost-effectiveness of nursery education and the programme has been introduced in many countries worldwide, including the UK. The most recent follow-up study has shown continued positive effects of the programme for adults at 40 years of age. Interested readers can find the details of this research from the website of the High Scope Education Research Foundation (www.highscope.org).

The programme sees children as active learners, encouraging them to become independent problem solvers and decision makers. It is not a rigid programme but provides a framework for children's learning. Although it has much in common with traditional nursery practice, the authors consider that it places greater responsibility upon children for planning and executing their own activities.

Working on a philosophy of *plan*, *do* and *review*, the environment is arranged so that it optimises children's learning, using key experiences to observe and plan for the individual needs of children, for example adult–child communication strategies, partnership with parents, observation and record keeping.

The key experiences implicit in the High Scope concept of active learning are:

* using language – describing objects, events and relationships;
* active learning – manipulating, transforming and combining materials;
* representing ideas and experiences – role playing, pretending;
* developing logical reasoning – learning to label, match and sort objects;
* understanding time and space – recalling and anticipating events, learning to find things in the classroom.

These key experiences not only provide the framework for planning and evaluating activities but also enable the staff to guide children from one learning experience to another. They suggest questions to put to the children and enable staff to assess children's development and provide a basis for discussion with the parents.

The daily routine provides adults and children with a consistent framework in which to work. It is planned to accomplish three main goals:

1   A sequence of plan/do/review. This process allows children to explore, design and carry out activities and make decisions in their learning.
2   Providing for many types of interaction. For example, small- and large-group work, adult to child, child to child, and times for both adult-initiated and child-initiated activities.
3   Providing the opportunities/time to work in a variety of environments, both indoors and outdoors.

The High Scope Curriculum is dependent upon careful planning and staff discuss the needs of both individual children and the group as a whole before a decision is taken on which aspect of the curriculum they must emphasise first. This consultation is termed 'team teaching' and is a feature of the High Scope classroom. Strange as it may seem to early childhood educators in the UK, in many parts of the world this is a new concept as cooperation among early years staff is not the norm.

Although the authors of this approach have been influenced by the work of Piaget, the conversations that children engage in with adults during the plan/do/review cycle embody the principles of Vygotsky's effective instruction within the zone of proximal development. The adult challenges children's thinking and helps them extend their ideas further. The High Scope Curriculum encourages children to develop mastery orientation and persistence in the face of failure. If a plan did not materialise as the child had hoped, then the feedback from an adult should help to increase the likelihood of a more successful outcome on the following day.

Developmentally appropriate curriculum

According to Kelly (1994), the term 'developmentally appropriate practice' indicates that the focus of the early childhood curriculum must be on the child and its development rather than on subjects and knowledge.

A developmentally appropriate curriculum must be based upon active forms of learning, on enquiry and discovery. It places emphasis on the process rather than the product. This approach is not new as it is similar to that advocated by the Hadow Report (1933), which put forward the view that the curriculum needs to be framed in terms of activity and experience rather than knowledge to be acquired and facts to be stored. In the United States, the developmentally appropriate approach was supported by the National Association for the Education of Young Children, who published curriculum guidelines based on this philosophy (Bredekamp 1987).

Developmentally appropriate practice is based on universal and predictable sequences of growth and change. It advocates that the teacher should take account of the age of the child and of its individuality in terms of growth pattern, personality, learning style and family background, and that children learn best through play that is:

- self-initiated;
- self-directed;
- self-chosen.

The teacher's role is to:

- provide a rich variety of activities and materials;
- support the children's play;
- talk with the children about play.

This view of the curriculum is based upon a specific understanding of children's learning and development and upon a child-centred philosophy steeped in the deep-rooted beliefs and ideals widely shared among Western-educated specialists, and is based entirely upon Western psychological theory.

Since the 1980s psychologists and educators have challenged this type of programme, arguing that what is 'appropriate' in one setting may be 'inappropriate' in another cultural context. It has been argued that this approach is insensitive to the cultural diversity in children's family experiences and parenting practices and it risks, according to Woodhead (1996), resurrecting discredited judgements about deprived environments and the need for compensation. Criticism from a growing number of sources led the National Association for the Education of Young Children (NAEYC) to look again at its earlier document and it has now been revised by Bredekamp and Copple (1997). The new document incorporates greater attention to the role of families and culture in children's development. It also highlights the role of the teacher as decision maker and curriculum developer. However, there are critics who still point out that it refers to 'developmentally appropriate practice' without defining 'appropriate' or 'inappropriate'. The American research has also pointed out that although many teachers subscribe to the child-centred philosophy, they frequently take a didactic approach to teaching and learning. This is a criticism that can also be made of some educators in the UK.

Research into the value of this approach has indicated that where children are in programmes that are developmentally appropriate they are less likely to develop signs of stress and anxiety in test situations. Equally there have been a number of studies that have looked at motivation and achievement and these have found that young children in developmentally appropriate programmes were more likely to have higher expectations of their own success than those in academic programmes (Stipek *et al.* 1995).

Te Whariki: the New Zealand early childhood curriculum

New Zealand is one of the increasing numbers of countries that is carrying out longitudinal research into the effects of early childhood programmes. An ongoing study carried out by the New Zealand Council for Educational Research is still showing positive results as the children move into secondary schooling.

In 1996, the government published a national early childhood curriculum that incorporated the Maori curriculum and was designed to form the basis for a bicultural education programme in that country. It has drawn upon the different philosophies available worldwide and recognises the diversity of early childhood education in New Zealand. The curriculum emphasises the critical role of socially and mediated learning and recognises the importance of responsive relationships for children with people, places and things. In the introduction it is written that 'children learn through collaboration with adults and peers, through guided participation and observation of others, as well as through individual exploration and reflection' (Ministry of Education, New Zealand 1996).

There are four main principles at the heart of the early childhood curriculum: empowerment; holistic development; family and community; and relationships. Five strands and goals arise from these principles, which together form the framework for the curriculum. Each strand has associated goals with specific learning outcomes.

Strand 1: well-being

Children experience an environment in which:

- their health is promoted;
- their emotional well-being is nurtured;
- they are kept safe from harm.

Strand 2: belonging

Children and their families experience an environment in which:

- connecting links with the family and the wider world are affirmed and extended;
- they know that they have a place;
- they feel comfortable with the routines, customs and regular events;
- they know the limits and boundaries of acceptable behaviour.

Strand 3: contribution

Children experience an environment in which:

- there are equitable opportunities for learning, irrespective of gender, ability, age, ethnicity or background;
- they are affirmed as individuals;
- they are encouraged to learn with and alongside others.

Strand 4: communication

Children experience an environment in which:

- they develop non-verbal communication skills for a range of purposes;
- they develop verbal communication skills for a range of purposes;
- they experience the stories and symbols of their own and other cultures;
- they discover and develop different ways to be creative and expressive.

Strand 5: exploration

Children experience an environment in which:

- their play is valued as meaningful learning and the importance of spontaneous play is recognised;
- they gain confidence in and control of their bodies;
- they learn strategies for active exploration, thinking and reasoning;
- they develop working theories for making sense of the physical, natural, social and material worlds.

The guidelines apply to all children in whatever educational setting and include children with special educational needs. Where appropriate, an Individual Development

Plan (IDP) is developed for children who require special resources. The programme has given rise to considerable interest among early childhood educators worldwide.

The Reggio Emilia approach

Reggio Emilia in Northern Italy has been the scene of an innovative programme for early childhood education for over 30 years. The *scuole dell infanzia*, for children aged from three to six years, and the *asili nido*, for children aged three months to three years, were established in close collaboration with parents and aim to offer children a comprehensive education in which the rights of the child are paramount. The pre-schools in this affluent region have been visited by many thousands of interested early childhood educators from all over the world and the method has been copied and adapted in many countries. Many others have seen 'The Hundred Languages of Children', the travelling exhibition that has visited many countries worldwide. The main feature of the approach is that it advocates communication between adults and children and considers that early childhood education involves children, teachers, parents and the community.

Loris Malaguzzi, the educator behind this idea, postulated a theory of early education based on social relationships. He wrote that:

> Our image of children no longer considers them as isolated and egocentric, does not only see them engaged in action with objects, does not emphasise only the cognitive aspects, does not belittle feelings or what is not logical, and does not consider with ambiguity the role of the affective domain. Instead our image of the child is rich in potential, strong, powerful, competent and most of all, connected to adults and other children.
>
> (1993: 10)

He stressed repeatedly the notion of the child as part of a community of adults, who lives and learns as part of the wider community.

> We must know that children, although naturally inclined, do not acquire the art of becoming friends or teachers of one another, by finding models in heaven or manuals, rather children extract and interpret models from adults, when the adults know how to work together, discuss, think, research and live together.
>
> (1993: 3)

This is a society that believes that it is possible to combine education and social services for the community. It is a kind of education that focuses on the child in relationship with the family, the teacher, the other children and the broader cultural context of society. For the educators in Reggio Emilia, early childhood institutions are places for dialogue, places of participation and places of education in a process that involves children, teachers and families. This is a social constructivist view of education that considers that children have the right to be 'connected to others'.

Supporters of this philosophy have an image of the child as a person who experiences the world, and feels part of the world from birth. The child is full of curiosity, the desire to explore and has the ability to communicate from birth. In this respect the approach is not unique, as it is one that is fully accepted by a number of other societies. In any community, institution or family, it is not only the adults who effect changes in the child, but the presence of the child also effects changes in the family, school and the wider society. We are all aware that some children have a greater impact upon their environment than others – some are troublesome, some are less demanding, but each and every one in their way leaves their mark upon their home, school and community.

The six stated principles of the Emilio Reggio approach are:

1   the study of child development as central to practice;
2   the importance of the teacher–child relationship;
3   the need for children's experiences to be taken into account when building the curriculum;
4   the importance of a rich environment in developing children's learning;
5   the importance of ongoing professional development for teachers;
6   the importance of the role of parents in the life of the school.

The centres are of a high aesthetic quality and reflect the culture of the region. Great value is placed on the role of the environment as a motivating force and emphasis is placed upon integrating each classroom with the rest of the school. Each classroom opens onto a central area, where all the materials for dressing up and imaginative play are stored, as well as access to the outside play areas. This central area has wall-sized windows to let in the natural light and link the school with the local community. A feeling of community is further encouraged by connecting the rooms with telephones for the use of both adults and children. The Reggio Emilia approach aims to give children time and space to develop their interests and a wide range of materials and tools are provided to help them develop their skills and abilities. Other elements of the environment include a workshop and ample space for storage. Malaguzzi speaks of the need for the child to be away from the ever-watchful eye of the adult – and certainly in some of the nurseries there are many areas where the child can play away from the adult's gaze.

Each institution has an *artelierista*, a specialist art teacher, and a cook, as well as the regular educators and a *pedagogista* who may work with several institutions.

The children are grouped chronologically with 25 children and two teachers in the class. The children stay with the same staff members over the three years but have regular sessions with the *artelierista*, who is heavily involved with all the projects. During their last term in the *scuola infanzia* the school leavers prepare a booklet for the new intake of children about their school and the activities they carry out. Thus the sense of connectedness and communication is passed on to the new children about to enter the school.

Throughout the school year, teachers, parents and members of the larger community meet to discuss any problems associated with the programme. At these meetings the 'pedagogical documentation' produced by the teachers is used to inform discussions. This documentation is more than teacher observations but includes children's work and drawings, and photos and videos of the various projects that have been carried out.

The documentation not only records the final outcomes of the project but also incorporates the ideas of the children, their experiences and their observations of the teachers. The documentation serves three main functions:

1   to provide the children with a permanent record of what they have said and done and helps them to understand what they have achieved;

2   to provide educators with an insight into the children's behaviour and learning, thus enabling them to reflect upon and support later learning;

3   to provide parents and the community with detailed information about what happens in the school and encourage better relationships between home and school.

There is no prescribed programme or curriculum, the children work on projects that have arisen from their own interests. These may be short or long term and involve all or just a small number of the children in the class, but *pedagogistas* use this pedagogical documentation to discuss, analyse and reflect with the staff on the practice in the institution. In this way the quality of the educational environment is maintained. The *pedagogistas* have time allocated within their working week for analysis and reflection.

The work of Loris Malaguzzi has been both a stimulus and challenge to early childhood educators in many parts of the world and many are working to introduce his ideas into their early childhood institutions. However, the uniqueness of this approach and the fact that there is no prescribed programme or curriculum means that there could be difficulties in transferring this type of practice to other cultures. Merely copying a project or using some of the ideas is not the same as adopting the philosophy. Educators need to believe that they can respond to the children's ideas and interests appropriately and ensure that the children are sufficiently challenged. Furthermore, this may not be an approach that is suitable to all children, for example, those who need more structure and guidance. Before any institution adopts this approach the adults involved must accept *and* understand the underlying principles and philosophy in the light of their own culture.

Pre-school education in Sweden

Many English educationalists have looked at pre-school education in Sweden over the last few years and ponder how it is that Swedish children progress so well and lead the literacy tables in Europe when the pre-school education is so informal. The Swedish approach to teaching young children is very relaxed and, although there has been a national curriculum for children from birth to five since 1998 with emphasis on learning, this focuses upon the traditional child-development-based approach where there is little structured learning, play is paramount and children are encouraged to help with cleaning and catering.

Specifically, the curriculum for pre-school states that:

- children have with rights of their own;
- children are respected as citizens;
- childhood is a valuable time, rich in opportunities;
- children are active, competent and curious for knowledge, co-constructors of knowledge;
- pedagogues reflect and observe, following and promoting the child's own learning processes;
- working approaches are project- and theme-oriented;

- pedagogical documentation is used to evaluate and improve ECEC work;
- no assessment of the child.

Swedish children have a year of kindergarten as a preparation for primary school, but most that leave pre-school at the age of six cannot read or write and yet within three years of starting formal schooling at the age of seven, these children lead the literacy tables in Europe. Sweden's overall policy towards families and young children is one that should give us food for thought.

Age of entry into school

Compared with most other countries in Europe, children in the UK start primary school at least one, if not two, years earlier than their European counterparts. The current trend for children to be admitted into reception classes at the beginning of their fifth year is unique to the UK, although in Luxembourg there is compulsory pre-primary education from four to six years. In the Netherlands, compulsory education starts at five and there is provision for four-year-olds in the primary schools, and in Hungary all children must attend one full year of kindergarten education in the year before they commence primary schooling. However, as Table 10.2 shows, in most European countries children do not enter primary schooling until six or seven years of age.

As you can see from the table, the UK alone feels that full-time primary education should commence at the beginning of the academic year in which the child will be five, even though statutory school age does not begin until the term after the child's fifth birthday. European children are still in pre-school settings or at home for two or more years than those in the UK.

During the last decade, the early admission of UK children into primary classes led to heated debates in the Scandinavian countries, resulting in the reduction of the school admission age to six years in Norway. In Denmark, the school admission age was not reduced but 98 per cent of the children attend kindergarten classes under the Ministry of Education, and in the Netherlands almost all children attend pre-primary classes at four years of age which are under the Ministry of Education. Under the 1997 Kindergarten Law in Hungary, attendance in kindergarten is compulsory for all children from the age of five. Greece was one country that has moved against the trend as, after a short period of lowered entry age to 5.5 years, the limit has once again been raised to six.

What effect does the later start to school have for parents, children and for the curriculum? Most of our European counterparts believe it is beneficial for entry into primary education to be deferred until at least six, although many of them offer special 'educational' classes in the last one or two years of the kindergarten, but this does not include the teaching of reading or writing. Early entry is not regarded as a viable alternative to quality early childhood care and education. The recent publication of the league tables for literacy where the UK came very low and the results of the study by Sylva (2007) raises questions as to the merits of early entry into primary school.

However, Sharp's (2007) findings suggested that there was no conclusive evidence concerning the benefits of starting school at different ages, but there is some evidence to suggest that an early introduction into formal schooling may have a negative impact on children's motivation to learn. What we do know is that well-qualified early years staff will provide the most appropriate experiences to extend children's learning.

Table 10.2 Age of entry into school

Country	Compulsory school age	Ministry responsible 0–3	Ministry responsible 3–6/7
Austria	6	Regional Health/Welfare	
Belgium	6	Social Welfare	Education
Bulgaria	7	Health/Welfare	Education
Czech republic	6	Health/Welfare	Education
Denmark	7	Social Welfare	Education(5/6–7)
England	5	Children, Schools and Families	
Estonia	7	Social Welfare	Education
Finland	7	Social Welfare	Education (6/7)
France	6	Social Affairs	Education
Germany	6	Social Affairs	Social Affairs*
Greece	6	Social Affairs	Education
Hungary	6	Health	Education
Iceland	7	Education**	Education
Ireland	6	Health	Education
Italy	6	Health/Welfare	Education
Luxembourg	6	Family Affairs	Education(4–6)
Netherlands	5	Social Welfare	Education (4+)
Northern Ireland	4	Education	
Norway	6	Children and Family Affairs	
Poland	7	Health/Welfare	Education
Portugal	6	Social Welfare	Education/Welfare
Rumania	7	Social Welfare	Education
Russia	7	Social Welfare	Education
Scotland	5	Education and Training	
Slovak Republic	6	Health	Education (2–6)
Spain	6	Education	
Sweden	7	Education	
Switzerland	6	Varies+	Education+
Turkey	6	Health/Welfare	Education
Wales	5	Education	

Notes
*In Bavaria the Ministry of Education is responsible for classes for some 5-year-olds.
**Childminders are the responsibility of the Ministry of Social Affairs.
+Responsibility according to the Cantons.

Reflect upon …

1   Children in the UK enter primary school earlier than their counterparts in many European countries. Consider the advantages/disadvantages of early entry into primary school.
2   To what extent and in what ways should parents be able to influence their children's early education?
3   Many practitioners fear that the new EYFS will result in a formal programme for children under three. Look at the standards and consider whether there is any justification for this concern.

References

Ball, C. (1994) *Start Right*, London: Royal Society of Arts.

Bredekamp, S. (ed.) (1987) *Developmentally Appropriate Practice in Early Childhood Programs Serving Children from Birth through Age 8*, Washington DC: National Association for the Education of Young Children.

Bredekamp, S. and Copple, S. (eds) (1997) *Developmentally Appropriate Practice in Early Childhood Programs* (revised edition), Washington, DC: National Association for the Education of Young Children.

Bruner, J. (1956) *Studies in Cognitive Growth*, New York: Wiley.

Consultative Committee (Hadow) (1933) *Report on Infant and Nursery Schools*, London: HMSO.

Curtis, A. (1998) *Curriculum for the Pre-school Child*, second edition, London and New York: Routledge.

Curtis, A. (1999) 'Evaluating early childhood programmes: are we asking the right questions?', paper presented at Early Childhood Conference, Santiago, March 1999.

DfEE (2000) *Curriculum Guidance for the Foundation Stage*, London: QCA.

DfES (2007) *The Early Years Foundation Stage*, London: QCA.

Drummond, M.J., Lally, M. and Pugh, G. (1989) *Working with Children: Developing a Curriculum for the Early Years*, London: National Children's Bureau.

Edwards, C., Gandini, L. and Forman, G. (eds) (1998) *The Hundred Languages of Children*, second edition, London: Ablex Publishing Corporation.

High Scope Education Research Foundation (2008) www.highscope.org.

HM Government (2003) *Every Child Matters*, www.everychildmatters.gov.uk.

Isaacs, S. (1930) *Intellectual Growth in Young Children*, London: Routledge.

Isaacs, S. (1933) *Social Development in Young Children*, London: Routledge.

Kelly, A.V. (1994) 'Beyond the rhetoric and discourse', in G. Blenkin and A.V. Kelly (eds), *The National Curriculum and Early Learning*, London: Paul Chapman.

Lilley, I. (1967) *Friedrich Froebel: A Selection from his Writings*, Cambridge: Cambridge University Press.

Love, J.M., Kisker, E.E., Ross, C.C., Brooks-Gunn, J. and Brady-Smith, C. (2002) *Making a Difference in the Lives of Infants and Toddlers and their Families: The Impacts of Early Head Start*, Washington, DC: US Dept of Human Sciences.

McMillan, M. (1919) *The Nursery School*, London: Dent.

Malaguzzi, L. (trans L. Gandini) (1993) 'For an education based on relationships', *Young Children 9*, 1: 10.

Melhuish, E.C. (2004) *Literature Review of the Impact of Early Years Provision on Young Children with Emphasis Given to Children from Disadvantaged Backgrounds*, London: National.

Ministry of Education (1996) *Te Whariki: Early Childhood Curriculum*, Wellington, New Zealand: Learning Media.

Montessori, M. (1964) *The Absorbent Mind*, Wheaton, IL: Theosophical Press.

Montessori Association (2008) *Guide to the Early Years Foundation Stage in Montessori Settings*, London.

National Association for the Education of Young Children (1991) 'Guidelines for appropriate curriculum content and assessment in programmes serving children ages 3 through 8 years', *Young Children* 46, 3: 21–38.

Pascall, C. and Bertram, T. (eds) (1997) *Effective Early Learning*, London: Hodder and Stoughton.

Schweinhart, L.J., Montie, J., Xiang, Z., Barnett, W.S., Bellfield, C.R. and Nores, M. (2005) *Lifetime Effects: The High/Scope Perry Preschool Study through Age 40*, Ypsilanti: High Scope.

Sharp, C. (2002) *School Starting Age: European Policy and Recent Research*, paper presented at LGA Conference, London.

Stipek, D., Feller, R., Daniels, D. and Milburn, S. (1995) 'The effects of different instructional approaches on young children's achievement and motivation', *Child Development* 66: 209–23.

Sylva, K. (2001) *Summary of Research Evidence on the Age of Starting School*, DfES brief no. 17–01 (September).

Sylva, K., Melhuish, E., Sammons, P., Siraj-Blatchford, I. and Taggart, B. (2004) *The Effective Provision of Pre-school Education Project: A Longitudinal Study 1997–2004*, London: Department for Education and Skills.

Vygotsky, L.S. (1962) *Thought and Language*, Cambridge, MA: MIT Press.

Wilson, A. (2003) *Special Educational Needs in the Early Years*, London: Routledge Falmer.

Woodhead, M. (1996) *In Search of the Rainbow*, Netherlands: Van Leer Foundation.

11 The primary curriculum at KS1

In this chapter the primary curriculum at KS1 is considered with special reference to the Foundation Subjects. Particular attention is drawn to the controversies surrounding the teaching of reading.

In July 1988, the Education Reform Act became law, 62 years after the control of the curriculum had been lifted. Two generations of primary-school teachers had devised their own educational programmes based on a child-centred approach and many were much affected by the introduction of the National Curriculum and its accompanying programmes of study that introduced a subject-based curriculum for children from five to 16 years.

The National Curriculum applies to all pupils of compulsory school age, including grant-maintained schools, and is organised on the basis of four Key Stages. Primary school covers KS1 and KS2 of the programme, while KS3 and KS4 involve children aged from 11 to 16.

Since the introduction in 2000 of the Curriculum Guidance for the Foundation Stage for children between the ages of three and six years, children in the reception class were not officially involved in the National Curriculum until the end of the summer term, when the teachers were required to implement the National Literacy and Numeracy Strategies. However, since September 2008, when the new Early Years Foundation Stage was introduced for children from birth to five years, there is no longer an overlap between the two phases.

A new vision of primary education was promulgated in 2003, with the publication of *Excellence and Enjoyment: A Strategy for Primary Schools*. The new framework enabled primary schools to take greater control of their curriculum and to be innovative in how they teach and organise the school, the aim being 'for every primary school to combine excellence in teaching with enjoyment of learning'. Emphasis is now placed on offering pupils the opportunity to:

- develop their knowledge and understanding of the world and the skills they will need to flourish in it;
- experience the excitement of learning by trying new things, learning from their mistakes and recognising their achievements;
- develop the confidence they need to continue as lifelong learners;

- build on what they already know;
- become partners in their own learning.

It was anticipated that the Primary Curriculum would enable all schools to develop a rich and broad programme to meet the individual learning needs of their children.

Core and foundation subjects

At KS1 there are three core subjects, English, mathematics and science, and in each of these areas the children are assessed during Year 2, although since 1993 science is no longer assessed in the same way as mathematics and English. Other areas of the curriculum include design and technology; information and communication techno-logy; history; geography; art and design; music; physical education; religious educa-tion; and personal, social and health education and citizenship.

There is a programme of study for each area of the curriculum that provides the basis for planning schemes of work. However, since 2007, the original detailed frameworks for Numeracy and Literacy have been removed and there is now a Primary Framework for literacy and mathematics. Although it is recognised that lit-erary and numeracy are key skills, the document emphasises that teaching in these areas should not be detrimental to a broad and balanced curriculum.

Although the programmes of study are given as specific subjects, it is anticipated that teachers will deliver the curriculum in a cross-curricular manner as it is recog-nised that, for young children, learning is not compartmentalised and that they learn in a variety of ways. Details of these programmes are available on the government websites: www.dfes.gov.uk and www.dfsc.gov.uk.

English-literacy and oracy

Probably the subject that causes most worry for parents is English, and reading in particular. Ask a random sample of parents anywhere in the country and you will find that their greatest concern is that their children should learn to read and write – to become literate members of our society. This concern begins almost from birth and although we want to see children 'bathed' in books from an early age, I am hor-rified at the amount of pressure that is currently being placed on practitioners in the nurseries and play groups to 'get the children reading and writing'. So many of our three-year-olds seem to be spending a great deal of time completing work sheets and copying letters and shapes; although hopefully the EFYS programme will encourage more learning through play. Every time I return from my visits to early years institu-tions in other parts of the world I ask myself, is this really the best way to support children's literacy?

What is literacy? According to the National Literacy Strategy framework:

> Literacy unites the important skills of reading and writing. It also involves speaking and listening skills. Good oral work enhances pupil's understanding of language in both oral and written forms and of the way language can be used to communicate. It is also an important part of the process through which pupils read and compose texts.
>
> (DfEE 1998: 3)

Literacy is an essential competence for success in school, and the Effectiveness Provision of Pre-school Education Project (EPPE) study (2005), has shown that pre-school children who have access to books in the home perform better throughout KS1 regardless of their parent's education. Learning to turn the pages of a book and talking about the pictures helps to develop a child's literacy and oracy. However, we need to consider seriously the work of Locke and Ginsberg (2002), who have found that over-emphasis upon early literacy is delaying oracy. Putting children onto a reading scheme as soon as possible and pushing them into formal writing and reading exercises may damage the development of both literacy and oracy.

These are obviously the anticipated outcomes for children at the end of the primary school years, but readers taking a close look at this document will realise that many of these skills and competences are introduced during the EYFS. These were discussed in an earlier chapter in relation to the early learning goals for communication, language and literacy. However, research by Clark (2002) shows that there is a growing tendency towards formality and teacher-led didactic approaches in early years classrooms that can be attributed to the Primary Literacy Strategy and there is a danger that this will continue now that the EYFS is separated from the primary curriculum.

In Western society children are born into a literate world and from the moment they can focus upon print they become aware of written language as part of daily life. Even children who come from homes where they do not have access to books are exposed to the printed word through advertisements, junk mail, shops, buses, etc., as well as the labels on food and packaging.

Although the vast majority of children enter school with the ability to communicate and use language effectively, each child will enter school with a very particular and personal understanding of the purpose of reading and writing. Literacy is part of the social and cultural practices for which is it used and therefore each child's experience of literacy will be closely linked to their family and community. The studies of Bryce-Heath (1983), Schieffelin and Cochran-Smith (1984) and Minns (1990) all point to the ways in which children learn about literacy from their family life.

Schools, early childhood classrooms and families are each dynamic cultural environments with unique views about literacy. Family views of literacy are dependent upon a range of factors including socio-economic levels, ethnicity, educational history, family stability and health. Hannon (1995) has pointed out that the literacy values and practices of families shape the course of children's literacy in terms of opportunities, recognition and models available to them. There is a great diversity of literacy practice among families and the failure of educators to acknowledge anything other than the 'mainstream' approach to literacy may, albeit unwittingly, contribute to academic failure (Makin *et al.* 1999).

Literacy, reading and writing finds its foundations in communication and talk. Enjoying books and understanding that the marks (such as letters and numbers) carry messages is a crucial step in children's reading development. Literacy is generally embedded in many activities, although frequently it is centred on story reading and discussion using the language of the dominant groups. Teachers are expected to provide a curriculum that offers equal opportunities for all children and that necessitates offering literature and discussions appropriate to minority groups. Otherwise, it could be argued that teachers perpetuate social inequalities by determining what is read and ways of being literate. We have long been aware of the importance of parental involvement in children's education and there is substantial evidence to show that the most academically successful children are those where the family literacy practices are most congruent with those of the school. Clay (1993) pointed out the importance of the degree of match between literacy practices of family and services especially in the period from birth to six. This knowledge makes it even more important that children coming from homes with different family literacy values and practices are not marginalised and develop into 'academic failures'.

As children learn to communicate with others, so they come to make meaning of the world around them and psycholinguists like Goodman (1967) and Smith (1988) have demonstrated that children's experience of learning to talk is fundamental to their development as readers and writers. Children appear to use similar strategies to make sense of written language as they did when learning to talk. Researchers like Bissex (1980), Ferreiro and Teberosky (1982) and Minns (1990) have shown how children learn from opportunities to see written language in real contexts.

Hearing narratives and stories also plays an important part in helping children to make sense of reading and writing. Fox (1993) has shown that access to narrative writing helps children to gain sensitivity to the distinctive forms of grammar like the use of the past tense as well as an introduction to more complex forms of language. Children are often helped to take on abstract ideas from stories and poetry.

One of the first ways in which children have an understanding of the written language is when they learn to recognise their names and those of their friends and family. Names mean something to children as they relate to real people and Minns (1990) has argued that by seeing their names in print, young children begin to develop an awareness of the value and use of the written word. However, although they begin to understand the nature of written language from reading and writing, the underlying processes involved in encoding meaning as a writer is different from those involved in decoding meaning as a reader.

Reading and writing are mutually supportive activities, although they make very different demands upon children.

Writing

The foundations of writing are to be found in the scribble patterns of the toddler. Vygotsky (1978) has suggested that drawing assumes particular importance as children come to realise that they can draw speech as well as objects. This understanding presents an enormous intellectual leap for young children. However, they also need to understand the difference between spoken and written language if they are to understand the power and purpose of writing.

When we are talking about writing it is important to remember to differentiate between composition (the expression of ideas) and transcription (the secretarial aspects of writing). Young children's compositional skills are far in advance of their motor writing skills, which is why teachers need to act as scribes for very young children or encourage them to write independently to free them from the pressures of 'getting it right'. The first compositions of children include symbols they recognise such as numerals, letters from their names and invented letter-like shapes. It is important that parents realise that this is normal development and that the child has really composed a piece of writing even though it may be indecipherable to the adult. Parents have to be helped to understand that if disproportionate attention is given to presentation skills, children will think of writing as another motor skill, not as the composing of text.

The Primary Framework draws attention to the need for children to be able to spell correctly and includes high-frequency word lists for the children to learn. However, in the early stages of writing, the younger children will develop ways of coping with the complexities of spelling by looking for regularities and patterns in exactly the same way as they looked for patterns when they were younger in dealing with the past tense (see Chapter 4). Bissex's work provides excellent examples of a young child's search for pattern.

Reading

By the end of the Early Years Foundation Stage children are expected to be able to 'read a range of familiar and common words and simple sentences independently'. These are very high expectations of young children and as a result many nurseries are now expecting children to carry out formal work on letters and words so that they are 'not falling behind' when they enter the reception class. David *et al.* (2002) asked a group of early years educators their views on literacy. She found that there was an almost 50–50 split, with half believing that children should not be involved in literacy activities until after the age of five, the other half believing that children were surrounded by print from birth and that most of them would be learning about it anyway.

The observations of these researchers were that those who advocated play as a vehicle for learning about literacy, in reality called children away from their play activities singly or in small groups to carry out a task that was totally unrelated to what they had been doing throughout the session.

By the end of KS1, most children are expected to be able to:

- read simple texts with understanding and general accuracy;
- express opinions about events or ideas in stories, poems and non-fiction;
- use a variety of strategies such as phonic, graphic, syntactic and contextual in reading unfamiliar words and establishing meanings.

It is intended that these aims will be achieved by offering children structured guidance and direction mainly during the literacy hour, although reading and writing skills will be developed throughout the school day. This hour normally takes place in the morning and includes whole class, group and independent learning. Since 2003 teachers have been given greater freedom to organise the time in the way most appropriate to the children.

What do we know about how children learn to read?

Reading is a process that begins as soon as children can focus on print. The first print to which children are exposed is environmental print and many would argue that it plays as large a part in learning to read as the reading books they are given at the early stages of reading. At home children will look at cereal packets and other packaging and point to the logos that identify them. At this stage, children are dealing with the pattern of the whole word, decoding comes later. As children become more aware of the printed word they show an interest in detail and will start looking at and commenting on letters of the alphabet. Frequently, the first one is the initial letter of their name. Around the same time many children start to notice the rhymes in songs and nursery rhymes.

The value of rhyming language is stressed by many as it has been found that texts that incorporate rhyme and recurrent tunes and contain language that is rhythmic and memorable make it easier for children to predict and anticipate the rest of the verse. Goswani and Bryant (1990) drew attention to the importance of offering young children opportunities for engaging in songs, rhymes and alliteration. They found that chanting and singing and playing with language gave children a sensitivity to rhyme that provided the basis for the development of phonological awareness and was strongly related to later success in reading.

Methods of teaching reading

Traditionally, teachers had used a variety of methods to introduce children to the skill of reading, including the phonic approach, whole-word method and a method based on using the child's experience of print, knowledge of stories and the language that children bring with them to school. When the National Literacy Strategy was introduced in 1998, the searchlights model was put forward, encapsulating what was then accepted as 'best practice in the teaching of reading'. It was a holistic approach to teaching reading, assuming that the reading process involves four strategies – phonic knowledge; grammatical knowledge; word recognition and graphic knowledge; and knowledge of context – the 'searchlights'. The best practice of the time drew heavily on the work of Clay (1972, 1985), who argued that the child needs four cueing systems in order to read. The cueing systems are: phonological (the sounds of oral language); syntactic (word order); visual (graphemes, format and layout); and semantic (text meanings). Clay's research suggested that the child uses all four cueing systems to develop multiple strategies to help process texts.

Although some progress was being made in raising reading standards, it was felt that the searchlights model was perhaps not as effective as had been hoped.

Newer psychological research, based on the work of Gough and Turner (1986), had suggested a simple view of reading in which, it is argued, there are two essential components: 'decoding' and 'comprehension'. Decoding is the ability to recognise words out of context combined with the ability to apply phonic rules and linguistic comprehension, which they define as 'the process by which given lexical (word) information, sentences and discourse are informed'. Based on this evidence, the government announced in 2005 an overhaul in the teaching of reading, the searchlights model was abandoned and all schools had to follow the recommendations of the Rose Report (2005) and introduce the teaching of synthetic phonics to children at the age of five. Although the teaching of phonics has always been an integral part of the National Literacy Strategy, the promotion of synthetic rather than analytic phonics came as a result of the findings of the Clackmannanshire Study, a seven-year longitudinal study, in which it was found that children following the synthetic phonics programme were more advanced in their reading compared with the other two experimental groups. Although it is admitted that there are flaws in this study, Rose advocated this method along with ensuring that children have good language and listening skills, and that educators should promote positive attitudes to reading for pleasure and for information. This involves the teaching of all the necessary strategies and skills, such as decoding and comprehension and the teaching of a sight vocabulary, when and where appropriate.

Synthetic and analytic phonics defined

Synthetic phonics refers to an approach to the teaching of reading in which the phonemes (sounds) associated with particular graphemes (letters) are pronounced in isolation and blended together (synthesised). For example, children are taught to take a single-syllable word such as *cat* apart into its three letters, pronounce a phoneme for each letter in turn /k/, /æ/, /t/, and blend the phonemes together to form a word. Synthetic phonics for writing reverses the sequence: children are taught to say the word they wish to write, segment it into its phonemes and say them in turn, for example /d/, /?/, /g/, and write a grapheme for each phoneme in turn to produce the written word *dog*.

Analytic phonics refers to an approach to the teaching of reading in which the phonemes associated with particular graphemes are not pronounced in isolation. Children identify (analyse) the common phoneme in a set of words in which each word contains the phoneme under study. For example, teacher and pupils discuss how the following words are alike: *pat*, *park*, *push* and *pen*. Analytic phonics for writing similarly relies on inferential learning: realising that the initial phoneme in /p i g/ is the same as that in /p æ t/, /p a: k/, /p u ?/ and /p e n/.

Sound sense 2003

There are still those who disagree with synthetic phonics, particularly as the chief evidence is flawed. However, it remains to be seen whether or not this method will produce higher reading levels and still maintain children's interest in books.

Children need many opportunities to practise reading, which is where the shared and guided reading practices recommended in the Primary Literacy Strategy are effective, as part of the literacy hour should be spent with the teacher reading to the children and the children reading to each other. For the child who has already a grasp on reading, silent reading is an important next step.

What are some of the factors that contribute to successful reading?

A summary of the literature reveals that the following have an effect upon children's reading success.

Family literacy practices:

* story-book reading at home;
* environmental print experiences;
* home–school links/mutual respect between home and school;
* opportunities for talk and discussion.

Classroom-based literacy practices:

- social context of classroom literacy experience;
- teachers foster a desire to read;
- opportunities for challenge;
- opportunities for choice;
- opportunities for collaboration;
- story-book reading in the classroom – including examples of good literature;
- shared reading in the classroom – reading to and by the teacher.

Literacy (reading and writing) is integrated across the curriculum

We no longer believe that children are not 'reading ready' until the age of six. Children are individuals who have different strengths and weaknesses and whose interest in learning to read will vary, nevertheless most learn to read and write conventionally within the first years of school. Schickedanz (1999) argues that these achievements represent the end result of years of literacy learning that begin the moment the very young child is able to focus on print.

Dyslexia

Although this edition of the book does not contain a section on communication disorders it was decided to include a short section on dyslexia and dyspraxia, very common communication disorders. Every school will have children suffering from dyslexia, who will need specialised attention if they are not to experience later school failure. There has been a great deal of discussion about the topic and in spite of the evidence, there are still those who regard it as a middle-class syndrome and a useful cover up for 'lazy children'. Watch a child who has this difficulty and you will soon appreciate that this is a child who is experiencing a learning disability. If not dealt with at an early stage, dyslexia can result in failure to gain competence in literacy, resulting in a child who is severely handicapped in today's society.

What is dyslexia? The term *dyslexia* comes from the Greek and literally means 'difficulty with' (*dys*) 'words' (*lexis*). It refers to difficulties with words read, spelled, pronounced and written, and also with the association of meaning with words. Not every child experiences all these disorders and they will be found in varying degrees of difficulty, but dyslexia is a syndrome that cuts across class, age and intelligence. Children with this syndrome may also be referred to as having a 'specific learning disability' or being 'learning disabled'.

Many teachers are loath to identify children with these terms as they feel that by labelling a child they are drawing attention to the disability. On the other hand, speech and language experts argue that it helps these children to understand why they are not keeping up with their peers. Children need to understand that there are some things that we are good at and some things we have difficulty with, and that dyslexic children have difficulties with reading and spelling. They need to understand that they can begin to get on top of the problem with help, *if* they work hard. Most teachers find that with hope and help, children are willing to work hard.

What are some of the characteristics of dyslexia and how do they affect learning?

Poor visual recall. Many children have poor visual memories and are unable to recall the word even if they see it again and again on the same page. This is particularly disastrous if their introduction to reading is through the 'whole-word' method instead of one that involves recognising the words that have to be decoded. Spelling also presents a challenge when there is little or no visual recall, particularly if accompanied by a lack of knowledge of phonics and language structure, as the children have no idea what to write. Likewise, both handwriting and numeracy will be affected as without an image of the letters/numbers it is impossible to know how to form these letters or numbers; even copying is very difficult for these children.

Phonological difficulty. This is difficulty in building up an awareness of speech sounds and linking them to the written word, making an analytic-phonic approach to reading inappropriate, although many children seem to gain success with a systematic synthetic-phonic programme.

Sequencing. Some children suffering from this syndrome experience difficulties with sequencing, not only with letters and numbers that they write in the wrong order (for example, string may be spelt as stirng, or the number 1476 may be copied as 1764), but also with the days of the week and the months of the year. The ability to sequence verbal and symbolic material correctly is a crucial skill. Although many people may have minor problems with sequencing, for example knowing the difference between right and left when map reading, the difficulties of the dyslexic leaves them in great confusion, often resulting in a great deal of loss of self-confidence and self-esteem. Imagine the child who cannot sequence the days of the week. She will not know which day of the week it is when she wakes up in the morning. Children need good directional awareness and to understand that in our culture we read from left to right; for those with sequencing problems these skills are difficult to acquire.

Orientation. Spatial relationships are particularly difficult, for two possible reasons. Language-based difficulties may lead to an inability to understand words like 'left' and 'right' or 'further' and 'nearer', and for a more severely affected group there are those who are totally confused in both time and space. Our sympathy and support is certainly needed for this small disadvantaged group of children.

Learning difficulties. These may well be aggravated by ear infections and high- and low-frequency hearing losses that make it difficult for the child to hear properly. Likewise, the child may have eye defects that can affect progress in reading. Visual defects can affect reading, writing and spelling. Eye and ear problems may be the cause of reading difficulties for non-dyslexic children, but they are additional factors with which the dyslexic child has to contend.

Poor visual and auditory memories. A dyslexic child may experience these as the result of an inability to form a mental image or retain a sequence of words or numbers. For the dyslexic child, learning must be multi-sensory and the programmes offered should use auditory, visual, olfactory and tactile senses. Concentration span is often short for these children.

Language processing. It is generally accepted that dyslexic children have a weakness in language processing. Many have difficulties in understanding simple questions like 'What is this colour?', even though they can match and sort colours accurately. These children also have difficulties with understanding time and verb tenses. For example a seven- or eight-year-old child may say 'I have done it soon' or 'I will do it yesterday', long after her peers have sorted out issues of time and tense.

There are two types of language-processing difficulties, expressive language and receptive language. Expressive-language difficulty results in the individual having problems putting thought into words, while the person with a receptive-language difficulty is unable to follow adequately the language of others. Some children and adults may have both an expressive and receptive language difficulty.

It is not always recognised that speech and language processing are a problem for some children and adults, as often speech problems are only considered if articulation is poor. The more subtle difficulties of expressive and receptive speech and language are often overlooked, particularly as the child may have developed some early ability to read, even though there is no progress beyond this basic level.

Dyspraxia is another form of communication difficulty that affects dyslexic children. Here the child has difficulty with the acquisition of patterns of movement. This can affect not only speech and language but also eye/hand coordination, especially handwriting and organisation. Such children do not necessarily have difficulties with reading and spelling, but with physical activities, including handwriting, and will probably be labelled 'clumsy'. Some research has indicated that the incidence of clumsiness occurs in as much as 5 per cent of the population.

Poor motor control will lead to poor handwriting and for these children when they are writing under stress it will deteriorate even more. The advent of the computer in the classroom was a boon for such children, as they can now produce a piece of work of which they can be proud.

Most dyslexic children eventually learn to read, but require highly trained specialist teachers who can diagnose their specific difficulties and offer a programme to meet their needs. Research has suggested that about 40 per cent of dyslexic children have difficulties with maths, reading and spelling, and most of these children quickly learn to feel school failures. Many are highly intelligent and it requires a lot of skill and support both from parents and from the school to ensure that these children develop a positive self-image and realise early that the problems they have are not due to laziness or stupidity. The best prognosis for children suffering from dyslexia and/or dyspraxia is early intervention and the positive support and understanding of parents and teachers.

Mathematics

Sparrow (1998) argues that mathematics is not just a collection of skills, it is a way of thinking. It lies at the core of scientific understanding and of rational and logical argument.

Mathematics is not just about computation, traditional number problems and numerical algorithms, it is about how children develop their mathematical understanding. The mathematics curriculum builds on the early learning goals that have required children to:

- count and use numbers to at least 10 in familiar contexts;
- recognise numerals from 1 to 9;
- talk about and create simple patterns;

- begin to understand addition as combining two groups of objects and subtraction as 'taking away';
- describe the shape and size of solid and flat shapes;
- use everyday words to describe position;
- use early mathematical ideas to solve practical problems.

The curriculum for children in KS1 focuses on:

1   the use and application of number, the number system, calculations, using both mental methods and symbols, problem solving and representing and interpreting data;
2   the use and application of shape, space and measures. Pupils are to be taught to use and apply shape, space and measures, to solve problems and understand the patterns and properties of shape, position and movement as well as understand measures.

The poor performance of British children compared with other countries led to the setting up of the National Numeracy Project whose initial concerns were:

1   the level of children's arithmetic skills;
2   the dominance of published schemes in schools, reducing teacher to scheme manager;
3   over-emphasis on standard written algorithms introduced too early.

From their findings, this group suggested that there should be:

- dedicated mathematics lessons every day;
- direct teaching and interactive oral work with the whole class and with groups;
- an emphasis on mental calculation;
- controlled differentiation, with all pupils engaged in mathematics related to a common theme.

These recommendations have now been incorporated into classroom practice in KS1 classrooms.

The National Curriculum is heavily weighted towards number with mental methods for calculation in the first years of schooling. Use of calculators is restricted to use in Years 5 and 6, but only for calculations and not for concept development and problem solving. Rousham and Rowland (1996) argue that it is surprising that the government was so adamant about the use of calculators, making them the scapegoat for disappointing mathematical performance, when there is ample evidence to show that calculators in the hands of children with competent and imaginative teachers can promote the learning of mathematical concepts and stimulate mental calculation (Shuard *et al.* 1991). Is this a message about the competence of teachers?

The mathematics curriculum requires early childhood educators to include specific content in their planning and teaching and to ensure that children have the necessary knowledge and understanding of and mastery of skills. However, in order to help children develop this knowledge and understanding, teachers need to be very aware of how children develop their mathematical thinking. Recent research has highlighted some of the important factors that need to be considered (Steffe and Wood 1990; Nunes *et al.* 1993; Nunes 1998).

Children enter the education system with a wealth of mathematical experiences and knowledge that they have gained from home and their environment. It is not always recognised as mathematical knowledge when a two-year-old complains that her brother has more sweets than she does. Unfortunately, so many adults still see mathematics as separated from everyday life and something that is carried out by mathematicians in their ivory towers. Although children can function mathematically from an early age, they do not intuitively understand mathematical ideas in an abstract formal way, nor do they appreciate that what they are doing or saying is mathematics. They may not be able to count accurately or recognise conventional symbols but, as Hughes (1986) has demonstrated, they are able to add and subtract even though they cannot represent these operations on paper in a recognisable form.

Part of the task of the early years educator is to introduce young children to the conventions of mathematics, particularly number. The Cockcroft Report suggested, as long ago as 1982, that one of the important roles of early years teachers is to 'open the doors of mathematical discovery' to the children in their care.

Aubrey (1997) has shown that reception class children bring into school a rich informal knowledge of counting, recognition of numerals, skills in simple addition and subtraction and social sharing, but there was very little evidence that teachers built on this knowledge in the classroom.

Mathematics involves children being active investigators with children 'doing' mathematics rather than just learning about it. Young children are constantly forming a sense of pattern and order and refining their abilities to think logically and compare, contrast and match what they know with the challenges of their environment. The role of the educator is to build on these developing strengths and help them to become actively involved in the learning process so that children can make meaningful connections within their existing frameworks and also to make changes in their frameworks. One task of the teacher is to ensure that she develops in children the skills associated with knowledge about and the manipulation of our number system. However, there is a danger that too great an emphasis on number fails to take into account the wealth of mathematical knowledge that children bring into school. Calling the mathematics aspect of the national curriculum the 'numeracy hour' reinforces this approach.

From the nursery throughout the first years of schooling, we introduce learning to young children by the use of practical activities and materials, but we need to consider what the child makes of the representations we offer. Does a line of ten bricks really help children to understand '10', or are we simply offering a concrete example of an abstract idea that remains abstract however many concrete representations we make? Children will bring their own interpretation to any concrete representation and that can sometimes result in more complexities rather than conclusions, as every teacher knows well.

Piaget put forward an activity-based model of learning that has been extended by researchers like Donaldson (1978) and Hughes (1986), who have pointed out that more effective learning takes place when it is presented to children within a context that is both familiar and meaningful. As we have seen, Bruner has criticised Piaget's model of development, arguing that the teacher must set challenges for the child. He proposed a spiral curriculum maintaining that any topic can be taught to a child at any age in an intellectually respectable form.

Vygotsky, like Bruner, was an interventionist who stressed the importance of the adult taking an active part in children's learning. His identification of the 'zone of proximal development' has helped to focus attention upon the importance of open questioning in facilitating children's learning.

Number

'She knows her numbers and can count up to 100', is the sort of statement that many reception class teachers hear from parents when their child enters primary school. Indeed, children come into school having made some attempt to come to terms with our number system. As Ginsberg (1977) has pointed out, children struggle to understand the apparent arbitrary nature of numbers in our culture. We say one, two, three, not three, one, two. He sees learning to count as a song that has no end as a new part is always being introduced, and there is always one number larger than the one before. Counting is endless.

For the young child, this task must seem overwhelming and yet they do learn to count, some even before they enter the nursery. Ginsberg (1977) has identified two important strategies necessary to succeed in this task – those of looking for order and pattern and coping with a little of the task at a time. For example, children manage one, two, three before they attempt four, five, six. The search for pattern takes longer as our counting numbers do not reflect any pattern until we pass 12 and then 20. There is an identifiable rhythm in the tens, 20, 30, 40, etc., and within the tens, but there is usually a need for prompting when the child reaches 29 to go on to 30, but they can then go on easily from 30 to 39. These problems are ones of our culture, as in some societies, like China or Korea, the number symbols have a clear regularity as do the number names. Fuson and Kwon (1992) reported that speakers of some Asian languages do not seem to have the same difficulties and are able to cope with the conceptual structures earlier than the English-speaking cohort. In our multicultural society, the different counting systems of other cultures should all be used to help support children's mathematical development. The Swann Report (1985) was the first official report to make teachers aware of the need to introduce a multicultural approach to mathematics in the classroom. The use of the Rangoli and Islamic patterns will add another dimension when making children aware of symmetry and tessellation.

Children need to make the transition from counting by ones to counting by tens, hundreds, thousands, etc., in order to develop effective problem-solving strategies and meaning for place value. Successful manipulation of the symbols within computational problems does not imply this transition, as many researchers have found that children can compute accurately without understanding (Kamii 1989; Kamii and Joseph 1988).

There is strong evidence to show that although most children have few problems with reading and writing numbers from 0 to 9, the higher numbers, which involve an understanding of place values, can be more difficult. A common error is for children to write the number two hundred and sixty-one as 200601, until they have a real understanding of place value.

However, learning to count involves more than learning number names and symbols. Gelman and Gallistel (1978) in a classic experiment identified five criteria that must be fulfilled before it can be said that counting has been successfully achieved:

1   *the one-to-one principle* – each and every item is given one, and only one, number name;
2   *the abstraction principle* – what the objects are is irrelevant, what matters is that they all belong to the collection being counted;
3   *the stable-order principle* – the number names are used in an unvarying order, for example, one, two, three, four, etc., not two, three, four, one;
4   *the cardinality principle* – the final number name denotes the number in the collection. For example, if there are five in a set, when the number five is reached, this gives the number in the set;
5   *the order-irrelevance principle* – it does not matter in which order the items are counted as long as all the other criteria are met.

Through this exercise, Gelman and Gallistel have shown that what is a simple exercise to an adult, is in fact a complex task for the young child.

Children use numbers in a variety of ways besides counting, for example: 'I live at number 89', 'I have four buttons on my blouse', but teachers are most concerned with the aspect that deals with 'one and one equals two'. It is this use of number that ought to lead to the child's understanding of number in the abstract world of mathematics. Hughes (1986) argued that there is a gap between children's abstract understanding of number and their ability to represent this understanding in the formal language of mathematics. He urges that teachers make links between the knowledge based on concrete experiences that the child is sure of and the abstract nature of the language or arithmetic. Piaget has argued that children need to attain the concept of conservation of number before they can see number as a property of a set. However, it may be that children need to be able to make a connection between their experiences of number and the representation of number in the world of concrete objects in order to deal with abstract mathematical ideas effectively.

There has been considerable research to show that the meaning of addition, subtraction, multiplication and division is complex and that children can only be said to understand these operations when they fully understand all the various interpretations. Experience with concrete objects is essential before children can make sense of the symbolic representations, although it is essential for teachers to listen carefully to the explanations children give so that they can understand the child's meaning. As has been said earlier, manipulation of concrete objects does not necessarily imply understanding.

Space, shape and size

If mathematics is perceived as the search for order, pattern and relationships to characterise ideas and experiences, then spatial concepts are central topics in children's understanding of mathematics. They are also important for the science and IT programmes of study. Constructivist theories of learning have as a fundamental tenet that children learn through their interaction with the environment. The development of spatial concepts is a gradual process and, according to Piaget, children had little understanding until there were around seven years of age. However, Donaldson's findings revealed that when the children were placed in a context that was meaningful to them they had greater understanding. This research has highlighted the importance of providing the appropriate tools in the classroom to enable children to explore and develop the concept of space. One of the most appropriate ways is during structured play sessions where the availability of open-ended situations in a meaningful setting will help children to develop this understanding.

Measurement

Measurement has many different aspects and is difficult for children to understand as we measure in different standard units, each one having been arbitrarily determined. We use linear measurement for some situations, measurements of capacity for others, and so on. Piaget's investigations led him to argue that the principle of invariance is associated with conservation and transitivity. According to Piaget, children at KS1 have not reached the stage of conservation of weight, time, mass and volume, although most will have achieved the concept of length at around six or seven years. Although there has been criticism that Piaget may not have been entirely correct, there is no doubt that young children cannot handle concepts of measurement effectively until further up the school. However, the varied experiences that they are offered in the Foundation Years and in KS1 will provide the basis for the development of understanding these concepts.

A dictionary definition of the verb 'to measure' is to 'ascertain the extent or quantity of x by comparison with a standard or fixed unit or object of known size'. This includes three important ideas, each of which needs to be considered when discussing measurement with young children:

- extent or quantity;
- comparison;
- fixed unit or object of known size.

The first idea relates to the purpose of measuring – how long, how thick, how heavy, how much is contained? When children are engaged in any form of measuring they will be required to make connections between shape and size, size and number (of units), number and order, and ordering and shape.

By making these connections children begin to see the relationships within mathematics and between mathematics and other areas of knowledge. So ascertaining extent and quantity is not a simple operation for a child.

The second idea relates to comparison. This is an important notion and it is crucial for children to understand that it is an inexact one. For example, we may use two different weighing machines and find that they measure different amounts. From discussions on comparison children can then be encouraged to think about the ideas of estimation and approximation and to making judgements about appropriateness and efficiency. In the early stages of measuring, non-standard units may be used and in this way children can quickly come to understand the need for a fixed unit of measurement. It is soon realised that two of the teacher's hand-spans measure more than two of a six-year-old's. They also need to realise that any unit of measurement is purely a social convenience.

Language and mathematics

Perhaps the most important part of the early mathematics curriculum is that children understand the language of mathematics and that they are engaged in problem solving, discussion and questioning with their teachers. The young child's first mathematical experiences are centred on oral language, both listening and speaking. We know that young children search for patterns and order among their experiences and often find confusion in the language of mathematics. For example, when we ask a child 'What is an odd number?', we are referring to something specific and do not mean the same as when we say, 'I saw something odd today'. Likewise, the word 'different' causes difficulties for many children. The term 'difference' in 'What is the difference between a monkey and an elephant?' is not the same as 'What is the difference between eight and five?'.

Children also become confused with the ambiguity of words in English. For example, a child is asked by the teacher to make her model 'twice as big' – does this mean in all directions, or only in height, length or width, or in two of these dimensions?

Talking with children involves the adult using precise, accurate language if we are not to increase their confusion. Some examples of this were given in Chapter 4, Language and Language Development.

Value of problem solving

In looking at children's mathematical development, we must consider it in the context of the child's development as a whole. Mathematics is not just for the 'numeracy hour'. Hughes *et al.* (2000) have found that there was not sufficient emphasis placed on problem solving and creative thinking at KS1 due to the emphasis on number knowledge and calculation skills in the programme of study. Many opportunities for problem solving and creative thinking arise during play. We should not underestimate the value of play in children's mathematical development, although the inspectors have pointed out that many schools fail to make good use of the opportunities for the development and extension of mathematical understanding that arise during play situations.

When children are given the opportunity to solve problems, frequently they develop strategies within the social construct of the classroom as they share their ideas with other children. This is not just discovery learning, as the teacher must pose questions and tasks that may stimulate appropriate conceptual reorganisation by the children. This requires the teacher to understand the expected developmental sequence of mathematical understanding as well as the current levels of mathematical understanding held by the children.

Many argue that place value cannot be learned by the use of concrete materials, but there is growing evidence to support the view that when arithmetic concepts and procedures are approached as problem solving, children's invented strategies foster number sense and understanding of multiple-digit addition and subtraction (Carpenter *et al.* 1998). When children are given problems to solve they should be presented with a variety of ways and with a variety of mathematical language. There is evidence that when the problem is set in a meaningful context for children, they can often solve problems mentally before they can use the written symbols correctly.

When talking with children, educators should:

- use open-ended and challenging questions;
- provide a focal point for discussion;
- allow children time to develop their own ideas;
- encourage children to develop their own ideas;
- encourage children to share and compare ideas;
- keep the children involved;
- ask questions to assess understanding;
- ask helpful questions to aid progress.

Children often learn numbers in everyday life but schools have the role of getting them to think about different sorts of number. As Nunes (1998) puts it:

> Numeracy is not just about learning, numbers and computations, it is first and foremost a matter of understanding the framework for thinking that mathematicians have developed over time. It is more likely that we understand these frameworks for thinking when we use them to solve problems.

Will the national numeracy strategy work in the long run? Only time will tell, but at least it has addressed some of the issues such as the neglect of mental mathematics and the use of the Vertical Arithmetic Syndrome (VAS) that had caused such problems for many children. It has challenged teachers in classroom mathematical thinking and teaching, but many would argue that there is still a high dependence on textbooks that favour the VAS as they are seen as surrogate teachers. A real challenge to policy makers is to ensure that during the Foundation Stage as well as KS1, written work is postponed for as long as is appropriate. Parents may want to see worksheets covered in numbers and 'sums', but educators must convince them that it is in the best interests of the child to learn to problem solve mentally.

Science

An awareness of the poor level of science teaching in primary schools resulted in a number of government initiatives in the 1980s designed to raise standards and support the teachers, many of whom had little knowledge of the subject themselves. By 1989, the HMI reported considerable improvements in primary science teaching, although it was still a weak area in many infant classrooms where few teachers had any scientific knowledge of the physical sciences.

When the National Curriculum was introduced, science was designated one of the core subjects, although less time is devoted to it than to mathematics and English. At KS1, the Programme of Study aims to provide the children with knowledge, skills and understanding in four main areas:

- scientific enquiry;
- life processes and living things;
- materials and their properties;
- physical processes.

It is expected that scientific enquiry is taught in the context of the other three sections, children being encouraged to observe, explore and ask questions about scientific ideas.

Throughout the document it is recommended that cross-curricular links are made, particularly with mathematics and IT. Teachers are also required to consider health and safety aspects and to encourage children to use simple scientific language to communicate and describe ideas.

Science is an exciting subject that interests and stimulates young children. From a very young age children are enthralled by many of the activities going on in the world around them. One has only to observe a young child watching a bee collect pollen from a flower to realise how much we take for granted what, for her, is a totally new experience. Children will have been introduced to many of the ideas encapsulated in the programme of study during the Foundation Stage, as the early learning goals related to 'Knowledge and Understanding of the World' make an excellent basis for the science curriculum at KS1. For example, cooking, which is a fundamental part of the nursery curriculum, will have provided opportunities for children to discuss with an adult the effects of the properties of heat on some materials. Naturally, the understanding of the seven-year-old will be much greater than that of a three-year-old, but the seeds of scientific understanding will have been sown.

Although the concepts that are needed to understand most scientific activities are not fully developed in children at KS1, nevertheless the skills of observing, questioning and evaluating can be fostered during these early years. Some have argued that by defining the specific scientific content in the programme we are preventing children from 'learning through discovery'. However, it has been pointed out that sometimes children need to be helped to make their discoveries. Children can learn to carry out simple experiments that will help them to understand their world, but their limited conceptual understanding may prevent them from making scientific judgements without the help of an adult to 'scaffold' the situation.

When educators are helping children to investigate and explore they are inculcating in them a scientific way of thinking that can be used on many other occasions. By encouraging the development of scientific skills like observing, questioning, communicating, measuring, classifying and recognising patterns, educators are helping to foster scientific attitudes and scientific concepts. Children need to talk with an adult and with other children and these discussions help them to find out about their surroundings and to make sense of the environment. Research has suggested that young children's progress in science depends upon the abilities and knowledge of staff who can stretch children and challenge their scientific thinking. It appears that teachers are often unaware of the amount of scientific knowledge that children learn from home and their environment.

Foundation subjects

Each of the foundation subjects has a detailed scheme of work for children at this stage, building on from the EYFS programme. However, many teachers believe that it is very difficult to introduce all the areas of study appropriately due to the predominance given to English and mathematics, and parents often complain that the foundation subjects are neglected.

Art

The primary curriculum for this area includes art, craft and design, children being encouraged to express themselves using a variety of skills, methods and materials. They learn to make representations of the world around them and the techniques that will produce surface effects like shade and pattern and the mixing of colours. Children are also encouraged to plan their work and evaluate the finished product.

The other aspect of the programme relates to the study of the work of artists and craftspeople from different cultures, traditions and times. In considering the work of others, it is hoped that, where possible, children are able to see paintings, sculpture and other objects for themselves, not just gain their experiences from two dimensional pictures. I would hope that more schools would follow the example of Bulgaria, where I saw artists and craftsmen working with children of five and six years in school on a regular basis.

Music

Music is another area of the curriculum that is marginalised in some schools, primarily due to the fact that there is no member of staff well-qualified to teach the subject. In early years settings, music, in the form of songs and the playing of simple instruments, educators encourage the development of music but this does not always continue at KS1. The scheme of study states that children should learn to express themselves both by singing and playing an instrument. They explore rhythm, tempo and the qualities of sound, leading on to learning the skills of musical notation and reading music, and schools should be encouraging an appreciation of music by introducing music from all over the world and encouraging listening to different kinds of music that reflects different places, cultures and times. Children who develop musical abilities usually acquire these skills during out-of-school activities.

Geography

Although children at KS1 are only expected to investigate the local environment in and around their school, they should be encouraged to ask geographical questions such as 'What is it like?', 'Where is it?' and 'Why is it like that?'. In the hands of skilled teachers, this is a subject area that can be exciting to children, when there are so many whose families come from places far afield, and others who holiday in distant places. Maps, posters and TV programmes can generate a great deal of discussion among the youngest primary-age children.

History

An understanding of the past and of how the world we live in has changed is of vital importance. In their science programme, children will have studied how they have changed since they were babies, and this is one of the ways in which they can be helped to appreciate how changes occur as time passes. At this stage, history is closely linked to family – grandparents are from the past and can talk about 'when things were different'. Talking about lifestyles in the past fascinates young children, particularly when they hear from the older generation that when they were young there was no TV and very few cars. It is also a time when children enjoy hearing stories about famous people and historical events, although it will be several years before they have a real understanding of chronology. Like art and music, this is a subject that can become marginalised in primary schools, but, as Cooper (2006) has demonstrated, it is an area that lends itself to cross-curricular learning.

Physical education

In recent years there has been a great interest in health and the problem of obesity in young children, and the importance of exercise for both physical and mental development has been mentioned in an earlier chapter. However, although there is a programme of study that helps children to develop good movement skills, become confident physically and learn to compete and cooperate, many parents and educators complain that insufficient time is devoted to this aspect of the curriculum. The one or two lessons a week for games, dance and gymnastics do not provide the necessary exercise for children who will probably go home to sit in front of the TV or computer for several hours each day. Many teachers give up their time to supplement the school programme with after-school physical activities; likewise, many parents enrol their children in clubs and classes so that children can benefit, but this should not be seen as a substitute for finding more time in the school day.

Information technology

At KS1, Information Technology involves familiarising children with the use of computers and hardware like CD-ROMs, and other electronic equipment such as video recorders and DVD players. Children are encouraged to use text and produce tables and images to develop their ideas. This is a subject area that is linked closely to all other areas of the curriculum as it provides a useful tool but, as it is clearly stated in the programme of study, 'information technology is not intended to replace reading, writing and basic maths skills, but to complement them'.

Design technology

From the earliest stages of nursery education, children are encouraged to design and make things. In the first three years of primary schooling children continue to explore materials, develop their design skills and evaluate their products, not only by discussing them with their peers and teachers but also writing about what they have made and the problems they have encountered. It is often in these sessions that children have an opportunity to put their knowledge of science, maths and information technology to practical use and to begin to see the relevance of these subjects to everyday life.

Personal, social and health education and citizenship

This subject area was not included in the original National Curriculum, but it is now fully recognised that emphasis must be placed on helping children to learn the basic rules and skills for keeping themselves healthy and safe and for behaving well. Children learn the skills of sharing and cooperation, how to resist bullying, resolve arguments and how, as members of a community, they have both rights *and* responsibilities.

This area of the curriculum permeates all aspects of school life, both in school and in the playground, and there are many interesting examples on the website of the ways in which some primary schools have tackled these issues.

Religious education

Religious education must be taught in all schools and children are required both to learn about different religions and to learn from religion. Children are encouraged to respect the beliefs of others and to understand the shared values of all the major religions: honesty, caring, justice and forgiveness. In most schools there is an emphasis on teaching about Christianity, but children also learn about other faiths present in the UK, such as Buddhism, Hinduism, Islam, Judaism and Sikhism. Parents have the right to withdraw their children from these classes.

Primary curriculum under review

In 2006, the government set up a Primary Review under the aegis of Jim Rose, to consider whether or not the existing programme was appropriate in the twenty-first century. One of the reasons for this review is that, as with any subject-based programme, the importance placed on the teaching and assessment of the core subjects could tempt teachers to deliver the curriculum without taking into account the knowledge we have about how children learn and develop during the early years of schooling.

At the time of going to press, the review has not yet reported its findings, but some of the preliminary reports, which have looked at the aims of primary education and compared the quality and approaches of our education with other countries, are indicating that we are exerting unnecessary pressure on our young children. The emphasis on testing and league tables may not be producing the hoped-for quality education for young children.

Reflect upon ...

1   Discuss the effect that separating the EYFS and the Primary Curriculum may have on children entering the reception class at the age of four.
2   The Primary Curriculum is currently under review; what changes would you make for children at KS1?
3   It is argued that the emphasis on the core subjects is detrimental to other areas of the curriculum. Do you agree?

References

Aubrey, C. (1997) *Mathematics Teaching in the Early Years: An Investigation of Teachers' Subject Knowledge*, London: Falmer Press.

Bissex, G.L. (1980) *GYNS AT WRK: A Child Learns to Write*, London: Harvard University Press.

Bryce-Heath, S. (1983) *Ways with Words: Language, Life and Work in Communities and Classrooms*, Cambridge: Cambridge University Press.

Carpenter, T.P., Franks, M.L., Jacobs, V.R., Fennema, E. and Empson, S.B. (1998) 'A longitudinal study of invention and understanding in children's multidigit addition and subtraction', *Journal for Research in Mathematics Education* 29: 3–20.

Clark, L. (2002) 'Lessons from the nursery: children as writers', *Reading* 34, 2: 69–74.

Clay, M.M. (1972). *Reading: The Patterning of Complex Behaviour*, London: Heinemann Educational Books.

Clay, M.M. (1985) *The Early Detection of Reading Difficulties*, Auckland: Heinemann.

Clay, M.M. (1993) *An Observation Survey of Early Literacy Achievement*, Auckland: Heinemann.

Coltheart, M. (2006) 'Dual-route and connectionist models of reading: an overview', *London Review of Education*, 4, 1: 5–17.

Cooper, H. (2006) *History in the Primary School*, lecture given at the second Institute of Historical Research Conference, London.

David, T. *et al.* (2002) *Making Sense of Literacy*, Warwick: Trentham Books.

DES (1982) *Mathematics Counts*, London: HMSO (Cockcroft Report).

DfEE (1998) *The National Literacy Strategy*, London: DfEE.

DfEE (1999a) *The National Curriculum*, London: DfEE/QCA.

DfEE (1999b) *The National Numeracy Strategy*, London: DfEE.

DfEE (2003) *Excellence and Enjoyment: a Strategy for Primary Schools*, London: DfEE.

Donaldson, M. (1978) *Children's Minds*, Glasgow: Fontana/Collins.

Ferreiro, E. and Teberosky, A. (1982) *Literacy before Schooling*, Exeter, NH: Heinemann Educational.

Fox, C. (1993) *At the Very Edge of the Forest: The Influence of Literature on Story and Narrative by Children*, London: Cassell.

Fuson, K.C. and Kwon, Y. (1992) 'Learning addition and subtraction: effects of number words and other cultural tools', in J. Bideaud, C. Meljac and J.P. Fischer (eds), *Pathways to Number*, Hillsdale, NJ: Lawrence Erlbaum Associates.

Gelman, R. and Gallistel, C.R. (1978) *The Child's Understanding of Number*, Cambridge, MA: Harvard University Press.

Ginsburg, H. (1977) *Children's Arithmetic: How They Learn it and How You Reach it*, Austin, TX: PRO-ED.

Goodman, K.S. (1967) 'Reading: a psycholinguistic guessing game', *Elementary English* 42: 639–43.

Goswani, U. and Bryant, P.E. (1990) *Phonological Skills and Learning to Read*, Hove: Lawrence Erlbaum.

Gough, P.B. and Turner, W.E. (1986) 'Decoding, reading and reading disability', *Remedial and Special Education* 7: 6–10.

Hannon, P. (1995) *Literacy, Home and School: Research and Practice in Teaching Literacy with Parents*, London: Falmer Press.

Hughes, M. (1986) *Children and Number: Difficulties in Learning Mathematics*, Oxford: Blackwell.

Hughes, M., Desforges, C. and Mitchell, C.L. (2000) *Numeracy and Beyond*, Buckingham: Open University Press.

Kamii, C. (1989) *Young Children Continue to Reinvent Arithmetic*, New York: Teachers College Press.

Kamii, C. and Joseph, L. (1988) 'Teaching place value and double column addition', *Arithmetic Teacher* 35, 6: 48–52.

Locke, A. and Ginsberg, J. (2002) *Report in Nursery World*, 10 January 2002.

Makin, L., Hayden, J., Holland, A., Arthur, L., Beecher, B., Jones-Diaz, C. and McNaught, M. (1999) *Mapping Literacy Practices in Early Childhood Services*, second edition, DET and DOCS.

Minns, H. (1990) *Read it to Me Now: Learning at Home and at School*, London: Virago.

Nunes, T. (1998) *Developing Children's Minds through Literacy and Numeracy*, London: Institute of Education.

Nunes, T. and Bryant, P. (1996) *Children Doing Mathematics*, Oxford: Blackwell.

Nutbrown, C. (1997) *Recognising Early Literacy Development: Assessing Children's Achievements*, London: Paul Chapman.

QCA (1999) *Early Learning Goals*, London: QCA/DfEE.

Richards, R., Collis, M. and Kincaid, D. (1986) *Early Start to Science*, London: Macmillan Educational.

Rousham, L. and Rowland, T. (1996) 'Numeracy and calculators', in R. Mertens (ed.), *Teaching Numeracy*, Leamington: Scholastic Press.

Schickedanz, J. (1999) *Much More than the ABCs*, Washington, DC: NAEYC.

Schieffelin, B. and Cochran-Smith, M. (1984) 'Learning to read culturally', in H. Goelmann, A. Oberg and F. Smith (eds), *Awakening to Literacy*, Portsmouth, NH: Heinemann.

Shuard, H., Walsh, A., Goodwin, J. and Worcester, V. (1991) *Calculators, Children and Mathematics*, London: Simon and Schuster.

Smith, F. (1988) *Understanding Reading: A Psycholinguistic Analysis of Reading and Learning to Read*, fourth edition, Hillsdale, NJ: Lawrence Erlbaum Associates.

Sparrow, C. (1998), quote from National Curriculum: 61.

Steffe, L.P. and Wood, T. (eds) (1990) *Transforming Children's Mathematics Education*, Hillsdale, NJ: Lawrence Erlbaum Associates.

Vygotsky, L.S. (1978) *Mind in Society*, Cambridge, MA: Harvard University Press.

Appendix

Outcomes

Be healthy

- Physically healthy
- Mentally healthy
- Sexually healthy
- Healthy lifestyles
- Choose not to take illegal drugs
- Parents, carers and families promote healthy choices

Stay safe

- Safe from maltreatment, neglect, violence and sexual exploitation
- Safe from accidental death and injury
- Safe from bullying and discrimination
- Safe from crime and anti-social behaviour in and out of school
- Have security, stability and are cared for
- Parents, carers and families provide safe homes and stability

Enjoy and achieve

- Ready for school
- Attend and enjoy school
- Achieve stretching national standards at primary school
- Achieve personal and social development and enjoy relaxation
- Achieve stretching national standards at secondary school
- Parents, carers and families support learning

Make a positive contribution

- Engage in decision-making and support the community and environment
- Engage in law-abiding and positive behaviour in and out of school
- Develop positive relationships and choose not to bully and discriminate
- Develop self-confidence and successfully deal with significant life changes and challenges

- Develop enterprising behaviour
- Parents, carers and families promote positive behaviour

Achieve economic well-being

- Engage in further education, employment or training on leaving school
- Ready for employment
- Live in decent homes and sustainable communities
- Access to transport and material goods
- Parents, carers and families are supported to be economically active

Glossary

This glossary contains the terms that are not explained in the text and any other that the authors feel may be helpful.

blend (vb.) To draw individual sounds together to pronounce a word, e.g. s-n-a-p, blended together, reads *snap*.

bonding The formation of stable attachments between the child and its primary carer/s.

Children's Workforce Development Council (CWDC) This is a Council set up by the UK government to oversee the employment and qualifications of people who work with children, particularly those in early years settings. It only deals with qualifications below Qualified Teacher Status (QTS).

cluster Two (or three) letters making two (or three) sounds, e.g. the first three letters of 'straight' are a consonant cluster.

digraph Two letters which together make one sound, e.g. *sh, ch, th, ph, ee, oa*.

dispositions Defined by Lindon (2007) as the area 'where feeling meets thinking. Learning is not all intellectual or rational; feelings are equally involved'.

Early Years Foundation Stage (EYFS) This is the curriculum for all provision catering for children from birth to five years of age and became compulsory from September 2008.

Early Years Professional Status (EYPS) A new qualification for early years workers who have a relevant degree. Their role is to lead the curriculum within the setting.

English 'stiff upper lip' The cultural aspect associated with Englishness, whereby it is not the done thing to express one's emotions in public.

grapheme A letter or a group of letters representing one sound, e.g. *sh, ch, igh, ough* (as in 'though').

home visit When a key worker is assigned a new child coming to the setting, they visit the home of the child and their parent/s in order to establish a relationship with the family.

key worker/person An early years worker who is assigned to a specific child to be their main carer and liaison person with the child's parents.

mnemonic A device for memorising and recalling something, such as a snake shaped like the letter 'S'.

National Occupational Standards (NOS) These are the standards laid down by the Children's Workforce Development Council which all qualifications for early years workers in the UK must conform to. They range from Level 2 to Level 4 qualifications.

object permanence When a child understands that although they can no longer see the object they were playing with they know that it still exists although it is out of sight.

Office for Standards in Education (OFSTED) The government office responsible for the inspection and registration of early years settings.

PEAL Project Parents Early Years and Learning Project which supports early years practitioners in involving parents.

persona dolls These provide an effective, non-threatening and enjoyable way to raise equality issues and counter stereotypical and discriminatory thinking with students, early years practioners and young children. Visit www.persona-doll-training.org/ for further information.

phonemes The phonological units of speech that make a difference to meaning. Thus, the spoken word rope is comprised of three phonemes: /r/, /o/, and /p/. It differs by only one phoneme from each of the spoken words *soap*, *rode* and *rip*.

phonics Instructional practices that emphasise how spellings are related to speech sounds in systematic ways.

phonological A more inclusive term than phonemic awareness and refers to the general ability to attend to the sounds of language as distinct from its meaning. Noticing similarities between words in their sounds, enjoying rhymes, counting syllables, and so forth are indications of such 'metaphonological' skill.

segment (vb.) To split up a word into its individual phonemes in order to spell it, e.g. the word 'cat' has three phonemes: /k/, /a/, /t/.

separation anxiety The stress which children can undergo when they are separated from the adults they are attached to, such as when the parent leaves them in their first day care setting or playgroup.

sibling rivalry When one child in a family is jealous or envious of their brother or sister.

social construct A sociological term for something that is constructed by a society, for example, 'childhood' is a social construct in most western societies but may not be the case in other societies and cultures where there may be child labourers, child soldiers, etc.

travellers' children Children from families that may be of Romany or Gypsy extraction or they may be a collection of extended family members who travel together living in caravans and moving from place to place. In more recent years there have been specific sites where travellers' families are able to stay either permanently or for long periods of time. This has helped their children to have access to regular health and education facilities.

UNESCO United Nations Educational, Scientific and Cultural Organisation established in 1945.

UNICEF United Nations International Children's Emergency Fund established in 1946.

Index